Willa Cather as Elektra in a Greek play at the University of Nebraska
Photograph by courtesy of the Willa Cather Pioneer Memorial Collection,
Nebraska State Historical Society

WILLA CATHER AND
CLASSICAL MYTH

The Search for a New Parnassus

Mary Ruth Ryder

Studies in American Literature
Volume 11

The Edwin Mellen Press
Lewiston/Queenston/Lampeter

Library of Congress Cataloging-in-Publication Data

Ryder, Mary Ruth.
   Willa Cather and classical myth : the search for a new Parnassus /
by Mary Ruth Ryder.
      p. cm. -- (Studies in American literature ; v. 11)
   Includes bibliographical references.
   ISBN 0-88946-113-9
   1. Cather, Willa, 1873-1947--Knowledge--Folklore, mythology.
2. Mythology, Classical, in literature. I. Title. II. Series:
Studies in American literature (Lewiston, N.Y.) ; v. 11.
PS3505.A87Z819 1990   90-34815
813'.52--dc20   CIP

This is volume 11 in the continuing series
Studies in American Literature
Volume 11   ISBN 0-88946-113-9
SAL Series ISBN 0-88946-166-X

A CIP catalog record for this book
is available from the British Library.

The Edwin Mellen Press   The Edwin Mellen Press
Box 450   Box 67
Lewiston, New York   Queenston, Ontario
USA 14092   CANADA, L0S 1L0

The Edwin Mellen Press, Ltd.
Lampeter, Dyfed, Wales
UNITED KINGDOM SA48 7DY

Printed in the United States of America

For my parents,
Ruth and Bernard Ryder

CONTENTS

Preface

The seeds of this book were planted a long time before I embarked upon a career in literary studies. I first read a novel by Willa Cather in my early teens, a time at which I was also introduced to classical studies, and the two have since been linked for me. That Cather had drawn heavily upon classical literature, history, and arts had long been apparent to me from the allusions sprinkled liberally throughout her novels. But, this study began to take shape only after intensive reading of the Cather canon and the resultant recognition of multiple literary traditions at work in her art. This enlarged vision allowed me to uncover the full import of Cather's translation of classical myths into her own time and place. Sharing with Cather a classically-trained consciousness, I began to understand how extensively these myths directed her thought and molded her art. This book is the product of that understanding.

This book also owes its existence to several scholars who encouraged my efforts and offered invaluable insights. I wish to express my indebtedness to Nina Baym for her continuing guidance and for her careful reading and thoughtful response to parts of this study in its seminal form. I gratefully acknowledge Susan Rosowski and Marilyn Arnold for their extensive commentaries on this manuscript as it developed and express appreciation for the support of numerous other scholars, including Richard Dammers, Margaret Dickie, and George Hendrick.

I also thank the Willa Cather Pioneer Memorial and Nebraska State Historical Society for their ready assistance in obtaining sources and the University of Nebraska Press, Houghton-Mifflin, and Alfred A. Knopf[1] for permissions to quote from

1.   Excerpts from *My Antonia* by Willa Cather. Copyright 1918 by Willa Sibert Cather. Copyright renewed 1946 by Willa Sibert Cather. Copyright 1926 by Willa Sibert Cather. Copyright renewed 1954 by Edith Lewis. Copyright 1949 by Houghton Mifflin Co. Copyright (c) renewed 1977 by Bertha Handlan. Reprinted by permission of Houghton Mifflin Co.

Excerpts from *Song of the Lark* by Willa Cather. Copyright 1915 and renewed 1943 by Willa Sibert Cather. Reprinted with permission of Houghton Mifflin Co.

Excerpts from *Obscure Destinies, My Mortal Enemy, Youth and The Bright Medusa, A Lost Lady, Sapphira and the Slave Girl, Lucy Gayheart, The Old Beauty and Others, Death Comes for the Archbishop, Shadows on the Rock , The Professor's House*, and *One of Ours* by Willa Cather. Reprinted by permission of Alfred A. Knopf, Inc.

Cather's works. I am indebted to the growing community of Cather scholars, who shared their ideas both formally and informally at the national seminars. Perhaps most important among those scholars was the late Mildred Bennett, whose enthusiasm for Cather studies and whose easy friendship invigorated me to explore new aspects of Cather's writings.

These acknowledgements would not be complete without mention of Bernice Fox, my undergraduate instructor in the Classics, who provided me with the tools to see what I otherwise would not have seen in Cather's work. I extend deep appreciation to my colleague and friend John C. Shields for long hours of discussion and continuing confidence in this project. My final debt is to the two people most important to the completion of this book- my parents, who gave unfailingly of their time, their encouragement, and their love.

WILLA CATHER AND CLASSICAL MYTH

The Search for a New Parnassus

CHAPTER I

INTRODUCTION

From her earliest stories and poems through the novels which mark the height of her career, Willa Cather employed references to the Classics, especially myth. Yet, the degree to which Cather's works are mythically based has been underrated, and a close examination of the Cather canon shows that her appropriation of myth was deliberate and an integral part of her work. Although she used only a limited number of myths, they served to reinforce her belief that only two or three human stories go on repeating themselves, in spite of changes in time and place. Cather rarely followed the ancients' account of a myth in all its details, but instead identified classical archetypes which illustrated the dilemma of the artist or the struggle of the pioneer. The intent of this study, then, is to explore Cather's use of myth, although not always overt, as it becomes a pattern for structuring her art, expressing her understanding of the human experience, establishing a stronghold for values, and defining the heroic dimensions of life.

Careful readers of Cather's works have long noted, but merely noted, references to Graeco-Roman myth, and occasionally a critic has focused on the importance of a specific myth to a single work (e.g., Bernice Slote and the "moon myth" in *Alexander's Bridge*). Moreover, Antonia's stature as an Earth Mother has been suggested repeatedly, while Sister Peter Damian Charles' discussion of Thanatos and Eros in *O Pioneers!* has become a "classic" interpretive study of that novel. As of yet, however, no full length study has explored in what ways references to classical myth work together to provide direction for and a reflection of Cather's thought. Only L. V. Jacks' 1961 article "The Classics and Willa Cather" (*Prairie Schooner*, Vol. 35), Evelyn Thomas Helmick's "Myth in the Works of Willa Cather" (*Midcontinent American Studies Journal*, 9[1968]), and Donald Sutherland's essay "Willa Cather: The Classic Voice" (in *The Art of Willa Cather*, 1975), focus exclusively on Cather's mythic sources.   Whereas Jacks provides an introductory look at Cather's inspiration from Greek and Latin sources, Sutherland deals largely with her style and the Latin writers.   Helmick focuses her study on Cather's efforts to shape a modern *Aeneid*, particularly through *My Antonia* and *O Pioneers!*.   These three articles, coupled with more recent influence studies, like Susan Rosowski's on Vergil's *Eclogues* and *O Pioneers!* (see *The Voyage Perilous*) and John J. Murphy's "Euripides' *Hippolytus* and Cather's *A Lost Lady*," offer scattered but useful insights into the larger issue of myth as a structuring principle for Cather's art.

What this book, then, hopes to provide is a comprehensive study of Cather's integration of classical myth into her allusive art and a suggestion why such mythic allusions gradually are subsumed to Christian myth. It is not the intent of this work to provide a biographical or cultural study but to draw upon those details of Cather's life and times only as they are needed to establish the basis of her classical training or to clarify shifts in her mythic emphases. Synopses of the less known, earlier stories are designed to aid the reader in recognizing the interplay of classical allusions and plot details. Considerably less attention is paid to the later, so-called "Catholic" novels since the scope of this study does not include an in-depth look at Christian myth.   Rather, in setting a direction for this largely chronological study, I intended to demonstrate that a growing dialectic developed between classical and Christian myth in Cather's fiction.

Cather's background and education indicate that she was familiar with and sensitive to the works of Greek and Roman writers and to the myths they related. Although early in her career Cather made a conscious effort to include mythic references in her writing, classical myth became a part of her unconscious thought and led her to describe her own aesthetic yearnings in mythic terms. In her early works, Cather focuses on the mythic struggle between Dionysian and Apollonian impulses as questers of beauty, like barbarians outside the gates of Rome, are lured by the bright Medusa of art. Cather often pictures this Medusa as an enchantress who embodies a Dionysian eagerness for life as well as an Apollonian devotion to pure art. What Cather discovered about her own artistic quest, her characters also discover: One cannot serve both Dionysus and Apollo.

As Cather embarked on a career in journalism, she realized that the Greek spirit of art was fast disappearing in a world governed by deadlines and profit. Cather described this realization with a growing sense of regret and irrecoverable loss, and her poems of *April Twilights* pointed to a world deserted by Apollo, ruled by a monstrous Medusa who fails to enchant and will not allow an alliance of art with life. Those who attempt to regain paradise, like Margie Van Dyck and Douglass Burnham in "The Treasure of Far Island," are only playing a game they are bound to lose.

In what might be considered the second phase of her writing, Cather redirected her gleaning from classical myth to the traits of independence and resolve that had characterized the Golden Age of epic heroes. Reworking the epic tradition, her Bartley Alexander strives to create the remarkable and the enduring, but the marriage of freedom and order eludes him. The authentic creative force for Cather becomes instead a female one, an Alexandra Bergson, who can direct her passion toward an inhuman object, overcoming all odds and imposing a matriarchal order like that of Demeter in pre-Olympian days. Cather's epic hero is often female, challenging a patriarchal order and preserving the past while succeeding in the present, and these thematic interests led Cather to other mythic structures in her early novels, namely the triumph of the goddess-woman. Wedding memory to desire, Cather describes the Orphic quest of Thea Kronborg, who does battle with those forces inimical to art, including her own passion, and achieves a kind of Pyrrhic victory. She becomes goddess-like and a Muse of

Song, but at a price. Having discovered the power of her femaleness in Panther Canyon, Thea redirects her creative energies into art. In reconciling desire with possibility, she becomes a devotee to Artemis, art's purity, but breaks her ties to Aphrodite, life's passion.

Whereas Thea emerges as defender of the purity of art, Cather celebrated, in the character of Antonia Shimerda, the eternal feminine as defender of civilization itself. Antonia is the archetypal Great Mother, establishing an affinity with the earth by immersing herself in it. Antonia's experiences echo the seasonal cycle defined by Persephone's descent and re-emergence, and in this cycle Cather finds the enduring and permanent, the very things long sought by her epic figures.

But, the aura of a Golden Age which surrounded the writing of *My Antonia* decayed before the reality of war, and the Georgic mood of that novel deteriorated as Cather moved into the third phase of her "organic" use of classical myth. Cather depicted the upheaval of World War I and the crass materialism of the Twenties as a struggle between mythic powers, between Aphrodite and Artemis. Those few lone questers of artistic purity and classical ideals, figures like Claude Wheeler and David Gerhardt in *One of Ours*, find no sympathetic mother-goddess to whom they can turn. For Cather, the modern world worshiped Aphrodite – glamour, success, and pleasure –, and this goddess was the ally of the Olympian patriarchy. In such a world, Cather's questers assume Hippolytean roles, but, as devotees of Artemis, they are doomed. Likewise, the mother-goddesses were doomed to extinction unless they, like Eden Bower of "Coming, Aphrodite!", were willing to compromise in their struggle against the patriarchy. In *A Lost Lady*, Cather further explores this problem. Niel Herbert's Hippolytean candor and naivete are shattered when he learns that Marian Forrester is not the untainted goddess of chastity but is a woman who must use the powers of Aphrodite to survive.

The passing of a matriarchy and its devotion to the ideals of art was of great concern to Cather, and the mythic allusions of *The Professor's House* and *My Mortal Enemy* indicate Cather's growing pessimism about their passing. The Professor searches for paternal roots in order to recover a strong time of Olympian order. He turns to Tom Outland, a potential Vergilian epic hero, but Tom has no place in a world unresponsive to eternal beauty and to the ideal. Like Claude Wheeler, Professor St. Peter does not succeed in his search. Myra Henshawe, too, lives without joy and substitutes the cruel guise of an aging Hera to cover her failings as both a follower of Aphrodite and worshiper of Artemis. In both *The Professor's House* and *My Mortal Enemy*, Cather combines these classical, mythic allusions with Christian myth as St. Peter looks for something or someone with whom he might become "outward bound" and as Myra Henshawe finds her final solace in Catholicism.

In the final phase of her work, Cather found increasingly satisfying the Christian mythos. Still retaining concepts from ancient myth, like the seasonal cycle, the epic adventure, and the Orphic quest, Cather integrated religious and classical imagery into aesthetic images. Father Latour becomes the Aeneas of the New World and Euclide Auclair preserves the religion of his fathers on a new frontier in *Shadows on the Rock*. These final works support a cultural tradition within which lay the ideals of the classical world. Merged with the moral teachings of Christianity, these ideals could fashion a novel of forgiveness like *Lucy Gayheart* or *Sapphira and the Slave Girl*, novels by which Willa Cather makes a truce with her world.

Cather's use of classical myth, then, spanned her entire career, beginning with a somewhat amateurish display of names and events from ancient accounts. But, as her skills as a writer progressed and as her concerns with modern civilization deepened, so did her references to myth assume greater significance. The epics were a major source of myth for Cather, but she also drew upon Greek lyric poets and playwrights, Hesiod, Ovid, and even Lucretius in interweaving references to those myths which best described the dilemmas facing her contemporaries. Nor did the ancients alone shape Cather's mythic allusions. As a student of English literature, Cather was also greatly influenced by intermediary sources, particularly by Shakespeare and Romantic and Victorian writers, whose works added new dimensions to classical myth. Her work was liberally sprinkled with references to the Fates, Persephone, Medea, Hephaestus, Hades, Athena, and numerous other figures. Her color imagery and landscapes reinforce the traits of immortals and locales of mythic activity. Nor did Cather limit herself to one mythos in her fiction. Images from Christian myth work together with classical myth from the earliest stories like "Jack-a-Boy" and "A Resurrection" to the final stories in *The Old Beauty and Others*.

The scope of this book is limited to an exploration of the classical myths Cather knew and incorporated, either overtly or subtly, into her work. The direction of my study was not to uncover the extent to which classical thought (i.e., philosophy and views of history), as opposed to classical myth, influenced Cather. That analysis, together with a full investigation of Cather's use of other mythos (Christian, Norse, Native American), I leave to others. I would hope that this study will prove useful to beginning students as well as to experienced scholars by illuminating in what ways classical myth lends significance to the body of Cather's writings.

Cather was always, like her artists, searching for the permanent or the enduring. Truth was the repository of the immutable, and myth, whether classical or Christian, had much to offer in recovering the truths of human experience. Everett Carter in *Howells and The Age of Realism* contends that "one of the major forces in modern fiction has been the reassessment of these stories [myths], rescuing them from the status of either superstitious lie or literal historical truth, awarding them their rightful title of aesthetic truth – of significant forms which express verities not articulated before."[1] For Cather, these verities had not changed throughout time, and classical myths grew from and defined universal experiences while serving as an expression of the memory of the race, as a fundamental link to "the precious, the incommunicable past."

---

[1]   Everett Carter, *Howells and The Age of Realism* (New York: J. B. Lippincott Co., 1954), p. 220.

CHAPTER II
CATHER'S CLASSICAL BACKGROUND

Biographers and critics have long noted that Willa Cather was introduced to classical studies at an early age through the tutelage of her grandmothers and that her interest in the ancient world continued to grow throughout her school-age years.[1] Although such early exposure to the history, legend, myth, and literature of Greece and Rome was in no way unusual as an educational foundation in the late nineteenth century, what may have been unusual was Cather's degree of assimilation of such material. Not only does a plethora of references to the ancient world appear in her works, but these references are more than literary embellishment. The ancient civilizations of Greece and Rome, and particularly their myths, became an integral part of Willa Cather's thought and artistic expression.

Cather's preschool education lay largely in the hands of her grandmother Boak who read to her from the Bible, *Pilgrim's Progress*, and

---

1. E. K. Brown in his early biography states that young Willa Cather did not attend school in Virginia but was taught by Grandmother Boak who had "read much and carefully" and had "an alert mind" [*Willa Cather: A Critical Biography* (1953; rpt. New York: Avon Books, 1980), p.15]. In *The Kingdom of Art*, Bernice Slote notes that, in childhood, Cather "learned the heroic literature of Homer, Virgil, the Norsemen" and knew the epics, myths, and ancient histories well [Lincoln: Univ. of Nebraska Press, 1966, pp. 35-36]. A more recent biographical study by Sharon O'Brien stresses that Cather's early reading with her grandmother provided "models of heroism she never forgot" and gave her reason "to associate the acquisition and mastery of language with a maternal presence" [*Willa Cather: The Emerging Voice* (New York: Oxford Univ. Press, 1987), p. 26]. James Woodress' definitive biography confirms that Cather's grandmother Boak "took charge of her preschool education" and that these early readings shaped Cather's taste in literature and influenced her writing throughout her career [*Willa Cather: A Literary Life* (Lincoln: Univ. of Nebraska Press, 1987), p. 23].

Peter Parley's Universal History. This latter work was a favorite of Willa Cather and was probably one of the first sources from which she learned of the exploits of heroes like Jason and Menelaus and heard the names of the great Greek poets–Anacreon, Pindar, Theocritus, and Homer. Little attention has been paid to the influence this "parlor" book may have had in shaping Cather's imagination, even before she began to attend school. Indeed, Parley's volume is designed for family reading, to protect young minds from the knowledge of historical evils and wickedness, but the author confesses that his chapters are nonetheless "spiced...with tales and legends,"[2] quite selectively chosen. One chapter is devoted to the major Olympian gods, with two special paragraphs describing Apollo and with engravings of male deities modestly garbed. Yet, about the goddesses Parley says little, merely naming the daughters of Cronus, except for Venus. In three sentences he identifies the goddess of love as the goddess of beauty and mentions her son Cupid. Willa Cather's introduction to an image which would later dominate many of her works is a censored one, the goddess' amorous exploits carefully avoided and her role diminished drastically. So fully did she absorb the ancient legends and myths, though, that, as a small child, she could be amused and quieted if allowed to sit in her chariot of inverted chairs and to reenact the triumph of Scipio on his return from Carthage,[3] a story recounted in some detail in Parley's *Universal History.*

Abruptly uprooted from Virginia at age nine, Willa Cather carried with her to the harsh Nebraska tablelands an already classically-developed consciousness and her memories of the Virginia countryside. Parley's history of the ancient world went with her, too, and surely became dearer to her as she read that "In the southern part of Greece, and among the islands, the climate is as mild as Virginia, and here the country abounds in all sorts of delicious fruits."[4] The genius of the land into which she had come must have seemed alien and inimical to a girl whose reality had been that of an almost

---

2. Samuel Griswold Goodrich, *Peter Parley's Universal History, on the Basis of Geography* (Boston: American Stationers' Co., 1838) I, viii.

3. Woodress, p. 23.

4. Goodrich, p. 188.

Edenic land where heroes triumphed and gods strode among men. In Nebraska, Willa Cather continued to learn at home, reading the English classics with her grandmothers, and she may also have learned to read Latin at this time.[5]

Life on the prairie soon took on epic dimensions for Cather, as she and her brothers explored the country whose red grass was the color of wine-stains, a description Cather would later use in *My Antonia*. In her dedicatory verse of *April Twilights*, Cather recalls in Homeric terms these childhood odysseys on her own wine-dark seas:

Let us pour our amber wine and drink it
To the memory of our vanished kingdom,
To our days of war and ocean venture,
Brave with brigandage and sack of cities;
To the Odysseys of summer mornings,
Starry wonder-tales of nights in April. [6]

Nor did the move into Red Cloud in September, 1884, put an end to Cather's love affair with the ancient world. Sleeping in a dormitory-like loft with her two oldest brothers, Cather often entertained them by repeating and sometimes embellishing stories which she had heard from childhood – stories of the Arabian Nights, of Greek and Roman mythology, of ancient heroes.

The family library also provided ample sources for reading on classical subjects. Among the Cather collection were a few translations of Latin authors, ranging from Caesar's *Commentaries* to satires by Juvenal and the letters of Pliny. Works by British writers, however, dominated the bookshelves, and Cather's perception of the ancient world was filtered through her reading of the Victorian and Romantic writers, who often drew heavily upon classical subjects. Among these were Tennyson, whose works appear in various editions in the Cather collection, including a copy of the complete works, endorsed in 1881 by Jennie B. Cather. Cather's childhood exposure to the English classics was extensive, ranging from the poetry of

5.   Edith Lewis, *Willa Cather Living: A Personal Record by Edith Lewis* (New York: Alfred A. Knopf, 1953), p. 14.

6.   Willa Cather, "Dedicatory," in *April Twilights (1903)*, introd. Bernice Slote, rev. ed. (1968; rpt. Lincoln: Univ. of Nebraska Press, 1976), p.3.

Thomas Campbell and Lord Byron, the novels of Charles Dickens and William Thackeray, to the essays of John Ruskin and Thomas Carlyle. Among American authors whose works were in the Cather family library were three of Willa's favorites – Poe, Hawthorne, and Emerson. Her penchant for the Gothicism of Poe, romanticism of Hawthorne, and transcendentalism of Emerson undoubtedly shaped her literary vision and appealed to her classical and romantic literary preferences.

What she could not find at home she eagerly searched out in the neighboring Wiener home (the Rosens of "Old Mrs. Harris"). The Wiener household offered an old world perspective, a sense of timelessness in which the historical past and myth became one. Here Cather absorbed a sense of European tradition, as did Vickie Templeton in the house that was "the nearest thing to an art gallery and museum" that Red Cloud could offer.[7] Willa Cather also began studying Latin and Greek with Mr. William Ducker, an Englishman whose passion for learning made him an unlikely prospect for success as a storekeeper in a small Nebraska town. With Ducker, Cather read portions of the *Iliad* and the *Aeneid*, the Odes of Anacreon and Ovid, although, as Mildred Bennett has pointed out, her interest in Latin was more "as a gateway to the classical world than as a study in itself."[8]

By 1888, Cather would record in a friend's album that the city she would most like to visit was Rome and that the inventor who did the greatest service toward the world's progress was Cadmus.[9] These answers may seem unusual for a fifteen-year-old girl living in a raw prairie town during an age which had already seen the invention of the dynamo, incandescent lighting, the telephone, and the phonograph. The influence of her classical training is clear: Rome was the seat of the eternal truths of human experience, and, as she had learned from Parley's *Universal History*, Cadmus was "one of the greatest benefactors of the Greeks, for he taught them the cultivation of the

---

7.   Willa Cather, "Old Mrs. Harris," in *Obscure Destinies* (1932; rpt. New York: Vintage Books, 1974), p. 103.

8.   Mildred R. Bennett, "The Childhood Worlds of Willa Cather," *Great Plains Quarterly*, 2 (Fall 1982), 208.

9.   Mildred R. Bennett, *The World of Willa Cather*, rev. ed. (Lincoln: Univ. of Nebraska Press, 1961), p.113.

vine, the manufacture of metals, and the use of the alphabet,"[10] the last surely being his claim to greatness for the teenaged Willa Cather.

In the Red Cloud schools Cather continued to study Latin, and by the time of her high school commencement, she had developed "a pure and classical literary taste," as she would later define it in a column for the *Nebraska State Journal*:

> As soon as a boy is old enough to read at all he is old enough to read the classics....The boy who is a confirmed devotee of the *Youth's Companion* and the child authors at ten will slight his Virgil and at twenty he will probably be reading Captain Charles King and Marie Corelli. Things were much better in the old days when a boy read only *Pilgrim's Progress* and *The Holy War* and Foxe's *Book of Martyrs* and was pounded through a dozen books of the *Aeneid*. He had the foundation then of a pure and classical literary taste.[11]

Her commencement oration, "Superstition vs. Investigation," was also studded with classical references, and her choice of studies at the University of Nebraska was predictable. Entering in the "second prep" for the study of elementary Greek as a prerequisite to the university program in "Literary, English, Philosophical" studies, Cather's interest was peaked and she subsequently studied the language for three years. She worked equally hard at her two years of Latin and found herself first in a class of fifty-three students.[12] The pedantic aspects of studying the ancient languages did not, however, appeal to her, and, instead, she found her excitement in the timeless tales the classical authors had to offer. Willa Cather was already embarking upon a journey in thought which would lead her to use classical images, and particularly those from myth, as links for joining her limited, provincial world to a greater and timeless one. She, like Carl Linstrum in *O Pioneers!*, must have believed that "there are only two or three human stories, and they go on repeating themselves as fiercely as if they had never happened before...."[13] How could one discover these truths in literature if all

10. Goodrich, p. 190.

11. Willa Cather, "The Passing Show," *Nebraska State Journal*, 12 April 1896, p. 13, in *The Kingdom of Art*, ed. Bernice Slote, p. 337.

12. Lewis, p. 30.

13. Willa Cather, *O Pioneers!* (Boston: Houghton Mifflin Co., 1913), p. 119.

12

one's time was used up conjugating verbs and learning declensions? Willa
Cather never became a scholar of Latin; the study was simply too meticulous
and time-consuming for her. In fact, errors in Latin phrases appear in
several of her works.[14]

But such mistakes do not indicate a disaffection for classical studies.
Even her living quarters in Lincoln had the appearance of a classical
scholar's study. She, like Jim Burden in *My Antonia*, decorated the walls with
a large map of Rome and a photograph of the Tragic Theater of Pompeii.
Her bookcases sported a copy of the *Odyssey*, Cicero's essays, and Ovid's
poetry, in addition to Thomas Seymour's translation of the first six books of
the *Iliad*. Her enthusiasm for classics surfaced in her coursework, as well.
In her remarkable freshman essay on Carlyle, for example, Cather drew
allusions from both Greek and Norse mythology. She compared Carlyle to a
true Orpheus, unlike the modern writers who strove only to satisfy the vulgar
public taste: "When Orpheus sings popular ballads upon the street corners,
he is a street singer, nothing more. The gates of hell do not open at his music
any more, nor do the damned forget their pain in its melody."[15]

In other college essays, Cather recalled the myth of Orpheus,
graphically describing his death at the hands of the Bacchae in her
"Shakespeare and Hamlet." The Orphic myth, which would serve as the
underlying structure for *The Song of the Lark*, already weighed heavily on her
mind, and the theme of the artist's struggle for perfection would be central to
her fiction. Cather's articles in the *Hesperian* and the *Journal* throughout her
college career also show her continuing interest in classical writers as well as
her growing tendency to use mythic allusions to highlight comments about
the current day. For example, her defense of football as a worthy sport places
the game on an epic scale: "A good football game is an epic, it rouses the
oldest part of us, the part that fought ages back down in the Troad with

---

14. Donald Sutherland, in his essay "Willa Cather: The Classic Voice" [*The Art of Willa
Cather*, ed. Bernice Slote and Virginia Faulkner (Lincoln: Univ. of Nebraska Press, 1974), pp.
156-157], cites the most obvious errors from three works: "Lupibus vivendi non lupus sum."
(*The Song of the Lark*); "Auspice, Maria!" (*Death Comes for the Archbishop*); "Pater noster qui
in coelum est." ("Peter").

15. Willa Cather, Untitled Essay, *Hesperian*, 1 March 1891, pp. 4-5, in *The Kingdom of
Art*, p. 424.

'Man-slaying Hector' and 'Swift-footed Achilles.'"[16] In a lighter vein, Cather uses the Herculean myth to define the modern artist's purpose as something other than muckraking: "An artist should have no moral purpose in mind other than just his art. His mission is not to clean the Augean stables; he had better join the Salvation Army if he wants to do that...."[17]

Although after a cursory reading one might accuse Cather of a youthful tendency to embellish her work with classical references, a closer examination of the total work of her campus years reveals her absorption of the classical spirit. For instance, in characterizing Sappho as the only great woman poet, Cather does not merely string together names from the Greek world. The poetic ease with which she comments on Sappho indicates a familiarity with mythic and literary personalities which would rival the naturalness of naming her own brothers and sisters: "She could not sing of Atrides, nor of Cadmus, nor of the labors of Hercules, for her lyre, like Anacreon's, responded only to a song of love."[18] For Cather, art was based on strong feelings, and such feelings for the classical world had been developing within her since childhood.

Cather's freshman enthusiasm for the classics had hardly diminished by her senior year. On February 16, 1894, when students presented part of Plautus' *Captivi* in Latin and part of *Antigone* and *Elektra* in Greek, Willa Cather appeared in a tableau as Elektra. In reviewing these performances for the *Nebraska State Journal*, Cather acknowledged the audience's reluctance to accept these dramas in their original text:

> One thing that the scenes from the Greek plays did bring out was the immense distance, not only of time, but of nature, or emotional habit, that divides us from the Greeks....[I]n tragedy ideals have changed. We cannot appreciate the Hellenic love for calm, for dignity, for sorrow that is majestically self-contained.[19]

16.   Willa Cather, "Waste-Basket Waifs. Football." *Hesperian*, 15 Nov. 1893, p. 9, in *The Kingdom of Art*, p. 212.

17.   Willa Cather, "Utterly Irrelevant," *Nebraska State Journal*, 23 Sept. 1894, p. 13, in *The Kingdom of Art*, p. 406.

18.   Willa Cather, "As You Like It," *Nebraska State Journal*, 13 Jan. 1895, p. 13, in *The Kingdom of Art*, p. 349.

19.   Willa Cather, "With Plays and Players," *Nebraska State Journal*, 25 Feb. 1894, p. 9, in *The Kingdom of Art*, pp. 220-221.

14

The unmistakable tone of regret which would color many of her major works, is apparent here. With an almost Vergilian sense of an earlier golden age, Willa Cather, even as a college student, recognized the loss of things of traditional value as times changed. For consolation she would turn again and again to what R. W. B. Lewis in *The American Adam* calls "the invulnerable world of myth, as an enduring model for the actual."[20]

The summer vacations of her college years Willa Cather spent in Red Cloud reading Vergil with her brother Roscoe, but, following her graduation in 1895, she saw little future in her hometown where artistic and intellectual stimulation was basically limited to the Sunday sermon, travelling opera companies, and the summer Chautauquas. Occasional columns for the *Journal* and *Courier* allowed Cather to keep attuned to the artistic world which had captured her imagination and had provided a forum for voicing her critical opinions. These early journalistic writings show Cather's skill at blending mythical allusions and allegorical language in her criticism. Cather seemed not only eager to use her learning to bolster her work but also anxious to establish an identity for herself and her contemporaries which would place them within what Thea Kronborg would call a "continuity of life that reached back into the old time."[21]

Those performers, artists, and literary figures who she most admired Cather described in classical terms, placing them in a tradition of excellence, a heritage of mythic proportions. For Cather, Sarah Bernhart's acting was "a sort of Bacchic orgy"; Christina Rossetti wrote "with the mystic, enraptured faith of a Cassandra"; and in pursuing his Muse, Poe was "blind to all else, like Anchises, who on the night he knew the love of Venus, was struck sightless, that he might never behold the face of mortal woman."[22] For figures like Swinburne who, like Homer, delighted "in his own thunder,"

20. R. W. B. Lewis, *The American Adam* (Chicago: The Univ. of Chicago Press, 1955), p. 103.

21. Willa Cather, *The Song of the Lark* (1915; rpt. Lincoln: Univ. of Nebraska Press, 1978), p. 304.

22. Willa Cather, "As You Like It," *Nebraska State Journal*, 16 June 1895, p. 12, in *The Kingdom of Art*, p. 119; "As You Like It," *Nebraska State Journal*, 13 Jan. 1895, p. 13, in *The Kingdom of Art*, p. 347; "The Passing Show," *Courier*, 12 Oct. 1895, pp. 6-7, in *The Kingdom of Art*, p. 386.

Cather reserved her highest praise, tinged with the humor which only a thorough-going classicist could muster: "He is intoxicated with melody and drunk with sound. He is like a bacchant singing himself hoarse and scourging himself with rods at the Eleusinian mysteries."[23] Yet, this girl with the meat ax, as Cather was sometimes called, could use mythic allusion to attack as well as to praise. In using exclamations like "Sacred lyre of Apollo! and has he come to this...,"[24] Willa Cather not only bemoaned the decay of the once famous Italo Campanini, but also decried the decline of artistic creation in her own day. Cather similarly criticized Julia Marlowe's newest addition of *Romola* to a "collection of unplayable plays": "Great arms of Juno, what a repertoire! If Miss Marlowe would only revive *The Jew of Malta* and Wycherley's *Love in a Wood* and a few miracle plays she would be perfectly consistent."[25]

The notes of cynicism in her newspaper pieces of 1895-1896 reveal that Willa Cather was already searching for a defense against the decay of civilization, a search which led her to incorporate myth into the whole of her writing and thought. She may have considered herself to be like Ruskin, to whom she wrote a tribute in May, 1896:

> For Ruskin is perhaps the last of the great worshippers of beauty, perhaps the last man for many years to come who will ever kneel at the altar of Artemis, who will ever hear the oracle of Apollo.... He belonged to the age of epics and Ionian columns, of marble and fine gold, not to this papier-mache civilization... last of the priests of Artemis, last of the mourners of art.[26]

When, therefore, she had the opportunity in the spring of 1896 to move to Pittsburgh and to taste life beyond the Nebraska prairies, Cather unhesitatingly seized the chance to observe first-hand the way of the world.

---

23. Willa Cather, "The Passing Show," *Courier*, 30 Nov. 1895, p. 6, in *The Kingdom of Art*, p. 350.

24. Willa Cather, "The Passing Show," *Courier*, 12 Jan. 1896, p. 9, in *The Kingdom of Art*, p. 165.

25. Willa Cather, "The Passing Show," *Courier*, 7 Sept. 1895, pp. 6-7, in *The Kingdom of Art*, p. 210.

26. Willa Cather, "The Passing Show," *Nebraska State Journal*, 17 May 1896, p. 13, in *The Kingdom of Art*, pp. 400, 403.

Throughout her college career Cather had written stories as well as newspaper columns, but, curiously, few of those stories make use of the classical references and mythical allusions that abound in her journalism. Of those stories published between May of 1892 and June of 1896, only two ("The Fear That Walks at Noonday" and "A Night at Greenway Court") have a single, direct reference to the Greek world that Cather so admired.[27] "A Tale of the White Pyramid," printed in the *Hesperian*, December 22, 1892, is unique among the Cather canon for its setting in ancient Egypt, but an underpinning of mythic images neither sustains nor augments the narrative. Cather was clearly experimenting with both form and content during this period. Settings range from seventeenth-century Virginia to late nineteenth-century San Francisco, and dialogues range from southern drawls to the fractured English of immigrants. What appears to have been important to Cather in this stage of her career was simply to write a good story. Apparently, applying to fiction the historical view she had used in non-fiction still eluded Cather, and, with it, that sense of identity as an artist which would not come to fruition until the publication of *O Pioneers!*.

The move to Pittsburgh in the summer of 1896, however, initiated the reappearance of classical images in Willa Cather's fiction, and she used classical allusions throughout her tenure at both the *Home Monthly* and the Pittsburgh *Daily Leader*. One might assume that her immersion into a world of educated and aesthetically attuned people, like composer Ethelbert Nevin, actress Lizzie Collier, and musician George Seibel, rekindled an interest in the Classics. The stories of her first years in Pittsburgh (1896-1900) are, however, generally unremarkable in style or content, many merely pieces which would suit the taste of the sentimental readers of the *Home Monthly*.

But, in the August 1896 issue of the magazine, Cather published "Tommy, the Unsentimental," a story that clearly upset the stereotype of the young girl as depicted in popular magazines at the turn of the century. The

---

27.   In "The Fear That Walks by Noonday," Cather refers to the madness gods sometimes bring on those they wish to destroy, and in "A Night at Greenway Court," she describes Mr. Courtney as dwelling at Lord Fairfax's estate "like the suitors in the halls of Penelope." [*Willa Cather's Collected Short Fiction 1892-1912*, ed. Virginia Faulkner, rev. ed. (Lincoln: Univ. of Nebraska Press, 1970), pp. 511 and 485.]

story is important for other reasons as well. In it Cather harkens back to a classical model for her hero and begins to develop a portrait of women conquerors who will reappear in her works as Alexandra Bergson and Antonia Shimerda. Tommy's "masculine" behavior – assertiveness, physical endurance, and determination – places her in the company of those female figures in Cather's later fiction who lack sentimentality, even toward the land, and evolve into earth goddesses. Tommy, who returns to Nebraska after a year in an eastern school, finds an invigorating power in the landscape:

> "It's all very fine down East there, and the hills are great, but one gets mighty homesick for this sky, the old intense blue of it, you know. Down there the skies are all pale and smoky. And this wind, this hateful, dear, old everlasting wind that comes down like the sweep of cavalry and is never tamed or broken, O Joe, I used to get hungry for this wind! I couldn't sleep in that lifeless stillness down there."[28]

Like an earth mother, her energy is sustained by the earth, and she, in turn, puts aside her love for the ineffectual Jay Ellington Harper and accepts her role as a product and lover of a potentially hostile landscape. Her relationship to Harper, although only a youthful infatuation, is not unlike Alexandra's attraction to Carl Linstrum or Antonia's affection for Jim Burden. In each case, the strong and capable female loves a less effectual man, much as the mother goddess enfolds mere mortals in her protective care.

Yet, in describing Tommy's masculinity, Cather establishes another means by which she would draw upon classical models for her heroes. Tommy embodies the male myth of rescuing the weak and executing justice, but she does so as a woman. Cather here dismisses the traditional female image of passivity and vulnerability and generates, instead, new forms of classical myth. With almost superhuman strength, Tommy pedals furiously through "the sickening, destroying heat" under a sun "like hot brass" (p. 477) and comes to Harper's rescue. Tommy is, perhaps, more truly Theodosia than Tommy. Her given name resounds with antique magnificence and, like Alexandra Bergson's, is the feminine form of the name of an aggressive

---

28.   Willa Cather, "Tommy, the Unsentimental," in *Willa Cather's Collected Short Fiction 1892-1912*, pp. 475-476. All further references to Cather's short stories are from this source and will be cited parenthetically in the text by page number.

conqueror. With the sure and swift justice of the Roman emperor Theodosius, Theodosia intimidates the frail Jessica, reprimands the Bohemian farmers, and swiftly puts to right the financial mess Harper has created. Although she rejects Jay Harper's groveling admiration and claims to be "only flesh and blood" (p. 479), Theodosia is the first of Cather's super-women. Her name, like Thea Kronborg's, harkens back to the *theoi* of Greek mythology. Indeed, Theodosia seems to be a Titanic offspring, not a goddess, but a primitive power beyond the control of human beings. Such a role in myth is associated with masculine figures like the dark gods of death or the perpetrators of cataclysmic disasters. Her final lament has a definite Olympian ring as she resigns herself to the frailty of men and to their undeniable attractiveness: "They are awful idiots, half of them, and never think of anything beyond their dinner. But O, how we do like 'em!" (p. 480). Such a lament is less colored by her femaleness than by her power; she is as a "god" disappointed in the weakness of "his" finest creation. In this early but well-wrought story, then, Willa Cather toyed with two mythic themes which would resurface throughout her life work: the struggle of the woman-goddess to maintain her position in an increasingly masculine-dominated world, and the translation of the male myth into female forms.

In September of the same year Cather released "The Count of Crow's Nest," a two-part story which foreshadowed her thematic concern with exploiters and despoilers of art and civilization. Again drawing upon mythic references, she develops a sympathetic portrait of the Count de Koch, exiled from his homeland and living in a Chicago boarding house, but retaining the dignity of a world devoted to honor rather than to materialism. The aging Count with his patrician ways considers himself a nearly extinct type of man, "a sort of survival of the unfit" (p. 457):

> "An old pagan back in Julian's time who still clung to a despoiled Olympus and a vain philosophy, dead as its own abstruse syllogisms, might have felt as I do when this new faith, throbbing with potentialities, was coming in. The life of my own father seems to be as far away as the lives of the ancient emperors. It is not a pleasant thing to be the last of one's kind." (p. 457)

The Count is for Cather another Ruskin, "the last of the priests of Artemis," clinging to ideals not only in art but also in life. His dislike for the contemporary music, which his daughter sings in order to make a living, and his distaste for modern literature, which is mere imitation of art, make the Count a citizen of Republican Rome, as yet untouched by imperial greed and corruption. For the Count, honor is all, and he jealously guards a handful of letters whose contents could ruin those to whom he once owed allegiance. The Count retains respect for rank and privilege, but his world no longer exists. The letters also sing the chorus of both Ares and Eros (p. 455). When his daughter Helena and her greedy boyfriend steal these documents and attempt to sell them for a sizable profit, the Count discovers the plot, recovers the letters, and comes to understand that Helena's values are not his own. This conflict between traditional and modern values underscores other stories of *The Troll Garden* (1905), as well.

Helena, however, is not the innocent barbarian who, with savage strength, rushes in to destroy the corrupted Roman world as Charles Kingsley described it in "The Roman and the Teuton," the origin of Cather's inscription for her collection of stories. Rather, Helena is a resident of a decadent Roman world, a Troll Garden. As Bernice Slote describes the conflict, Helena lives in a world of distorted values where "there may be goblin fruit to desire, and trolls to guard their riches."[29] The Count's letters are the fruit, the key to wealth and power in a new society, but in "The Count of Crow's Nest" the garden remains unmolested. Helena embodies the cold, grasping nature of Aphrodite. In appearance alone she is a vulgar seductress:

> As the Count was speaking, they heard a ripple of loud laughter on the stairs and a rustle of draperies in the hall, and a tall blonde woman, dressed in a tight-fitting tailor-made gown, a pair of long lavender gloves lying jauntily over her shoulder, entered and bowed graciously to the Count. (p. 457)

Like her classical namesake, Helena is driven by passion and, as her father claims, has never known what honor means. Helena is the prototype for Cather's adventuresses, and rather than serving as the barbarian/forest child poised "to crush the defiled altars of Aphrodite into dust," as Cather had

---

29.   Slote, *The Kingdom of Art*, p. 96.

written in 1895,[30] she is herself the defiler. Thus, in an early story Cather has planted the seeds for a theme concerning art and for another mythic image of woman which would blossom in her later fiction.

Not until April of 1897 does another story appear in which Cather's classical training underscores the work. In the slight and conventional story "A Resurrection," Margie Pierson is a stoical hero who has become "as completely lost to the world as the last nine books of Sappho, or as the Grecian marbles that were broken under the barbarians' battle axes" (p. 426). Having devoted her life to raising the cast-off child of Martin Dempster and his hedonistic lover Aimee, Margie endures her own disappointed hopes for a life with Martin until his unexpected return to Brownville at Easter time. Cather describes Martin as one of the worshipers of the River Gods whose fates are "some of the saddest fables of ancient myth" (p. 433). His "intimate sympathy with inanimate nature that is the base of all poetry" (p. 433) is not unlike Tom Outland's or Claude Wheeler's, but Cather allows Martin a new beginning rather than an early death. The story loses its realistic flavor as she resurrects Martin's love for Margie and lets them escape from the town that had become "a little Pompeii buried in bonded indebtedness" (p. 430).

Perhaps the false note of "A Resurrection" stems from Margie's failure to declare and maintain her independence apart from Martin. She does not follow in the footsteps of Tommy, the Unsentimental, but, though serving as Martin's moral savior, she succumbs to the passion he arouses in her:

> She felt as though some great force had been locked within her, great and terrible enough to rend her asunder, as when a brake snaps or a band slips and some ponderous machine grinds itself to pieces. It is not an easy thing, after a woman has shut the great natural hope out of her life, to open the flood gates and let the riotous, aching current come throbbing again through the shrunken channels, waking a thousand undreamed-of possibilities of pleasure and pain. (p. 438)

Herein lies the potential tragedy of the tale. In becoming the unwilling victim of her own sexuality, Margie fails to achieve the translation of male mythic strength into female assertiveness. The story is disquieting to readers who

---

30.   Willa Cather, "The Passing Show," *Courier*, 2 Nov. 1895, p. 6, in *The Kingdom of Art*, p. 232.

expect more from Cather's central characters, and Cather herself must have been disgruntled to leave Margie as one of those "women who were made to rule, but who are doomed to serve" (p. 426).

Yet, in spite of the story's structural flaws, "A Resurrection" adds, by contrast, to the development of Cather's later heroes, like Alexandra Bergson, Antonia Shimerda, and Thea Kronborg, who, forgotten by or disappointed in love, maintain an epic stature and nobility which make them more than human and mythic in dimension.

In "The Way of the World" (1898), a fictional account of her own childhood games, Cather again utilizes mythic references to enhance her tale, references whose grandiose nature emphasizes the "tragedy" of events as the boys of Speckleville see them. More importantly, though, Cather again wrestled with the theme which would be the basis of the Troll Garden stories and with the role of the woman in a male-dominated society. The entrance of Mary Eliza into the "boys only" society of Speckle Burnham's packing-box town is not, however, a simple account of Eve as temptress in a child's Edenic garden. Although Cather foresees that Speckle's invitation to Mary Eliza to set up business in Speckleville is likely to end with the same "disastrous results" as the Romans' invitation to the Sabine women (p. 398), such insight she denies to her young narrator. With childish jealousy and resentment, Speckle blames the fall of his play world on the treacherous Mary Eliza, who then suggests that he and his friends patronize her new town: "It was as though Coriolanus, when he deserted Rome for the camp of the Volscians, had asked the Conscript Fathers to call on him and bring their families!" (p. 403). Cather is hardly aghast at the turn of events, as is Speckle Burnham, and seems to find amusing both Mary Eliza's audacity and her triumph. Upon reading the story, one is reminded that Cather had once been elected mayor of a similar packing-box town in her own yard.

But, Cather is not content to let the narrator perpetuate the myth of woman as despoiler of the Edenic garden and nemesis to man. The innocent residents of Speckleville become trolls by choice, eagerly devouring Mary Eliza's cream puffs, trading pins for her colorful neckties and hats, and admiring her blue tights and blonde locks. Cather herself had by 1898 observed enough of the way of the world to reject the account of Eve as temptress and Adam as victim. As she would demonstrate in works like *Alexander's Bridge* and *A Lost Lady*, the suffering in human relationships is a product of self-seduction as well. Niel Herbert is enchanted by his own image of Marian Forrester, and Bartley Alexander tempts himself in returning to Hilda Burgoyne. Just so did Speckle Burnham have "really no objection to granting Mary Eliza naturalization papers and full rights of citizenship" (p. 398), and he actually preferred her "to any boy on the street" (p. 397). His inability to deal with the fall of his petty empire naturally results in a feeling of persecution and desolation. He can do little more than sit down in the deserted town "as Caius Marius once sat among the ruins of Carthage" (p. 404). Carthage, too, had been a woman's city, but its ruin resulted from the faithlessness of a man, not a woman. By interchanging gender roles in the story of Speckleville, Cather does not diminish the stature of woman but elevates it, equating Mary Eliza's ingenuity and even her treachery with the masculine traits of epic heroes. In the guise of children's play, then, Cather embarks upon her exploration of the mythic temptress figure as it has arisen from the classical models of Circe, Medea, and the Sirens. Like their ancient counterparts, Cather's temptresses are enchanting but are often sympathetically portrayed as not alone responsible for the tragic results of the enchantments they weave.

After a virtual stoppage in her creative work during her busy years with the Pittsburgh *Daily Leader* (1897-1900), Willa Cather began to gain success at selling her short stories. Encouraged by the publication of six stories between April and July of 1900, Cather apparently decided to withdraw from her journalism career and to pursue some other employment that might allow greater time for writing fiction. Among these six stories was one remarkable for its power of setting and characterization. "Eric Hermannson's Soul" anticipates what would be Cather's greatest subject, the struggle of the sensitive and yearning individual entrapped by a powerful and unyielding environment. In this story, more than in any other work of her early period, Cather comes to grips with this problem and again turns to classical myth to develop her ideas. David Stouck suggests that this is the first of Cather's stories to create and sustain the epic feeling: "The two central figures in this story are both larger than life – the man for his vitality and primitive strength, the woman for her beauty and sophisticated enterprise."[31] Indeed, Cather encourages an epic interpretation by referring to Eric as a young Siegfried and by interrupting her narrative with exhortations of grandiose proportions: "...but ah! across what leagues of land and sea, by what improbable chances, do the unrelenting gods bring to us our fate!"(p. 362).

In addition, Cather again creates, in the character of Lena Hanson, a woman who recalls both Helen of Troy and the mythic female principle. Lena, "whose name was a reproach through all the Divide country"(p. 360), dresses in a pink wrapper and silk stockings, keeps her hands white and soft, and sings love songs to Eric. Her allure is undeniably sexual, placing her among the devotees of Aphrodite. "Lena," although a common name among Norse immigrants, is the diminutive form of "Helena" and seems to have been a favorite name for Cather to assign to similar figures in her works (Lena Yensen in "On the Divide" and Lena Lingard in *My Antonia*). As a Latinist, however, Willa Cather may well have been aware of the original meaning of the word "lena," a procuress or female pander. Lena Hanson is certainly Eric's temptation to moral turpitude, and the pointedly symbolic scene of Eric seeing a rattlesnake on Lena's doorstep has thematic implications. Cather makes clear Eric's revulsion at the idea of a fallen Edenic garden as well as his rejection of the classical earth mother figure, who is associated with serpent worship and procreation.

Eric's conversion to the Free Gospellers' strict denial of physical gratification is soon sorely tested by the arrival of the elegant eastern lady, Margaret Elliot. Again, Cather utilizes the barbarian-Roman motif; the primitive passions of Eric are aroused as are his artistic yearnings. He is one of the forest children who desire entry to the troll garden, wherein lie all the forbidden fruits of learning, beauty, and culture. He stands enchanted before Margaret's beauty, thinking her to be, at once, both goddess and woman:

> ...in [her beauty's] presence he felt as the Goths before the white marbles in the Roman Capitol, not knowing whether they were men or gods. At times he felt like uncovering his

---

31.   David Stouck, *Willa Cather's Imagination* (Lincoln: Univ. of Nebraska Press, 1975), p. 9.

head before it, again the fury seized him to break and despoil, to find the clay in this spirit thing and stamp upon it. (p. 370)

To assume that Eric's reawakening is the central point of this story would be to ignore the emphasis Cather places on Margaret's growing self-realization. Margaret, a product of an artificial culture which creates marble-like beauty and its accompanying coldness and remoteness, finds that she is not goddess but woman. Her discovery of a submerged self and uncontrollable desires is Cather's central focus. Margaret's suppressed animal passion is aroused by the stampede of the wild horses, and she soon begins to compare the refined and artificial attentions of her fiance to Eric's unrestrained and natural passion. Cather clarifies the distinction by referring to two paintings, one by Puvis de Chavannes and the other by Constant. Whereas Margaret's fiance prefers the de Chavannes in which a "pale dream-maiden sits by a pale dream-cow and a stream of anemic water flows at her feet," Margaret herself admires the Constant "in all its florid splendor" (p. 373). Constant, one of the school of Orientalist painters in the late nineteenth century, was well-known for his Moroccan scenes, bathed in light and color and sometimes depicting violence.[32] The painting which Margaret so admires is "dominated by a glowing sensuosity"; a female figure draped in "barbaric pearl and gold" is profiled against the "white, gleaming line of African coast" (p. 373). Although this image of primitive emotion stirs memories of Margaret for her fiance, he admits that the painting irritates him. Yet, the painting, like the wild horses and Eric's natural responses, arouses an unfathomable and fearful desire in Margaret: "Again she felt herself pursued by some over-whelming longing, some desperate necessity for herself, like the out-stretching of helpless, unseen arms in the darkness, and the air seemed heavy with sighs of yearning" (p. 374). Like Margie Pierson in "A Resurrection," Margaret grapples with desire she does not fully understand, a problem which will confront many of Cather's later characters.

Margaret also anticipates the moon goddess figures in Cather's fiction, for in Part III of the story, Margaret, who like Artemis is associated with pearl and gold, experiences "love's self" (p. 378) high on the windmill

---

[32]   Donald A. Rosenthal, *Orientalism: The Near East in French Painting 1800-1880* (Rochester, NY: Memorial Art Gallery of the Univ. of Rochester, 1982), p. 86.

platform under the moon's sanctioning light. The atmosphere of an ancient religious ritual dominates the scene. Faint sounds of music drift up from below, and the wind brings "the heavy odors of the cornfields," which Eric says must be "like the flowers that grow in paradise" (p. 371). The "pale, white light, as of a universal dawn" (p. 376), recalls Artemis' original role as mother of the Universe and a seducer of men. The classical scene is enhanced by Cather's description of Eric as a hero of old, a spear-bearing Doryphorus. He is "a giant barbarian" (p. 377), caught up in the Dionysian celebration of life which has made even the old men at the dance stamp the floor "with the vigor of old Silenus" (p. 374). The magic spell which Margaret casts over Eric likewise alleviates his suffering. Margaret, therefore, fulfills two of her Artemisian roles, one as the magical Selene and the other as the healing sister of Apollo. But, Margaret, too, is caught up in the spell she casts. Her kiss in this instance awakens herself as well as her beautiful Endymion. The fear she feels is a fear of succumbing to the passion she denies, and, true to her role as a maiden divinity who never falls victim to love, she leaves "All that she was to know of love... upon his lips" (p. 378).

In "Eric Hermannson's Soul," then, Cather introduces an epic scale to her Nebraskan setting through the use of subtle mythic references. Not only does she support her theme of aesthetic yearning through classical images of the barbarian attack on Rome, but she also supports her subject of struggling human emotions through references to Artemis, a goddess who refused to allow sexual passion to rule her existence. Both of these concepts would appear throughout Cather's fiction, and, as this early work testifies, she would continue to support her work with references to the mythos of the ancient world which she knew so well.

CHAPTER III
VANISHING ARCADIA, VANISHING GODS: THE EARLY
STORIES AND *APRIL TWILIGHTS*

The year 1900 was a turning point in Willa Cather's career as she gradually weaned herself from the security of a well-paying position on the Pittsburgh *Daily Leader* and redirected her efforts toward writing fiction. During this year she wrote at least two dozen items for the *Library*, a periodical designed to encourage literary talent. The periodical, however, published only twenty-six issues and, after a lengthy summer visit to the West, Willa Cather returned to Pittsburgh to begin free-lance work. Still not confident of her ability to earn a living in this way, Cather also decided to apply for a teaching position in Pittsburgh. After spending the winter of 1900-1901 in Washington, D.C., as a free-lance journalist and translator--an experience she found neither very remunerative nor enjoyable--she returned to Pittsburgh in March, began teaching at Central High School, and moved into the home of Judge McClung. Cather, who undoubtedly viewed herself much like the young journalist of *My Mortal Enemy*, hoped that the fewer demands of teaching would allow her time to write and that the quiet of the McClung home would provide better conditions for thought.

Indeed, during the "dry spell" of her last years on the *Leader*, Cather had produced little work of notable quality. Her most inspired writings evolved from visits to Nebraska or from anticipation of such visits, and two-thirds of her stories written between March and August of 1900 have prairie settings. While only two of the eight poems published in the same period

("Broncho Billy's Valedictory" and "Are You Sleeping, Little Brother?") make clear references to a western setting, all of these poems evoke a sense of loss and longing. These works, though, reveal a loss on yet another plane. Classical allusions and mythic images, which had underscored much of Cather's early journalistic work, are missing here. Only "Eric Hermannson's Soul" and the verse to her brother Jack— "Are You Sleeping, Little Brother?"— include references similar to those which had peppered her work since her campus years. Could this be evidence that Willa Cather had outgrown what L. V. Jacks believes was her "youthful inclination to parade her learning"?[1] Such an explanation is not satisfactory, for Cather's interest in the Classics did not diminish and her use of classical references was far from superficial. Cather had not abandoned this mode of developing her ideas; she had only submerged it while doing her newspaper work, work which apparently gave her little pleasure. In fact, within a year of abandoning journalism as her sole means of support, Cather again began to make prolific use of mythic allusions in her writing, a fact which might be accounted for as much by her association with the McClungs and their circle of friends as by her new career of teaching Latin and English.

Teaching Latin at Central High School was not as simple for Willa Cather as she had anticipated, for she found her language skills rusty. She eagerly accepted a position in the English Department for the fall term, yet it was not a dislike of the subject which led Cather to this move. E. K. Brown notes that, when asked in the 1930's why she had taught Latin as well as English, "she appreciated with a shock that her inquirer could not believe that it was because she liked Latin—the language and the literature."[2] As a beginning teacher, though, "brushing up" on Latin proved to be hard work and time-consuming. Cather later noted in *My Mortal Enemy* that teaching can be a cul-de-sac in which "'Generous young people use themselves all up....'"[3] Cather had no intention of using herself up, and, with the help of a

1. L. V. Jacks, "The Classics and Willa Cather," *Prairie Schooner*, 35 (1961), p 290.

2. E. K. Brown, *Willa Cather: A Critical Biography* (1953; rpt. New York: Avon Books, 1980), 221.

3. Willa Cather, *My Mortal Enemy* (1926; rpt. New York: Vintage Books, n.d.), p. 64.

theme reader, she found teaching quite satisfying. The students generally responded favorably to Cather, although she rarely gave a grade higher than 85 on a theme. Phyllis Martin Hutchinson, a student in Cather's class, pointed out that Cather's effectiveness as a teacher of English was enhanced by her classical background:

> She was steeped in the classics, and her knowledge of Latin was always evident in class. Invariably she tried to show us how to derive the meaning of English words from their Latin roots.... She always made us look up references to mythology, which helped us in our ancient history course.[4]

The "classics" in which Cather was steeped were not limited to the ancient authors, however. In her classroom Cather attempted to instill "a discriminating literary taste," and, as late as 1936, she argued that such a taste could not be acquired by teaching contemporary literature. Rather, students must have a "thorough knowledge of the great English authors and, when possible, the great Latin writers...."[5] But, what were the "classics" of English? In 1939, when corresponding with Henry Canby, Editor of the College English Association *News Letter*, Cather wrote that "No book can be called a 'classic' until it is a hundred years old, surely." Classics were not specialized works, like those of Sir Thomas Browne or De Quincy, she contended, but were "great books that still influence the life and thought and standards of English speaking peoples."[6] Her subsequent list of classic authors reads much like a sampling from a traditional course in British literature – Shakespeare, Milton, Fielding, Austen, Thackeray, George Eliot, Meredith, and Hardy. Noticeably missing from this late list are many of the poets, Victorian and Romantic, whom she had read and admired since childhood and her days at the University of Nebraska. Yet, her classes did read Tennyson's *Idylls of the King* and surely were exposed to works like Keats's "Ode on a Grecian Urn,"

4.   Phyllis Martin Hutchinson, "Reminiscences of Willa Cather as a Teacher," *Bulletin of the New York Public Library*, 60 (June 1956), 265.

5.   James Woodress, *Willa Cather: A Literary Life* (Lincoln: Univ. of Nebraska Press, 1987), p. 467.

6.   Willa Cather, *News Letter of the CEA*, Dec. 1939, rpt. in *Willa Cather in Person*, ed. L. Brent Bohlke (Lincoln: Univ. of Nebraska Press, 1986), p. 191.

which Cather cited as true art and able to satisfy aesthetic longings.[7] For Cather, exploration of fundamental human truths did not cease with the passing of the Graeco-Roman world. The classics of English literature examined these truths, too, truths which Cather knew "from experience" could not be taught "as Latin can be taught" but could, nonetheless, greatly influence young people.[8]

Cather not only drew upon these classics in her classroom but was also cognizant of her literary predecessors in her own writing. Her work, from even the earliest stories, is colored by a filtering of ideas through a western tradition, and, especially in her incorporation of myth, the influence of intermediary writers must be considered. As Cather continued throughout five years of teaching to expose students to the classics, both ancient and English, she also made greater use of this learning. Her indulgence in classical allusions was not, however, mere embellishment. Classical texts, and myth particularly, provided a shape and meaning to her work at this time as she expanded upon these themes she had touched in her earliest writings.

"Jack-a-Boy," a story packed with classical references, was published in the *Saturday Evening Post* even as Cather began her teaching career. "Jack-a-Boy" is a delicately wrought tale of a sprite-like child whose beauty and love of life reawaken the sensibilities of the lonely and forgotten residents of Windsor Terrace. Jack-a-Boy is certainly a portrait of Jack, Willa Cather's youngest brother, who served as the model for Thor in *The Song of the Lark* and provided the inspiration for her poems "My Little Boy," "Thine Eyes So Blue and Tender," and "Are You Sleeping, Little Brother?" The first two of these, published in 1896, shortly after Cather's move to Pittsburgh, indicated her homesickness and loneliness for the little brother whose eyes opened wide at her stories of high romance. Yet, in both poems Jack assumes a role as spiritual redeemer, a dimension more mythic than real:

---

7. Arthur G.Staples, "Willa Catha [sic] -- Novelist," rpt. in *Willa Cather in Person*, p. 162.
8. Cather, *News Letter of the CEA*, in *Willa Cather in Person*, p. 191.

And when all the world went wrong with me,
   And Nobody seemed to care,
I'd feel his dear little hand on my knee--
   And my little boy was there!
                ("My Little Boy")

Every sick soul has its comfort,
   That can make its weakness strong,
Or the cords would snap asunder
   Sometime, when the strain is long.

Every soul that doubts and wanders,
   Has its priest who intercedes,
Has its saint who brings God nearer,
   Mightier than all the creeds.
        ("Thine Eyes So Blue and Tender")[9]

The Jack-a-Boy of her story embodies these same traits but is described in classical terms. By 1900, Jack Cather had moved into Willa Cather's dormer room in the house on Cedar Street. Associated with that room were her memories of "high desire," her dreams "Of the tread of Roman legions/And the purple pride of Tyre" (*AT*, p. 73). As a result, when writing "Jack-a-Boy" in 1901, Cather created an image of the child as "one of the immortal boys from Parnassus" and "Cupid out of Psyche's arms,"[10] both natural consequences of her imagining young Jack Cather snug in her room beneath the eaves.

The finished story "Jack-a-Boy," however, proves to be more than a tribute to Jack and a fond remembrance of her own childhood. The story exudes a sense of loss, which is expressed in strictly classical terms. Perhaps Cather pictured herself at this time much like the professor of her story who lived only for Sanskrit roots and Greek meters. In struggling to recover her skill as a Latin grammarian, Cather may have felt she was losing an appreciation for the beauty of the antique world and its literature. Like the

---

9.   Willa Cather, *April Twilights (1903)* (1968; rpt. Lincoln: Univ. of Nebraska Press, 1976), pp. 64 and 66. [All subsequent references to Cather's poetry in this collection will be cited parenthetically in the text by abbreviated title (*AT*) and page number.]

10.   Willa Cather, "Jack-a-Boy," in *Willa Cather's Collected Short Fiction 1892-1912*, ed. Virginia Faulkner and Mildred R. Bennett (Lincoln: Univ. of Nebraska Press, 1970), p. 320. [All further references to Cather's short stories are from this source and will be cited in the text by page number only.]

Professor, she would have to learn to see again the beauty of Homer, not through illustrations as did Jack-a-Boy, but through teaching the old stories to her students. Jack-a-Boy becomes, therefore, much more than a portrait of her little brother. He possesses a Pan-like vitality which leads others to an appreciation of a world far removed from the meadows of Arcady.

Jack-a-Boy, with his precocious ways and marblesque beauty, becomes a favorite of the lonely and unsuccessful residents of his apartment house. The simple pleasure he finds in beautiful things, his fascination with the glories and heroes of ancient days, and his fondness for music endear him to the aging Professor, the spinster in Number 326, and even the Woman Nobody Called On. But Cather is doing much more than creating a story about a handsome lad whose death by scarlet fever brings together a group of lost persons in their rediscovery of life's beauty. Jack-a-Boy is one of Cather's first characters to embody the high ideals of pure and classical art, the ideals which the forest children think lie beyond their reach in the troll garden. At least one critic has pointed out Cather's reliance on the myth of Narcissus in making Jack-a-Boy the personification of art.[11] Jack-a-Boy is a Narcissus, but not in the egocentric role of the youth who spurned Echo. Rather, he is the youth who despised all that was ugly and was captivated by the reflection of beauty.

In delivering his May baskets in a pagan celebration of the rites of spring, Jack-a-Boy trips about like a faun from door to door under the sanctioning light of the moon goddess:

> There was just a pallid ghost of a new moon in the sky, a faint silver crescent curve, like Artemis' bow, with a shred of gauzy cloud on its horn.... Below, in the dusky street, I heard every little while the ring of a doorbell and the hurry of swift little feet down the steps and up the pavement, and sometimes a clear, silvery little peal of laughter, suddenly muffled. (p. 317)

Like the simple woodland creatures devoted to and protected by Artemis, Jack-a-Boy detested the paper flowers he had to use in his baskets. The Professor remarks, "ugly things hurt him;" he was "all gossamer and phantasy

---

11.   Richard Giannone in *Music in Willa Cather's Fiction* suggests that psychologically, Jack-a-Boy "has the personality of Narcissus" and that "The lad reflects the secret self. To the Professor he is antiquity incarnate...." (Lincoln: Univ. of Nebraska Press, 1968), p. 30.

and melody" (pp. 317-318). Artemis, protector of youth and lover of the chaste, enfolds in her protective care this boy whose idea of art is pure, simple, and natural. Unaffected by the loss of imaginative sympathy in the modern world and untouched by the drabness of daily existence, Jack-a-Boy is "not a human child, but one of the immortal children of Greek fable made flesh for a little while" (p. 318). He embodies the highest ideals of art and of the art of living, traits which Cather found in the classical worlds of Greece and Rome.

Jack-a-Boy exhibits not only an appreciation of unadulterated beauty, as protected by Artemis, but also an admiration of heroic action. His preference for the story of Theseus in the Centaur's cave rather than "Jack the Giant Killer" seems to the Professor proof that "he simply had that divinity in him, that holiness of beauty which the hardest and basest of us most love when we see it" (p. 312). For Cather, too, he represents that heroic ancient world where wrongs were avenged without loss of human compassion and tenderness. Although Jack-a-Boy spends hours admiring Flaxman's illustrations to Homer and never tires of hearing the story of Achilles' wrath, the touching picture of Hector taking his leave of Andromache is what he likes best of all. The kindness and magnanimity of the great hero touch the boy deeply and he says, "'...it was so kind of Hector to take off his gleaming helmet not to frighten his little boy'" (p. 321). This boy, who asks for the terrible story of the white horses of Rhesus with all its accompanying violence, can also describe the stars peeping into his crib as "the eyes of Golden Helen" (p. 321). This is the "Greek spirit" which Cather hopes lies within each person's secret self, a coupling of heroic ideals and humanness.

Yet, Cather recognizes that such beauty of spirit cannot continue to thrive in a world where the treasures of the troll garden have become tarnished. The "charming little airs" Jack-a-Boy plays for himself are "minor melodies, indefinitely sad" (p. 314). Even his heroic defense of a little girl against the cruel boy who has burst her balloon is "the frenzied, impotent revolt of a high and delicate nature against brutality and coarseness and baseness..." (p. 315). The spirit of Jack-a-Boy slowly withers under a cruel summer sun and the financial worries of his family. Protected by the goddess of purity in art, Jack-a-Boy receives the greatest blessing of the ancients--to die young. Cather describes his death in mythic terms with a handmaiden of Artemis ushering the child to an existence sympathetic to his nature: "Perhaps some wood nymph, tall and fair, came in and laid her cool fingers on his brow and bore him off with the happy children of Pan" (p. 320). Cather does not suggest, however, that the disappearance of such beauty from the earth is any more permanent in Jack-a-Boy's case than it was in the decline of the ancient civilizations. For those receptive to it, like the residents of Windsor Terrace, beauty exists, even if revealed only occasionally. Cather would return to this theme of the demise of ideal beauty in her poems written within the two years following the publication of "Jack-a-Boy" and collected in the volume titled *April Twilights*.

The concluding paragraphs of "Jack-a-Boy" illustrate Cather's attempt to show that the revelation of beauty serves as a redemption for all people whose lives the child had touched. A comparison of Jack-a-Boy to the Christian savior is obvious. The child is now "the greatest Revealer" (p. 322), the one for whom fishermen left their nets and whose feet the sinful woman wiped with her hair. Although the Christian allusions may seem incongruous and jarring in a story packed with classical references, Cather's primary concern in "Jack-a-Boy" has not changed. What she mourns is the fading of the classical ideals, the loss of the civilizing elements in society.

The Christian emphasis of the story's close is best understood when examined in light of Cather's sense of "the practical." Cather was still testing her talents as a writer to determine if she could earn her way on this skill alone. The publication record of "Jack-a-Boy" shows that the story was first printed on March 30, 1901, in *The Saturday Evening Post*, and the cover boldly reads "The Easter Number." Cather had spent enough time as a journalist to know how to sell a story. The resurrected spirits of the residents of Windsor Terrace make less tragic the sacrifice of Jack-a-Boy. With her ending, Cather met the needs of the publishers and satisfied the reading public. Although, as she gained self-confidence as a writer, Cather would cease manipulating her material for these reasons, she would continue to portray human problems in mythic terms.

In 1901, Cather published only one other story, "El Dorado: A Kansas Recessional," and this tale showed neither the artistry nor integrated use of classical myth which she had utilized in writing "Jack-a-Boy." Still clearly influenced by her teaching of Latin and its accompanying classical studies, Cather used mythic references to produce a story which has been variously described as "flat" and "unimpressive" or mere "hack work."[12] Indeed her efforts to develop a tale of "supreme irony" (p. 309) are flawed, and "El Dorado" deteriorates into predictable romance.

Such criticisms of the plot structure are warranted, but "El Dorado: A Kansas Recessional" does offer further insight into Cather's widening use of myth. The story unfolds in a western setting where Colonel Josiah Bywaters lives alone in the ghost town of El Dorado. He, like many others from Virginia and the East, had been duped by the Gump family, who had encouraged investment in a town which was to become "the Queen City of the Plains, the Metropolis of Western Kansas, the coming Commercial Center of the West" (p. 294). Influenced by the suave manners of the least despicable of the Gumps, Apollo Gump, Josiah invests his life's savings in a town whose land proves worthless and which the railroad bypasses. Of all the victims of this scam, only Josiah achieves just compensation when, long after the Gump family has fled with the investors' monies, Apollo returns to retrieve some personal mementos he has buried near the town. Apollo dies of rattlesnake bite while unearthing his treasure, and, after burying the swindler, Col. Bywaters takes the ten thousand dollars in bank notes found in Apollo's belt and turns his back on El Dorado.

Although the plot offers little different from the many "right always triumphs" stories popular in magazines of the day, Cather's choice of characters indicates her experimentation with the interweaving of Biblical and classical allusions. The Gump family name echoes "chump," which may describe the Gumps' opinion of those they entrap, but more significantly the first names of the Gumps show Cather's manipulation of her story. The oldest brother Isaiah is the greatest rascal and serves as minister in El Dorado. Cather uses his sermon on the rebuilding of Jerusalem as only one element of irony in the story. Unlike the Biblical prophet who stressed

---

12. David Stouck, *Willa Cather's Imagination* (Lincoln: Univ. of Nebraska Press, 1975), p. 75; Robert Edson Lee, *From West to East: Studies in the Literature of the American West* (Urbana: Univ. of Illinois Press, 1966), p. 125.

avoidance of alliances with earthly powers, Isaiah Gump is the embodiment of such powers. His brother Hezekiah, as president of the El Dorado Board of Trade, provides a parallel to the Biblical king under whom Isaiah's prophecies were treated with greater respect. But, rather than tearing down the temples of corruption as his ancient counterpart had done, Hezekiah Gump, the hardware merchant, provides the very means of building a city based on the worship of Mammon. Their brother Ezekiel, as namesake of the prophet, might be expected to offer a vision of a new Zion, where the fertility of the land will usher in a new age and even the trees can be used for healing (Ezek. 40:2, 36:29-30, 47:12). As real estate agent for El Dorado, Ezekiel does precisely this. Beside the waters of Babylon, the prophet Ezekiel sang of a new Zion; beside the waters of the sluggish and turbid Solomon River, Ezekiel Gump superintends the waterworks. The wisdom of Solomon eludes the immigrants to El Dorado; only nature itself, like the river, knows the truth of the land's unproductiveness:

> Nature always dispenses with superfluous appendages; and what use had Solomon Valley corn for tassels? Ears were only a tradition there, fabulous fruits like the golden apples of the Hesperides; and many a brawny Hercules had died in his own sweat trying to obtain them. (p. 294)

Even in naming Josiah Bywaters, Cather drew upon a Biblical name to serve her purpose. Just as the workmen devoted their energy and money to adorning the temple under the leadership of Josiah, king of Judah (II Kin. 22:4-7), so did the residents of El Dorado follow the lead of Josiah Bywaters, heavily investing in the plans he so innocently endorsed. Just as King Josiah was assured that God's threatened calamity would not descend upon Judah in his life-time (II Kin. 22:20), so Josiah Bywaters wonders "whether some day the whole grand delusion would not pass away...as a bubble bursts, as a dream that is done" (p. 303).

Cather extends her references from the ancient world even further in giving to the town architect, the would-be builder of the Academy of Arts and Sciences, the dubious name of Aristotle Gump. His sister is Venus Gump, dressmaker and milliner, a modern goddess of beauty who preys on the vanity of women displaced from the cultural refinements of their native regions. Cather's disgust with people like the Gumps is clear, and she

satirically uses their names to show the perversion of once admirable roles--
prophets, kings, educators, and even goddesses.

Central to the story is, of course, Apollo Gump. He harbors several
traits of the Greek god, appearing "finer and franker," with a kinder heart
than his relatives (p. 301). He wins over Josiah with his easy manner, refined
appearance, and "good-natured smile" (p. 296). Like the mythic Apollo, he
exudes radiance, is a model of manly beauty, and is a founder of cities.
Apollo Gump impresses Josiah by showing off his "blooded horses,"
reminiscent of those fiery steeds which drew the chariot of the sun. Apollo's
rooms are cluttered with mementos from his past, everything from boxing
gloves to pictures of theatrical celebrities. Cather may be consciously
fashioning her details here to reflect the god's association with the Pythian
games, as well as his patronage of the arts, particularly poetry and music, the
essentials of the theater. Also, like the pagan deity, Apollo has proved
unlucky in love, having made what his brothers call an "unfortunate
marriage," and he is still obsessed with the memory of this woman.

But in the closing scenes of the story Cather seems to enjoy fully the
possibilities which the naming of her characters allows. The sentimental
reader may applaud as Apollo dies in agony, alone on the rain-drenched
banks of the Solomon River. Cather, however, tempers the vengeful mood by
the unearthing of the tin-encased box, which contains only a woman's picture,
clothing, and the garments for a baby. Apollo, whose Greek name refers only
to the destructive power of the noonday sun, possesses some of the traits of
Phoebus, the loving and life-giving god. The means of his death, too, harkens
back to myth, to the beginnings of Apollo's power. Whereas the god Apollo
slew the Python at Delphi, an offense against nature and against Gaea
(Mother Earth), Apollo Gump is slain by the serpent. He is an offense
against mankind, and empathetic Nature exacts its punishment. Just as
Apollo buried the Python and established the Pythian games as a propitiation
for Gaea, Josiah Bywaters buries Apollo Gump in a conciliatory gesture:

> "Apollo, I like you mighty well. It cut me to the heart when
> you turned rascal – and you were a damned rascal. But I'll
> give you a decent burial, because you loved somebody once....
> The Lord knows you better than I do; there have been worse
> men who have lived and died Christians." (p. 310)

By using the inversion of the myth and by fashioning a liar out of the god of truth, Cather achieves the irony she hoped for in writing "El Dorado." Her final words hammer home her intent:

> In the spring the sunflowers grew tall and fair over every street and house site; and they grew just as fair over the mound beside the oak tree on the bluff.... The river creeps lazily through the mud... Year by year it buries itself deeper in the black mud, and burrows among the rotting roots of the dead willows, wondering why a river should ever have been put there at all. (p. 310)

The wary reader notes the appropriateness of the sunflower above Apollo Gump's grave. The water-nymph Clytie, rooted to the ground while admiring Apollo, became a sunflower, an outward symbol of Apollo's unresponsiveness to those who adored him. In Cather's story, the sunflower represents Nature's unconcern: "For if Nature forgets, she also forgives. She at least holds no grudge..." (p. 310).

In "El Dorado: A Kansas Recessional," Willa Cather exhibits her skill at handling allusions to both Biblical figures and mythic personalities. Yet, she also shows that she can employ these allusions in unexpected ways, significantly altering her tone. Willa Cather's technique was not to follow exactly the details of any myth, classical or Christian, but was to adapt those sources and to make them her own. Written immediately after the completion of her first and rather rigorous term of teaching, this story is as much a wry commentary on Cather's reabsorption into classical studies as it is an ironical account of the end of Apollo Gump. The story is not essential to understanding the Cather canon, but one can imagine on the face of the young writer the same smile that accompanied those early journalistic outbursts, "Great arms of Juno..." and "Sacred lyre of Apollo!"

Throughout her first full year of teaching (1901-1902) and prior to her summer visit to Europe, Willa Cather produced only four poems and one short story, "The Professor's Commencement." This story serves not only as a commentary on her feelings as a teacher but also as an indication of her growing use of the Homeric epics, which she had long admired. The story draws heavily upon Tennyson's poem "Ulysses" and reflects a fascination with the hero whose presence had colored her poetry since her university days. In 1892, for example, Cather had expressed her admiration for Shakespeare in

Homeric terms, making the "sun born bard" an incomparable Ulysses who dwarfs the children "of earth's sterile age":

> Within the great hall of our armory
> Where hang the weapons of our ancient chiefs
> And mighty men of old, there hangs a bow
> Of clanging silver, which today no man,
> Be he of mortal mother or the son
> Of some sea goddess, can its tense drawn cord
> Loosen, or bend at all its massive frame.
> Beneath it hang the bronze shod shafts which none
> Having cunning to in these days to fit thereto,
> Above it all the sun stands still in heaven,
> Pierced there long centuries with a shaft of
> song.
>   (*AT*, pp.61-62)

In the same year she wrote of her admiration for Columbus, characterizing him as a visionary who, unlike the ancient Ithacan sailor Ulysses, sailed not "for the love/ Of blue sea water, nor of the sweet sound/ Of surges smiting on thy vessel's prow/ Nor of the soft white bosom of the sail/ Swelling against blue heaven" (*AT*, p. 63). Although the two poems use the image of the great adventurer in distinctly different ways, Cather's admiration for the spirit and desire of Ulysses is clear. Even her Greek text of *The Odyssey*, which she dated December 1892, "opens to its most worn passages in Book 5,"[13] at which point Athena complains of the hard lot which the gods have doled out to Odysseus. Cather portrays this heroic endurance in her study of Professor Graves, and, perhaps, she projects a vision of what she may become if teaching were to be her life work.

In writing "The Professor's Commencement," though, Cather filters her image of Ulysses through the vision of Tennyson, a poet whom she, at age fifteen, had identified as her favorite.[14] As early as 1899, Cather echoed Tennyson in her poetry, calling for a return to the epic life, filled with adventure and gallantry:

    Lift high the cup of Old Romance,

---

13.   Bernice Slote, ed., *The Kingdom of Art: Willa Cather's First Principles and Critical Statements 1893-1896* (Lincoln: Univ. of Nebraska Press, 1966), p. 40.

14.   Mildred R. Bennett, *The World of Willa Cather*, rev. ed. (Lincoln: Univ. of Nebraska Press, 1961), p. 112.

> And let us drain it to the lees;
> Forgotten be the lies of life,
> For these are its realities!
> *(AT,* p. 69)

Tennyson's Ulysses, too, wished to "drink life to the lees" and to continue his pursuit of the romantic "lies" which were his life's realities. All aspects of the Ulysses myth intrigued Willa Cather, and in her poem "Asphodel" (1900), she drew upon Tennyson's "The Lotos-Eaters" to capture the atmosphere of a land where it also "seemed always afternoon" and where heroes rested "weary limbs at last on beds of asphodel."[15] Here in the meads of Asphodel the tired adventurer feels no impulse to rejoin his comrades in their frantic pursuit of life:

> But [he] feels no ache within his loosened knees
>   To join the runners where the course is set,
> Nor smite the billows of the fruitless seas, –
>   So I recall our day of passion yet,
>   With sighs and tenderness, but no regret.
> *(AT,* p. 8)

Similarly, Tennyson's weary mariners are content in their new-found Elysium:

> Surely, surely, slumber is more sweet than
> toil, the shore
> Than labour in the deep mid-ocean, wind and
> wave and oar;
> Oh rest ye, brother mariners, we will not
> wander more.
> ("The Lotos-Eaters")

Cather's early exposure to the myth of Ulysses, both in the Homeric epic and in the works of Tennyson, greatly affected her depiction of the heroic struggle of characters like Professor Graves, and Professor St. Peter after him, who strove to maintain aesthetic ideals before the onslaught of commercialism and industrialization.

"The Professor's Commencement" indicates that, at this time, Cather's interpretation of classical texts was largely influenced by her reading and teaching of the Victorian poets. She had just completed a full year as an instructor of British Literature, and her renewed acquaintance with the

---

15. Alfred Tennyson, "The Lotos-Eaters," in *Victorian Poetry,* ed. E. K. Brown and J. O. Bailey (New York: The Ronald Press Company, 1962), p. 17.

elegant style and rich language of the nineteenth-century writers colored her fiction. The tales of Homer and other ancient writers, as Tennyson, Morris, and Swinburne presented them, delighted Cather, and, as early as 1896, she had heralded these Britons as the only three worthy of holding a laureateship.[16] In their interpretation of the Classics, these writers often embellished details, as did Tennyson in imagining conversations between Paris and Helen or in recording the musings of an aged Ulysses. William Morris, for instance, wrote a song of homecoming for Orpheus to sing to the Argonauts, and Swinburne recreated even the erotic scenes of Euripides' long-lost drama of Atalanta. Yet, such writers were well-acquainted with the ancient texts, sometimes only fragmentary, from which they drew their inspiration. What Cather must have admired, in addition to poetic style, was their adherence to fundamental themes. Tennyson's Ulysses was still the unrelenting searcher, willing to strive with the gods; Morris's Jason was still the heroic champion, struggling against monstrous adversaries; and Swinburne's Meleager was still the defender of right, defying those who would rob a woman of her triumph. Echoes of Tennysons's verse are not, therefore, unexpected, but Cather integrates references to nineteenth-century texts with references to ancient texts in "The Professor's Commencement." Cather was attracted to the English poets' imaginative explorations of personalities from both myth and ancient literature, but, when dealing with underlying truths she turned back to original texts, to Homer, Vergil, Ovid, or the Greek tragedians.

Professor Graves in "The Professor's Commencement" is, then, very much a reflection of the young Willa Cather. His diction is influenced by his career of teaching British Literature, but his concerns are those recorded by the Greek and Roman authors whom he has studied and admired. "The Professor's Commencement" is set in the bustling and smoke-choked hills of Pittsburgh, where the Professor's high school stands as a fortress, "a stronghold of knowledge in the heart of Mammon's kingdom..." (p. 286). Having devoted himself to thirty years of teaching English literature to boys and girls

16.   Willa Cather, "The Passing Show," *Nebraska State Journal*, 19 Jan. 1896, p. 9 in *The Kingdom of Art*, p. 192.

"hypnotized by the glitter of yellow metal," he faces retirement while still committed to the very ideals which drove Ulysses forever onward: "...but his real work had been to try to secure for youth the rights of youth; the right to be generous, to dream, to enjoy; to feel a little the seduction of the old Romance, and to yield a little" (p. 287).

Cather's descriptions of the Professor confirm her intended parallel to Ulysses. Professor Graves had wandered in the Orient, "was truly a part of all that he had met" (p. 283), and had heard throughout his career many students pledge themselves, as Ulysses had done, "'to follow knowledge like a sinking star beyond the utmost bound of human thought'" (p. 287). At his retirement dinner the Professor even views his colleagues in terms of Tennysons's poem: they are "souls that had toiled and wrought and thought with him" (p. 289). Before attempting to recite again his own commencement address, the aged professor reminds the audience that "he had still some work to finish among them, which had been too long incomplete" (p. 290). The paraphrase of Tennyson's "Ulysses" is clear: "...but something ere the end,/ Some work of noble note may yet be done,/ Not unbecoming men that strove with Gods."

Cather compares the intellectual struggle, which had consumed both Prof. Emerson Graves' youth and desire, to Ulysses' struggle to regain his homeland and his kingdom. The Professor feels the urgency of his call to duty "on this morning when he was to lay down his arms" (p. 287), much as Ulysses re-entered his own house, ready to avenge himself on the suitors, before, with a glad heart, he lay down his arms before Athena (*Odyssey*, Bk. 24). Cather also describes in epic terms the Professor's prolonged struggle against the industrial wasteland of his world:

> To the west, across the river, rose the steep bluffs, faintly etched through the brown smoke, rising five hundred feet, almost as sheer as a precipice, traversed by cranes and inclines and checkered by winding yellow paths like sheep trails which led to the wretched habitations clinging to the face of the cliff, the lairs of the vicious and the poor, miserable rodents of civilizations. (p. 286)

The wording is strong and vindictive, but the scene mirrors that in *The Odyssey* when Ulysses, the Greek spirit incarnate, looks upon the cave of the huge and inhuman Cyclops, an exile from true civilization:

> When we got to the land, which was not far, there, on the face of the cliff near the sea, we saw a great cave overhung with laurels. It was a station for a great many sheep and goats.... This was the abode of a huge monster who... would have nothing to do with other people, but led the life of an outlaw. He was a horrid creature, not like a human being at all....[17]

The Professor had struggled for thirty years to defend aesthetics against such horrid creatures. He has become very like the inhabitants of the troll or Roman garden who strive to protect their artistic achievements from the attack of the barbarians.

Cather further describes this struggle by paralleling the Professor's position to the ancient legend of "Horatius at the Bridge." His students jokingly refer to him as "the bold Horatius," an epithet based on his inability some thirty-five years earlier to recite the poem at his own commencement. Yet, Professor Graves had served as captain of the gate for years, making a valiant stand against the Etruscans, those Philistine forces of modern society which had tried to invade the garden of delights. He had entered the fray as a gifted and resolute young man "with the strength of Ulysses and the courage of Hector" (p. 291), but, looking back, he realizes his defeat and self-deceit. He now feels "like a ruin of some extinct civilization, like a harbor from which the sea has receded" (p. 289). In looking about him at his retirement fete, the Professor believes he has wasted his efforts in fighting materialism. Like Tithonus, he and his comrades have become merely "spent warriors who could only chatter on the wall, like grasshoppers, and sigh at the beauty of Helen as she passed" (p.290). This early short story, then, lays the foundation for the Roman versus barbarian motif which would reappear in detail in Cather's 1905 collection *The Troll Garden*.

Yet, Cather shows her reader a last attempt on the Professor's part to redeem his past failures. He rises before the assembled students and his colleagues to attempt once more the recitation of "Horatius at the Bridge."

---

17.   Homer, *The Odyssey*, trans. Samuel Butler (New York: Washington Square Press, 1965), p. 91.

Again he founders on the same line. His defeat is complete. Professor Graves discovers that youth, once spent, is not recoverable and that "to cry the name of beauty so loud that the roar of the mills could not drown it" was an effort appreciated but destined to failure (p. 290). The tone with which the story ends is neither the conciliatory one of Homer's hero in accepting his destiny nor is it the resolute one of Tennyson's Ulysses in vowing "To strive, to seek, to find, and not to yield." "The Professor's Commencement" ends with a sense of regret and failure. The Professor realizes that, in his efforts to defend the arts before uninterested students, he has failed to meet his personal challenge as an artist. Likewise, Willa Cather must have viewed her teaching career as hostile to her work as an artist. Could she, after all, stand alone on the bridge, defending against the Etruscan hordes, "for motives Quixotic to an absurdity" (p. 285)? Agatha Graves, the Professor's sister, cautions that in high school teaching all a teacher's best tools may rust, and her admonition is certainly Cather's warning to herself: "You owe something...to your own name" (p. 285).

One of Cather's first steps in satisfying her debt to herself came in the summer of 1902 when she and Isabelle McClung departed for Europe. Having completed her first full year of teaching at Central High School, Cather was eager to visit those cultural centers about which she had read. Although she was anxious to observe modern life in the fabled streets and countryside of England, it was the Roman atmosphere that most excited her.[18] The influence of Imperial Rome, as she had studied it with William Ducker in Red Cloud, was very much a part of her, and many of her columns describing her journey are colored by references to this civilization and its lost glories.

She felt the impact of the Roman world especially acutely in Arles. Here she found the women "now and then strangely Roman" with a beauty which legendarily owed itself to secret vows to Venus. These people were not like the forlorn, gin-alley Londoners whose children she had described as seeming "to have sprung from a sowing of the dragon's teeth...."[19] They were,

18. Bennett, p. 124.

19. Willa Cather, *Willa Cather in Europe* (New York: Alfred A. Knopf, 1956), pp. 172, 178.

instead, the remnants of a civilization which could build an imposing amphitheater, "still as huge and white under its blue porcelain sky as it was in the days of Constantine." But it was the "stubborn, arrogant, defiant hugeness" of the Roman ruin that brought to Cather's mind a parallel to her own culture. Cather described the colonists of Arles as people who possessed "a sort of Chicago-like vehemence in adorning their city and making it ostentatiously rich."[20] Although she greatly admired a cornice which bore the image of a garlanded Roman eagle and was inscribed with the phrase "Rome Eternal," Cather recognized that piece of sculpture as a symbol of a beautiful but doomed culture. The same eagle represented her country, and Cather saw in the expansive and dynamic plans of the new-century American the same "self-devouring and suicidal vastness"[21] which had brought the eclipse of the Roman world.

Long before this European tour, Cather had equated America with Rome, for she had observed on the Nebraskan plains the decline of the creative impulses of the Latin races before the ascendancy of materialistic values among the northern peoples. In 1895, Cather had written in her "Passing Show" column, that Rome became a nation that ceased to create but "gleaned the world and gathered into its colossal city everything that was worth loading on its galley-- everything but taste...."[22] This was the very problem which led Cather in the same commentary to dub America "a strange country," where an Anton Shimerda or Spanish Johnny failed while a Bayliss Wheeler or Ivy Peters succeeded. Cather saw going on before her the Roman-Teuton struggle, and the trip to France merely confirmed what she believed to be inevitable. Just as wealth had diminished creativity and had undermined individual morality in the Roman world, thus corrupting the garden and inviting invasion by barbaric tribes, so the garden of the plains would be invaded and would not flourish. Three years after her excursion to France, Cather would return to the Roman-Teuton parable in compiling her

20. *Willa Cather in Europe*, pp. 173, 175.

21. *Willa Cather in Europe*, p. 176.

22. Willa Cather, "The Passing Show," *Nebraska State Journal*, 11 August 1895, p. 9, in *The Kingdom of Art*, p. 195.

first book of short stories, and a Charles Kingsley epigraph from "The Roman and the Teuton" would appear on the first page. For Cather, then, the lesson drawn from the classical world assumed mythic proportions and surfaced as a thematic concern, the disruption and the distortion of enduring values.

In her effort to recall the values she so admired, Cather often turned to childhood experiences which were untainted by materialism. In the last story she published prior to *April Twilights*, Cather described in mythic terms the striving of a successful playwright to return to the uncorrupted childhood Eden of Far Island. In "The Treasure of Far Island," Douglass Burnham returns to Empire City with the intention of unearthing a treasure box which he and his childhood companion Margie Van Dyck had buried on Far Island in their days of playing pirates on their own Ultima Thule. Douglass and Margie spend an afternoon on their island, and Douglass, who has made his living by his imagination, tries to recreate a romance in which he is the knight and Margie his lady. Margie, at first, denies "the dregs of the old enchantment" (p. 281) and accepts Douglass' attentions only after he admits that the pirate play is ended. Had Cather concluded her story at this point, she would have confirmed Donald Sutherland's contention that most of her work was composed on the basis of "long sad retrospect, the motif of absence of exile, and her very frequent device of having a person return home and find things changed...."[23] Douglass, however, finds only one major change in Empire City: Margie has become an enchanting woman rather than a freckled and defensive tomboy. The mule-drawn cars still take Douglass home, and, although a celebrity in his own right, his mother still does not trust him with the icebox. Empire City preserves childhood for Douglass, but in rediscovering it, he must reassert his rule, even over his childhood playmate.

The story's ending is, though, neither unexpected nor superficial if read in keeping with the mythic references scattered throughout the piece. From the outset, Douglass weaves a web of images from the Olympian world, a web in which Margie must eventually be caught, for she, like the reader,

---

23. Donald Sutherland, "Willa Cather: The Classic Voice," in *The Art of Willa Cather*, ed. Bernice Slote and Virginia Faulkner (Lincoln: Univ. of Nebraska Press, 1974), p. 177.

wishes to reenter the imaginative world and to "become as the gods, who dwell in their golden houses, recking little of the woes and labors of mortals, neither heeding any fall of rain or snow" (p. 282). Yet, Margie's power to enchant should not be underrated. Margie works her spell over Douglass from the moment of their meeting:

> A woman stood in the dark by the hall lamp with a lighted match in her hand. She was in white and very tall. The match burned but a moment; a moment the light played on her hair, red as Etruscan gold and piled high above the curve of her neck and head.... Then the match went out, leaving Douglass to wonder whether, like Anchises, he had seen the vision that should forever blind him to the beauty of mortal women. (p. 270)

Here Margie is clearly Aphrodite, identifiable by her beautifully molded neck and golden hair and the charm by which she persuaded Anchises to be her consort. Douglass more than once refers to her as a goddess, a being whom he would fear to accost on a city street (p. 271), a Venus de Milo unearthed in the sleepy Nebraskan town of Empire City (p. 275). She becomes for him "Helen of Troy, to the disaster of men" (p. 273) and a beautiful wood nymph, a Dryad who closes the tree behind her and will not admit a mere mortal to her secret world (p. 279). In her engaging beauty, Margie anticipates the powerful women of Cather's later works – a Lena Lingard or Eden Bower – who control their admirers while asserting independence.

She also assumes the proportions of an early earth spirit, embodying all the freedom and strengths of an ancient order:

> She started fleetingly across the glittering sand and Douglass fell behind to watch with immoderate joy that splendid, generous body that governed itself so well in the open air. There was a wholesomeness of the sun and soil in her that was utterly lacking in the women among whom he had lived for so long. She had preserved that strength of arm and freedom of limb that made her so fine a playfellow, and which modern modes of life have well-nigh robbed the world of altogether. (p. 278)

Cather's concern with the recovery of simple values is obvious, as she lays the groundwork for creating other characters like Antonia Shimerda, who will fashion her own Elysium on the windy Nebraska tablelands. Douglass is not immune to the deific power of Margie's beauty and imagines himself like an Actaeon, spying on Diana and her women as they speed down the slopes of Mt. Ida, brandishing spears and shouting. Margie even wears "her wonderful hair piled high on her head like a helmet of gleaming bronze" (p. 276). She becomes at once Athena, Diana, and Demeter, forces too awesome to resist. It is no wonder, then, that Douglass imagines himself as Orpheus, flayed by the Thracian women whose enticements he had spurned.

Although Douglass admits he has drunk with the Immortals of New York City, he also admits that he has not grown into an Apollo. Margie's assessment that he is a case of "arrested development" (p. 273) is not far from the truth. He is not only arrested in his growth from children's play, as she suggests, but he is also arrested in his growth toward deification. He seems hardly an equal or even likely consort for Margie. Douglass succumbs to the power of Margie's immortal beauty as much as she succumbs to his bewitching "fire and fancy" (p. 281). Just as both Speckle Burnham and Mary Eliza were responsible for corrupting their garden in "The Way of the World," both Douglass and Margie are responsible for reestablishing a childhood utopia. Both are individuals who live by the imagination, "not so unlike those Hellenic poets who were content to sing to the shepherds and forget and be forgotten, 'rich in the simple worship of a day'" (p. 280).

Margie's apparently sudden surrender to Douglass' spell, after her Penelope-like waiting, is not so predictable, however. In alluding to Margie's goddess-like qualities, Cather prepares her reader to expect a strength of character which commands Douglass' worship and will withstand his physical allure. Even within the last paragraphs of the story, Margie's eyes grow hard, and she pushes away Douglass' hand. She accuses him of having "taken on the ways of the world" (p. 281), a pointed reference to Cather's earlier story in which a childhood utopia is disrupted by a female playmate. In "The Treasure of Far Island," though, the situation is reversed. Margie has put aside childish romance and has asserted her role as woman, if not goddess. But, true to her natural impulses, she is filled with remorse and tenderness when she discovers that her refusal to be part of Douglass' "new play" has deeply hurt him. Unable to maintain her guise as an aloof but loving deity, she succumbs to forces like those that swept Margie Pierson back into Martin Dempster's arms in "A Resurrection":

> The fire and fancy that had so bewitched her girlhood that no other man had been able to dim the memory of it came furiously back upon her, with arms that were new and strange and strong, and with tenderness stranger still in this wild fellow of dreams and jests; and all her vows never to grace another of his Roman triumphs were forgotten. (pp. 281-282)

In opening that cache of pirate treasures, Margie opens a kind of Pandora's box. The precious memories of childhood engulf her, forcing her to relinquish womanly independence, her only protection against "the dregs of the old enchantment" (p. 281). This failure to maintain power as goddess and woman before male dominance anticipates the struggle of characters like Alexandra Bergson and Thea Kronborg, whose stories, to some degree, reflect the mythic matriarchal struggle against Olympian, masculine forces. But, in "The Treasure of Far Island," Cather is not yet convinced that such heroic stands are possible for women, and Margie falls back into the traditional role of submissive female.

The ambiguity of the final scene is largely due to the authorial voice. Nostalgic longings and references to legendary romances, to Paris and Helen, to Romeo and Juliet, do little to dispel the tone of irony. Margie, indeed, recoups the losses of childhood but gives up her independence. Cather herself seems troubled by the conclusion. She could only applaud Douglass' reestablishment of an imaginative realm in the adult world; she could only regret Margie's capitulation, for Margie will assuredly one day "wake and weep" (p. 281). The final lines are at once both an evocation of romance and a disquieting assertion of impossibility. Margie and Douglass look out over their world and see that it is good. The lines parody the creation story of Genesis, for readers know that the Edenic fall is yet to occur. And the glow of the moon that lighted Paris' trip over the blue Aegean and young Montague's way to the Capulet orchard shone just as brightly upon the sack of Troy and the suicides of two young lovers.

What appears, then, to be a conventional ending to "The Treasure of Far Island" is fraught with thematic concerns which would reappear in *April Twilights* and in *The Troll Garden*, Cather's first collection of stories. The

50

story becomes a crucial one to understanding the Cather canon, for it shows not only Cather's lament for a loss of classical Arcadia but also her skill in making classical myth her own, in refashioning the stories to serve in her own time and place.

The themes of lost youth and passing of a true age of art surfaced in Willa Cather's first book, *April Twilights*, a slim volume of poems, which were generally unremarkable in form and conventional in subject for the turn of the century. The importance of this first work, however, lies in moods, subject, and motifs which would shape her major work in the novel genre. Most of the poems are imitative of classical works or pastorals or reflect enthusiasm for Housman, an enthusiasm which was not squelched by Cather's disastrous visit with the poet during her European tour. Although Cather claimed, "I don't take myself seriously as a poet,"[24] she did take seriously the subjects about which she wrote. At the time of this collection's publication, Willa Cather was thirty years old and still teaching English in a high school. The elegiac tone, which underscores the poems, is surely an indication of the author's regret as she looks back to a lost youth and the passing of its opportunities. These poems, therefore, belie Rene Rapin's early criticism that they are not of much importance, "unoffending [to] ear or taste, at best picturesque, hardly ever impressive, betraying nothing of their author's personality."[25] Cather, who by 1912 seemed to have been embarrassed by her early poems, would probably have been the first to agree that her work was unimpressive. The quality could not measure up to the models she set before herself as great women poets: Christina Rossetti, who "wrote with mystic, enraptured faith of Cassandra, which is a sort of spiritual ecstasy..."; and Sappho, who "invented the most wonderfully emotional meter in literature...that short, sharp one that comes in like a gasp when feeling flows too swift for speech."[26] But, the poems, regardless of structural merit,

24.   Willa Cather, qtd. in Alice Hunt Bartlett, "The Dynamics of American Poetry--XI," *The Poetry Review*, 16 (Nov.-Dec. 1925), 408.

25.   Rene Rapin, *Willa Cather* (New York: Robert McBridge and Co., 1930), pp. 15-16.

26.   Willa Cather, "As You Like It," *Nebraska State Journal*, 13 Jan. 1895, p. 13, in *The World and The Parish*, ed. William M. Curtin (Lincoln: Univ. of Nebraska Press, 1970), I, 143 and 147. [Cather did occasionally employ the five-syllable Sapphic line as is evidenced in

express Cather's concern for an age in which April twilight was descending, an age in which the promise of creativity, the spirit of Apollo, was fading from view.

The poems of the 1903 edition of *April Twilights* grow directly from Cather's visit in Europe and her acquaintance with the ancient cultures. As Bernice Slote concludes, *April Twilights* shows an orientation to a "young Europe...the April time of childhood and the youth of the world; for she had first caught through the classics the sense of glory and habitation of the gods." Slote further notes that Cather had always liked the idea of poet as singer and the "'Greek' ideal of art that was high and pure, but also intuitive and natural."[27] The impending loss of this spirit provides the mythic dimension for the poems which comprise her first book. The poems owe a debt to both Vergil's *Georgics* and A. E. Housman's *A Shropshire Lad*, for the most common subjects are gods and god-like men performing legendary rites in ancient climes or acting their parts in medieval romances. The Homeric vision, too, continues to haunt Cather. In her dedicatory verse she longs for "the Odysseys of summer mornings,/ Starry wonder-tales of nights in April" (*AT*, p. 3). The wine-dark sea of Homer still draws her in "On Cyndus," and she turns to Odysseus in looking for a parallel for Marsyas:

> He will startle you no more
> When along the river shore
> Damsels beat the linen clean.
> Nor when maidens play at ball
> Will he catch it where it fall:
> Though ye wait for him and call
> He will answer not, I ween.
> (*AT*, p. 27)

Here Cather recalls a scene in Book VI of *The Odyssey* when Odysseus is awakened by the shouts of Nausicaa and her maids who, having gone to the

---

"Going Home," a poem in the 1923 edition of *April Twilights*.] Sharon O'Brien suggests that Cather's admiration for Rossetti was tempered by the implicit meaning of Cassandra's dilemma as "woman poet disempowered by the masculine aesthetic," a result of the prophetess' rejection of Apollo's suit. O'Brien further argues that Cather most admired Sappho as the model of a "poet who transcended the culture's polarization of feminine and masculine." [*Willa Cather: The Emerging Voice* (New York: Oxford Univ. Press, 1987), pp. 279 and 186.]

27.　　Bernice Slote, Introd., *April Twilights (1930)*, pp. xxxvi, xvi.

stream to wash their linen, relax by playing ball. "On Cyndus" warns, however, that Odysseus-like individuals no long wander along streambeds.

But, the absence of heroic virtues is not what Cather most mourns in *April Twilights*. The greatest loss for Cather is Apollo's absence. Arcadia is no more; the perfection of beauty, art, and song has vanished. The question Cather poses is, "Will Apollo ever return?"

The Apollo figure is central to these poems and appears in many guises, as minstrel, harper, troubadour, and god. But, in each case, the sense of absence or loss of the creative spirit is what governs the poems. As early as May, 1901, Cather had begun to wrestle with the loss of the ideal in art. Her poem "Winter at Delphi" could serve as the one piece most crucial to understanding the intent of *April Twilights* and to understanding the doubts of Cather herself. In the poem Cather pictures the Delphic Oracle lying silent in the cold of winter; Apollo's watchers have prepared the temple for his return but have fallen asleep in their waiting. Apollo has deserted those who wait to follow his call, and, perhaps, Cather also felt the artistic inspiration had deserted her after her relatively unproductive winter in Washington, D.C., and after a trying semester at Central High School. The second stanza strikes a very personal note:

> Sick is the heart in my breast,
> Mine eyes are blinded with weeping;
> The god who never comes back,
> The watch that forever is keeping.
> Service of gods is hard;
> Deep lies the snow on my pillow.
> For him the laurel and song,
> Weeping for me and the willow:
> Empty my arms and cold
> As the nest forgot of the swallow:
> Birds will come back in the spring, –
> But Apollo, the god, Apollo?
> (*AT*,p.22)

The tone of frustration is strong as Cather goes on to describe the vibrant signs of spring returning and to admit that "Pan will be drunken and rage – / But Apollo, the god, Apollo?" (*AT*, p. 23). Cather draws upon the ancient concept of Pan and Apollo as antithetical to one another, the pagan life-force versus the civilizing, creative force. Indeed, Cather's concern about her own ability to create a literary work of note is her concern for the entire culture. The April twilight which encompasses the poems is one of sadness, unfulfilled hopes, a true twilight of the gods.

When considering together "Winter at Delphi" and Cather's next poem "Arcadian Winter," the reader feels even more keenly the loss of a golden age, characterized by Apollo's absence from the earth. In "Arcadian Winter," winter winds blast upon the pastoral scene, and even Apollo's rival, the nightingale, has fled. Shepherd lads and maids, now silver-haired and no longer fair, reminisce with tales of summer and desire. The pastoral world of simple shepherds and song has long been gone from the earth, but Cather's grieving is immediate. In February, 1901, Ethelbert Nevin, a talented young composer and close friend of Willa Cather, had died suddenly. She had associated Nevin with the perfection of artistic creation, as one who must have resembled the shepherd boys in the Vale of Tempe and from whose youthful countenance "the lyric soul" shone forth. Cather had seen in Nevin the spirit of Apollo and, in 1898, had praised him as both poet and singer:

> That is the essential essence of his genius; that exquisite sensitiveness, that fine susceptibility to the moods of others, to every external thing. That is why he can interpret a poet's song better than the poet himself; that is why he can put the glory and melancholy of a Tuscan summer into sound; that is the all divining intuition.[28]

When Nevin died at thirty-nine years of age, Cather lamented his passing but also felt despair over her age's unwillingness or inability to respond to the voice from Delphi. "Sleep, Minstrel, Sleep" equates Nevin and Apollo, both of whom rest like "yellow" April, "buried deep and cold"(*AT*, p. 14). As she had written in "Winter at Delphi," the service of gods is hard in a world unresponsive to beauty. In "Sleep, Minstrel, Sleep," she reiterates this idea, now joining her theme of the vanished god with the theme of lost youth:

> Sleep, minstrel, sleep; in such a bitter night
>   Thine azure song would seek the stars in vain;
> Thy rose and roundelay the winter's spite
>   Would scarcely spare – O never wake again!
> These leaden skies do not thy masques invite,
>   Thy sunny breath would warm not their
> disdain...(*AT*, p. 14)

---

28.   Willa Cather, "The Passing Show," *Courier*, 5 Feb. 1898, p. 3, in *The World and The Parish*, II, 533-534, 538.

Cather envisions the world as hostile to youth and beauty and alludes to Nevin's death in terms of the death of Adonis, also a lover of ideal beauty who was destroyed by a wound "wet and deep" (*AT*, p. 14).

Death is omnipresent in these poems, too,[29] especially the untimely death of youths, a theme which must have attracted Cather to the poetry of Housman. Although Cather does include some poems based on personal experiences that illustrate this theme (e.g., "The Namesake" and "The Night Express"), she turns frequently to figures from the classical world to express her elegiac mood. In "Antinous," for instance, Cather questions the reasons for the death of the young Antinous, a favorite of the Emperor Hadrian and renowned for his beauty:

> Did the perfection of thy beauty pain
> Thy limbs to bear it? Did it ache to be,
>   As song hath ached in men, or passion vain?
> Or lay it like some heavy robe on thee?
>   Was thy sick soul drawn from thee like the rain,
> Or drunk up as the dead are drunk, each hour
> To feed the color of some tulip flower?
> <div align="right">(<i>AT</i>, p. 18)</div>

Drowned in the Nile, an apparent suicide, Antinous is afterwards sculpted with a "mortal misery in his eyes" or with the attributes of gods, but only gods of death--Hermes and Osiris (*AT*, p. 18). Antinous provides the classical model for characters like Claude Wheeler, Lucy Gayheart, and Tom Outland whose spiritual beauty is doomed in a world where, as Cather writes in "In Media Vita," the dead is under all. Moreover, Antinous' "mortal misery" prefigures that of Claude Wheeler and Tom Outland in another sense. They will share with Antinous homoerotic impulses which, along with their artistic sensibilities, set them apart from their society. The homosexual relationship between Antinous and Hadrian is well documented, and Cather accepted such relationships as part of the classical world whose artistic achievements she admired.

---

29.   In discussing *April Twilights* as a foundation for Cather's novels of a pastoral mode, David Stouck also stresses the importance of recognizing the dual nature of Arcadia as Cather portrays it: "The literary world of antiquity--Arcadia--provides a retreat in time and place for the poet, but she is aware that classical pastoral is also preoccupied with mutability: *et in Arcadia ego*," [*Willa Cather's Imagination*, p. 40].

In yet another poem Cather returns to Greek myth to describe the death of an aspiring artist, not at the hands of an unappreciative society, but at the hands of the god Apollo, a hard taskmaster. In "Lament for Marsyas," Cather recalls the story of the satyr Marsyas who, having taken up the flute discarded by Athena, fails to respond to the beating the goddess gives him and challenges Apollo to a music contest. The results of his rash presumption are disastrous; he is flayed alive by Apollo. During her stay in Arles, Cather had found "the most beautiful" of all remaining Roman sculptures, a bas-relief which showed in the middle panel the triumph of the poet, flanked on one side by Apollo whetting his knife and on the other by Marsyas hanging limp from an oak tree.[30] Cather recognized that dedication to art was, in many ways, self-destructive. To strive for perfection was the writer's, artist's, or musician's ambition, but the anguish involved in that pursuit Cather undoubtedly related to Marsyas' cry as Ovid imagined it: "Quid me mihi detrahis?" ("Why are you stripping me of my very self?") [*Metamorphoses*, Bk. VI, l.385]. In "Lament for Marsyas," then, Cather wonders if the artist is not wise to find ease in an early death:

> Marsyas sleeps: Ah! well-a-day,
> He was wise who did not stay
> Until hands unworthy bore
> Prizes that were his before.
> ....
> Whether summer come or go,
> April bud or winter blow
> He will never heed or know
> Underneath the daffodil.
> (*AT*, pp. 27-28)

The anxiety of a Marsyas, who realizes the death of self is the recompense one pays for the attainment of beauty, is an early version of the problem which Thea Kronborg confronts in her pursuit of artistic achievement in *The Song of the Lark.*

The passion of Marsyas is only one example of destructive passions as Cather pictures them in *April Twilights*. She incorporates images from the classical world to show the results of uncontrolled desire, another theme

---

30.   Cather, *Willa Cather in Europe*, p. 176.

56

central to the collection. In her Italian sonnet, "On Cyndus," Cather recalls the legend of Antony's yielding to passion, to the enchantment of Cleopatra. He, like a madman, casts away his worldly power like a pearl dissolved in wine. Whereas Antony is a victim of passion, Eurydice, in the short poem of that name, is victimized by Orpheus' anxiety of love. The poem dramatizes Eurydice's unfulfilled dream of returning to Arcadia with her husband, but, as the Vergilian version of the myth makes clear, Orpheus' excess of love prevents the couple's reuniting. Only the memory of his song can comfort Eurydice, and her desire must go unsatisfied:

> For all of him she yearned to touch and see,
> Only the sweet ghost of his melody;
> For all of him she yearned to have and hold,
> Only the wraith of song, sweet and cold.
> (*AT*, p. 33)

In light of these thematic concerns Cather aptly named her collection of poems, for she presents the agony of memory and desire in what T. S. Eliot would, some twenty years later, call the cruelest of months. Apparently even her publishers failed to recognize the yearning for perfection, the despair with the present, and the sense of loss of the classical Arcadia which underscored the poems in *April Twilights*. In their mail announcement, released in April, 1903, the Gorham Press seriously misinterpreted the title as well as the volume's content:

> The title of the collection is an especially happy one...but the tone of the whole collection is like that of a beautiful April evening, when the old world is young again, and the quiet charm of the clean, whole-some air and the twilight is at once restful and invigorating.[31]

Cather's friend George Seibel, however, understood and appreciated the intent of the poet. In his review for the Pittsburgh *Gazette*, he identified in these poems "a haunting melancholy": "Like the lament for the vanished god, unresponding, unreturning, there is an undertone of pensive sadness."[32]

31. A facsimile reprint of this announcement appears in Bernice Slote's introduction to *April Twilights (1903)*.

32. George Seibel, rev. of *April Twilights*, by Willa Cather, Pittsburgh *Gazette*, 26 April 1903, qtd. in Bernice Slote, Introd., *April Twilights (1903)* p. xxi.

The two poems Cather chose to end *April Twilights* indeed captured this very mood and surely reflected their author's personality. "Song" again mourns the absence of the troubadour (Apollo) whom, one winter night, Fortune held in her despite. The speaker in "Song" mourns the fading of Arcadia into the April twilight: "April yearneth, April goes;/ Not for me her violet blows,/ I have done for long with those" (AT, p. 50).

Cather ends her collection of poems in a manner which she may have borrowed from Rudyard Kipling, one of the few contemporary writers who she felt could continue the romantic tradition. By 1892, Kipling had composed four poems entitled "L'Envoi," three serving as epilogues for longer works — *The Seven Seas*, *The Story of the Gadsbys*, and *Soldiers Three*. Cather was apparently well-acquainted with these poems. In "The Treasure of Far Island" (1902), she had paraphrased two lines from Kipling's concluding poem in *The Seven Seas*:

> "We were artists in those days, creating for the day only; making epics sung once and then forgotten, building empires that set with the sun. Nobody worked for money then, and nobody worked for fame, but only for the joy of the doing." (p. 280)

Whereas Margie Van Dyck bemoans the passing away of her childhood utopia where artistic endeavors were undertaken for sheer joy, Kipling's poem suggests that a golden time will return for the artist, after "Earth's last picture is painted" and "the youngest critic has died":

> And only the Master shall praise us, and only the
> Master shall blame;
> And no one shall work for money, and no one shall
> work for fame;
> But each for the joy of the working, and each,
> in his separate star,
> Shall draw the Thing as he sees It for the God
> of Things as They Are![33]

For Kipling, the April twilight exists only briefly before a May dawning and Apollo's return. Cather's adaptation of Kipling serves as another instance of

---

33.   Rudyard Kipling, "L'Envoi," in *The Seven Seas* (New York: D. Appleton and Co., 1897), pp. 208-209.

58

her propensity for altering literary sources to suit her own purposes, a technique even more evident in her borrowings from classical mythology.

But, "L'Envoi" from *The Seven Seas* seems hardly the source Cather had in mind when writing her "L'Envoi." Her final poem reinforces the image of the lover of beauty, like Nevin and Marsyas and Eurydice, held fast in the arms of Darkness. Perhaps more than any other piece in the collection, "L'Envoi" echoes the insecurity that Cather felt as a struggling young writer:

> No matter when or how love did befall,
> 'Tis Loneliness that loves me best of all,
> And in the end she claims me, and I know
> That she will stay, though all the rest may go.
>   (*AT*, p. 51)

The twilight mood of April is here, not in its "quiet charm" but in its "pensive sadness." Cather found that same mood in Kipling's three earlier poems by the same title. In a December 23, 1894, article for the *Nebraska State Journal*, Cather praised Kipling's *Soldiers Three* (1888) and quoted from his epilogue of *The Story of the Gadsbys* (1888). She had, therefore, read, in the first instance, a poem in which a young sculptor questioned the value of his work:

> Lo, I have wrought in common clay
> Rude figures of rough-hewn race;
> For Pearls strew not the market-place
> In this my town of banishment,
> Where with the shifting dust I lay
> And eat the bread of Discontent.[34]

Cather could have identified easily with this artisan, and in sooty Pittsburgh she must have shared the struggling artist's weariness as "My wares ere I go forth to sell." In the same *Journal* article she chided Kipling for allowing his marriage to distract him from the kind of writing he did best and quoted from the *Gadsbys* "L'Envoi": "Down to Gehanna or up to the Throne, he travels the fastest who rides alone." Although slightly changing the original wording ("Down to Gehanna or up to the Throne/ He travels the fastest who travels alone"), Cather clearly endorsed the artist's work as singular, and sometimes even lonely. If one were to fail as a writer, if April twilight and

---

34.   Rudyard Kipling, "L'Envoi," in *Soldiers Three, The Story of the Gadsbys, In Black and White* (Garden City, NY: Doubleday, Page and Co., 1927), p. 107.

"the lips of Silence" were what awaited, then, as Kipling wrote, "One may fall but he falls by himself – / Falls by himself with himself to blame...."[35]

In composing her "L'Envoi," Cather harkened back to these ideas in the poetry of one whom she admired for possessing "the virility of the epic manner."[36] The feelings of loss throughout *April Twilights* were, perhaps, most evident in Kipling's earliest "L'Envoi," published in *Departmental Ditties* (1886). The poem offers close parallels to Cather's "Winter at Delphi," also alluding to a world abandoned by the gods and awaiting their return:

> The smoke upon your Altar dies,
> The flowers decay,
> The Goddess of your sacrifice
> Has flown away
> What profit then to sing or slay
> The sacrifice from day to day?
>
> "We know the Shrine is void," they said,
> "The Goddess flown –
> Yet wreathes are on the Altar laid--
> The Altar-Stone
> Is black with fumes of sacrifice,
> Albeit She has fled our eyes.
>
> "For, it may be, if still we sing
> And tend the Shrine,
> Some Deity on wandering wing
> May there incline:
> And, finding all in order meet,
> Stay while we worship at Her feet."[37]

If, as she wrote in an article on Kipling, "Poetry is retrospective; life precedes it always,"[38] then this "L'Envoi" confirms what Cather laments in *April Twilights*. Arcadia was gone, and the artists, striving to recover the pastoral world, could only work and wait. Kipling's poem suggests that such waiting

---

35.   Kipling, "L'Envoi," in *Soldiers Three, The Story of the Gadsbys, In Black and White*, p. 205.

36.   Willa Cather, "The Passing Show, *Courier* 4 March 1899, pp. 2-3, in *The World and The Parish*, II, 559.

37.   Rudyard Kipling, "L'Envoi," in *Kipling: A Selection of His Stories and Poems*, ed. John Beecroft (Garden City, NY: Doubleday and Co., 1956), II, 458-459.

38.   Willa Cather, "The Passing Show," *Nebraska State Journal*, 16 May 1897, p. 13, in *The World and The Parish*, II, 556.

might not be in vain, and that thought must have offered some comfort to the ambitious young author of *April Twilights*.

A close reading of *April Twilights* and its mythic allusions is, therefore, essential to understanding many of Cather's later works, particularly those colored with "inconsolable, passionate regret"[39] for the loss of a golden age, whether it be the Arcadia of childhood, the Nebraska frontier, or the European heritage. As *April Twilights* indicates, Cather's use of classical literature and myth shows not a Vergilian preoccupation with death, as L. V. Jacks claims,[40] but an acknowledgement of life's temporality, an acknowledgment tinged with regret.

---

39. Willa Cather, "The Enchanted Bluff," in *Five Stories* (New York: Vintage Books, 1956), p. 8.

40. Jacks, p. 293.

CHAPTER IV
MYTHIC STRUGGLE IN *THE TROLL GARDEN*

In her stories written between 1902 and 1904 and later collected in *The Troll Garden* (1905), Cather continued to confront the issues of an artist's relationship to art and his or her world. The collection's epigraphs from Rossetti's "Goblin Market" and Kingsley's "The Roman and the Teuton" set the stage for Cather's examination of the cyclical pattern of the rise and fall of civilization where the struggle for superiority lies between those who horde creative treasures (Roman or troll) and those who crave the treasures (Teuton or forest child). Unfortunately, those within the Troll Garden are often corrupt and their treasures false. The garden is protected by greed, and, for Cather, this is the one force most destructive to true art. Even those attempting to batter down the garden walls are driven by materialism, desiring equal share of the fruits inside.

In the mythic re-enactment of civilization's decay and a return to savagery the artist is central. In each of the seven stories of *The Troll Garden*, the artist is also a quester, an Orpheus figure. The Orpheus myth and its many musical adaptations had long been favorites of Willa Cather and would figure significantly in her novels, especially in *The Song of the Lark*, where the myth provides the structural basis for Thea's quest as a singer. In three early stories, however, the Orphic quest is thwarted, as often by cultural factors as by the individual's psyche. Like the mythic Orpheus, the would-be artists vacillate between worship of Apollo and Dionysus. As illustrated in *April Twilights*, Apollo, the epitome of true art, has absented himself from earth, and the Dionysian forces, representing false art, have entered the garden of which the naive forest children so desire to be a part.

The *Troll Garden* stories have been variously described as a warning against the false and potentially destructive attraction of art, a parable of the soul's inability to rise above human desires, and a study of the artist's failure to enchant self.[1] The underlying commonalities of such interpretations, though, are contradiction and struggle. In *The Troll Garden* all the protagonists struggle to reconcile art with life, and all meet defeat. As in the myth, the artist (Orpheus), separated from the source of sublime inspiration (Eurydice), falls victim to worshipers of false art and worldly desires (Maenads).

Of particular interest are those stories which draw most heavily upon allusions to classical mythology for illustrating this struggle. These stories—"Flavia and Her Artists," "The Garden Lodge," "'A Death in the Desert,'" and "A Wagner Matinee"—are also the four whose protagonists are female, a fact which may indicate Cather's efforts to define herself as a creative artist. Sharon O'Brien also suggests that "Cather is now writing about women who possess creativity—albeit creativity that is denied, distorted, or repressed by cultural pressures and psychological necessities."[2] Yet, these women provide a basis for figures like Antonia Shimerda, Alexandra Bergson, and Thea Kronborg, whose creativity will triumph and will return matriarchal order to a crumbling civilization. It is fitting, therefore, that many of the details associated with the female protagonists of *The Troll Garden* are mythic, for they anticipate the power of the earth goddesses who, when unthwarted, revitalize civilization.

"Flavia and Her Artists," the opening story of *The Troll Garden*, draws heavily upon the structural motif of the Roman-Teuton struggle. Flavia Hamilton, whose Midwestern background is without distinction, has

---

1.   Marilyn Arnold, *Willa Cather's Short Fiction* (Athens: Ohio Univ. Press, 1984), p. 46; Richard Giannone, *Music in Willa Cather's Fiction* (Lincoln: Univ. of Nebraska Press, 1968), p. 90.

2.   Sharon O'Brien, "Mothers, Daughters, and the 'Art Necessity': Willa Cather and the Creative Process," in *American Novelists Revisited: Essays in Feminist Criticism*, ed. Fritz Fleischmann (Boston: G. K. Hall & Co., 1982), p. 277.

established a country retreat for "interesting people" in an effort to become a patron of the arts and to be recognized as a culturally-attuned woman. Most of the individuals whom she invites to her temple for the arts are second-rate performers or intellects, but, when M. Roux agrees to spend a few days at the Hamiltons' house, Flavia is thrilled. After his departure and the publication of his scathing satire of Flavia, Arthur Hamilton, Flavia's quiet and perceptive husband, lambasts the guests and M. Roux as individuals with no "'ordered notion of taste'" (p. 168). This action at once disrupts the atmosphere Flavia has worked so hard to create. Unknown to Flavia, Arthur has acted in her defense, for she is very much like one of the forest children, innocent of the corruption within the very garden in which she lives.

In writing "Flavia and Her Artists," Cather further extended the troll garden image by relaying the events through the eyes of an intelligent young woman, Imogen Willard. Imogen's more than childhood fondness for Arthur makes her sympathetic to his silent suffering and disgusted with Flavia's treatment of her husband. Yet, Imogen herself is an Alice in Wonderland figure, a fact made clear by Cather's four direct references in the story to Lewis Carroll's well-known tale. Arthur wishes that his Alice had not grown up but could yet eat some of that magic cake and walk through the glass door into a truly magical garden. No magical garden exists in the Hamilton "infirmary for the arts"; the inhabitants are goblin men, "'mountebanks and snake charmers, people indispensable to our civilization, but wholly unreclaimed by it ...'" (p. 168).

In developing this idea Cather borrowed details from the ancient world, but she did so with ironic intent. The Roman name of her principal character – Flavia – is quite in keeping with the large number of classical allusions in the story, and Cather was surely acquainted with the historical aspects of the Flavian Gens as described in the works of both Tacitus and Suetonius.[3] Vespasian, the first of the Flavian emperors, was himself of

3. Mildred R. Bennett suggests in her article "How Willa Cather Chose Her Names" [*Names*, 10 (1962), 31] that Cather, in selecting her principal character's name, may have used the first name of Dorothy Canfield's mother, an artist whom Cather did not like. Sharon O'Brien also refers to Mrs. Canfield but interprets Cather's choice of the name as perhaps "Cather's first literary attempt at revenge against Dorothy, and perhaps also an exorcism of Flavia Canfield's influence over her younger self." [*Willa Cather: The Emerging Voice* (New York: Oxford Univ. Press, 1987), p. 266n.].

humble origins and had married Flavia Domitilla, of equally obscure beginnings. Vespasian, like Arthur Hamilton, was simple and frugal, quite in contrast to some of the luxury-loving earlier emperors, and he is said to have instigated more moral reforms in Rome than all his predecessors. Just as Arthur is unashamed of his name being "annually painted upon some ten thousand threshing machines" (p. 153), so Vespasian was never ashamed of his agrarian, Sabine origins. Nor were the reasons for Vespasian's affection for the freed-woman Caenis far different from Arthur's for Imogen Willard. Caenis was a woman of "vast and extensive genius...and the most discreet conduct."[4] Imogen, too, had distinguished herself in "certain esoteric lines of scholarship" (p. 149), and, like Caenis's close study of Vespasian's humor and inclinations, Imogen keenly observes Arthur, making an "inventory of speculations" about him (p. 157).

The subtle parallel of Flavia to her ancient counterpart is even further promoted in that Flavia bore two sons and a daughter to Vespasian, just as Flavia Hamilton did to her husband. In her treatment of her sons, however, Flavia Hamilton more appropriately recalls another Roman mother, Cornelia, the mother of the Gracchi, as Miss Broadwood points out in the story. The most well-known story of Cornelia tells of a lady's visit to the Gracchus home and of her conceited display of elegant jewels. Cornelia then pointed to her two sons, saying "These are my jewels." The boys are Flavia's jewels, too, and she longs for the time "when they will be intellectual companions for her" (p. 163). Although little more is known about the domestic life of Flavia Domitilla, her name was resurrected after her death when deification of emperors and their families had become accepted procedure in the Empire. As Bernard Henderson describes in *Five Roman Emperors*, the Flavian household established itself as an object of reverence and worship:

> The Imperial House became a "domus divina," the family home on the Quirinal hill a "templum," the Princeps "sacratissimus." Even the women of the house and the babies who died in infancy received divine honours after death. Only, curiously enough, the old Italian dame, Vespasian's wife, Flavia Domitilla, escaped deification....[5]

4.   Jacques Boergas de Serviez, *Lives of the Roman Empresses* (New York: William H. Wise and Co., 1935), p. 331.

5.   Bernard W. Henderson, *Five Roman Emperors* (1927; rpt. New York: Barnes and Noble, 1969), p. 29.

The historical events well fit Cather's purpose, for Flavia Hamilton's home is, in her eyes, a temple of worship for the gods of the arts, and she hopes to preside as the priestess.

Additionally, Cather's description of the Hamilton home is that of a sacred temple. A "large, square hall with a gallery on three sides" is flanked by music rooms, smoking rooms, and a library. The servants move silently through the halls "in response to inaudible bells, on felt soles, and in hushed voices, so that there was very little confusion about it" (p. 151). The religious atmosphere which caters to the "rarae aves," Flavia's chosen few, reminds the reader of the temple at Delphi where the true god of the arts communicated with mere mortals. There a suppliant directed his praise to Apollo in music and song (Flavia's music room), worshiped him as the source of knowledge (the library), and hoped to discover truth in the mutterings of a priestess, who was inspired by the smoke issuing forth from an underground chasm (the smoking room). Cather writes that Flavia "had at last builded her house and hewn out her seven pillars" (p. 152). The reference is pointedly to Apollo to whom seven was sacred, whose lyre boasted seven strings, and whose oracle was open only on the seventh day of each month. Miss Broadwood twice refers to the residence as "The House of Song," the same phrase Cather uses for the Delphic Oracle in her poem "Winter at Delphi."

Yet, the irony of the reference becomes clear as the story progresses. This house, paralleled to the temple for the god of healing, is called an "asylum for talent" and a "sanitorium of the arts" (p. 152). It is not, however, a refuge for sacred creators with refined tastes. Nor is Flavia's "temple to the gods of Victory" the triumphal arch she believes it to be. In fact, here guests are more accurately described as "that band of indigent retainers who had once fed at her board like the suitors in the halls of Penelope..." (p. 152). The nine current guests are hardly the Muses. Cather returns to Kingsley's Roman-Teuton conflict in describing those who have entered the "temple." Schemetzkin is a "short, corpulent man, with an apoplectic face and purplish skin...." Frau Lichtenfeld, "the German giantess," wears a gown of "barbaric splendor" and looks like a "refugee from Valhalla." Herr Schotte is "reminiscent of the Stone Age," having "absorbed something of the savagery of those early types of life which he continually studied." Others, less

Teutonic in their threat to the civilized arts, simply contribute to the demise of artistic standards. Wellington includes in his novels passages once considered improper for young minds, and Miss Jimmy Broadwood supports such broad-mindedness against the Puritanical judgment of Mr. Will Maidenhood. The chemist, Restzhoff, so twists traditional values that he compares children to "certain salts which need not be actualized" and sees the possibility of manufacturing ice cream from vegetable oils as more beneficial to society than children. Signor Donati, the Italian tenor, is an ineffectual little man, and Jules Martel's sharp tongue recalls the satire of Martial (pp. 157-158). All in all, Flavia believes she has a garden full of talent, but as Miss Broadwood comments, "'You see, it's all on an entirely false basis'" (p. 164). Unconscious of her inability to distinguish the true from the false, Flavia has admitted to her garden the Teutons who will leave her temple in ruins. Like Flavia Domitilla, deification is not to be hers, for, in her naivete, she worships false gods of art.

It is the Vespasian figure who stands as "'a Pillar of sanity and law in this house of shams and swollen vanities...'" (p. 171). He scoffs at placing vain artists on pedestals, but will not allow them to hurt with their maliciousness and bigotry one who is "pathetically unconscious of her nakedness" (p. 168). In an effort to save Flavia from further humiliation through M. Roux's newspaper article, Arthur Hamilton insults his guests, thrusts them from the garden they have tainted, and closes the gate behind him, content to sit like "'Caius Marius among the ruins of Carthage'" (p. 172), the same phrase Cather had used to describe another spoiled garden in her early story "The Way of the World." Cather also describes this unexpected turn of events in Homeric terms. Miss Broadwood tells Imogen that she is responsible for reinstilling the heroic spark in Arthur, a quiet but keenly observant man: "'It's you, *ma cherie*, you've brought Ulysses home again and the slaughter has begun!'" (p. 170). Indeed, Arthur Hamilton does battle against the false gods of art, and victory is his, even if it be temporary.

The irony of "Flavia and Her Artists" lies in the battle against the new Medusa. In her innocent pursuit of her epithet as "the Advanced American Woman," Flavia has created a monster. Unable to recognize the intrusion of the Teutons into the Roman world, Flavia not only misses deification as patron of the arts, but she also "'Transmute[s] us all into stone,'" as M. Roux so readily puts it (p. 159). The humane spirit of the artist is gone, and elevation to divine status awaits neither M. Roux nor Flavia. Only Arthur Hamilton, the practical businessman whose artistic tastes are underdeveloped, could, like Vespasian at the very instant of his death, jest at the idea of approaching divinity. Flavia, not Arthur, is the deluded quester of the fruits in the troll garden.

Yet, while her intent is ironic, Cather does not portray Flavia completely unsympathetically. Here is a woman with a creative spirit, who desires to become part of the world of art but is misguided in her devotion. In worshiping a male artist rather than developing her own creativity, Flavia becomes a pathetic figure to the men about her, including her husband, and loses her identity as potential artist. Flavia's plight is hardly new or unique, and Cather reveals in this story her own concerns with breaking away from the imitation and "worship" of the masculine literary tradition. For a female artist to fulfill her potential, she could not remain the lesser light, the consort of a Caesar, yet unworthy of deification beside him. Cather must have recognized that she, too, was still imitative of models set before her; indeed, "Flavia and Her Artists," as well as other stories in the collection, show Cather's tendency to follow the Jamesian method. Cather, although having great respect for the male authors of English literature, may have feared that she, like Christina Rossetti before her brother, might find her greatness absorbed in theirs, "drowned by [their] loftier themes and deeper cadences...."[6] Flavia Hamilton's fate is that of most would-be female artists, falling into "one rank morass of misguided genius and wasted power," as Cather wrote in 1895. Cather's subsequent comment that she did not have "much faith in women in fiction" because they have "a sort of sex consciousness that is abominable"[7] seems somewhat less scathing in 1905 when applied to Flavia Hamilton. In this story, Flavia is only partly responsible for her humiliation. She is also victimized by male artists who

---

6.   Willa Cather, "As You Like It," *Nebraska State Journal*, 13 Jan. 1895, p. 13, in *The World and The Parish*, ed. William M. Curtin (Lincoln: Univ. of Nebraska Press, 1970), I, 143.

7.   Willa Cather, "The Passing Show," *Courier*, 23 Nov. 1895, p. 7 in *The World and The Parish*, I, 276.

expect deference from women, feed upon their worship, and, like M. Roux, scorn their artistic yearnings. The classical allusions in the story reinforce this idea, leaving Flavia Hamilton's "House of Song" empty and her spirit crushed.

The lure of the troll garden is again Cather's subject in "The Garden Lodge," the next story of the collection whose protagonist is female. Caroline Noble, unlike Flavia Hamilton, does not make a career of inviting artists to her garden lodge, but, when the world-famed Raymond d'Esquerré spends a month at her lodge, Caroline finds reawakened within her all the desires and longings she has suppressed in her pursuit of a comfortable and secure life. Caroline's apparently "glorious garden" which "had burst into impassioned bloom" is the result of careful tending and not the magical result of "the witchery of Freya," the Nordic goddess whose dominion includes the blossoming of flowers and productivity of fruit-bearing trees (p. 187). Nor is the apple orchard in which Caroline spends hours with d'Esquerré an Edenic one complete with temptress and serpent. Rather, the garden becomes Proserpina's, an abode substituting for the imaginative delights which Caroline has denied herself. Caroline, "cool-headed...and disgustingly practical" (p. 187), has superintended her gardeners, like the mistress of her realm, creating an undeniably beautiful world through artifice.

Against this artificial, but comfortable, beauty Cather sets the shabbiness of Caroline's former existence as a girl growing up in a family of impractical artists dedicated to "the shrine of idealism" (p. 189). Caroline's life has been a constant effort to avoid bowing down in "mystic worship of things distant, intangible and unattainable" (p. 189). Such worship had brought only drudgery for her mother, dissatisfaction for her composer-father, and suicide for her brother who, like Icarus, heeded not the practical demands of life. Having experienced the pain of living for art, Caroline locks herself out of the garden of delights until d'Esquerré's music ushers her again into a fanciful world.

Cather develops much of her story of the lure of art through a reworking of the Orpheus myth. Caroline becomes a Eurydice, not unlike the women who pour into the Metropolitan to enter into enchantment with d'Esquerré: "His appeal was all the more persuasive and alluring that it was to the imagination alone, that it was as indefinite and impersonal as those cults of idealism which so have their way with women" (p. 193). Caroline comes to fear d'Esquerré not in those moments of ecstasy which he arouses in her but in the moments of dullness and lethargy. His "tacit admission of disappointment under all this glamour of success" is merely Orpheus' dilemma – "the helplessness of the enchanter to at all enchant himself" (p. 194). For two weeks after d'Esquerré's departure, Caroline visits the garden lodge daily, compelled by the memory of his song, much as Eurydice longed for the music of Orpheus' lyre. Cather describes the final stormy night Caroline spends in the lodge in terms reminiscent of the closeness of Hades:

> The storm had held off unconscionably long; the air within the lodge was stifling, and without the garden waited, breathless. Everything seemed pervaded by the poignant distress; the hush of feverish, intolerable expectation. The still earth, the heavy flowers, even the growing darkness, breathed the exhaustion of protracted waiting. (p. 195)

Even as Caroline wrestles with her own soul, she, clad in "thin drapery, diaphanously vague and white" (p. 195), appears like one of the shades of the Underworld. The echoes of her duet with d'Esquerré haunt the air, and Caroline finds that the ghosts of slain desires rise "as from a sowing of dragon's teeth" (p. 195), a phrase which recalls images of Medea, as well. But Caroline is no sorceress who can conjure up the image of d'Esquerré. Surrendering to her imagination, Caroline falls asleep and her dream slips away. After "such a night of sorcery" (p. 196), she awakens to the reality of romance. She has become a Eurydice, forever possessed by Orpheus' song, but living the only life feasible for her, a life regulated by order and self-control.

However, Caroline's end is, as her name implies, more noble than Flavia's. Caroline has likewise been deluded into worshiping a god of art, who will only drain creative vitality from her. When d'Esquerré sings "Thou art the Spring from which I sighed in Winter's cold embraces" and puts his arm about her, Caroline falls victim to his power, in spite of her belief that she is in control. She is like the goddess of Spring, Proserpina, who in accepting the cold embrace of the death god, surrenders her own desires to a life of silence and memory. She does not become a pathetic figure, though, and retains a degree of nobility by suppressing her pain. Caroline's emotional outburst in the garden lodge during the storm is not likely to occur again. Reconciling herself to the loss of her own creative powers, absorbed in the superior talent of her "god," Caroline Noble gives up her dreams of aesthetic fulfillment. She becomes another instance of thwarted potential, a woman whose creativity has no outlet. No nourishment exists in the troll garden, but only guilt and resignation. In "The Garden Lodge," then, Cather utilizes both the classical myth of the Orphic guest and the poetical image of the troll garden to illustrate that the goblin fruit of the imagination can destroy while it enchants.

In the apparently earliest story of *The Troll Garden* – "'A Death in the Desert'" (January, 1903) – Cather also deals with the fate of a woman whose life has been devoted to artistic achievement and to an artist. In developing the details of Katharine Gaylord's death, Cather extends her analogy of the troll garden and draws upon myths of Proserpina and Athena to emphasize the loneliness of this death in the desert. Katharine Gaylord, like Caroline Noble, had risen from a humble beginning and had struggled to achieve fame as a singer. Having formed an early acquaintance with both Adriance and Everett Hilgarde, she serves as a vocalist to Adriance while his career as a composer sky-rockets. Katharine never reveals her love for Adriance and, after contracting tuberculosis, returns to her Wyoming home to die. As the result of a chance meeting, Everett Hilgarde spends the last days of Katharine's life with her, comforting her in the isolation she feels from the world of art and acting as a substitute for his brother Adriance, who is unable to commit himself to Katharine or others because of the demands of his art. Cather ends her story with Everett again being mistaken for Adriance, a situation to which he has resigned himself while both resenting and admiring the success he cannot share.

Adriance is the forest child who, attracted by the goblin fruits, has entered the troll garden and thrived. His performances place him beyond the baser aspects of life as "a circle of flame [is] set about those splendid children of genius" (p. 209). Yet, even the residents of the troll garden find that devotion to art may drain one of life. Katharine describes his compositions as not just "tragedies of passion" but "the tragedy of the soul, the shadow coexistent with the soul" (p. 213). This shadow eventually consumes even the artist as well as those whose lives he touches. Katharine diagnoses Adriance's inexplicable illness, to which he succumbed while in Florence, as "'the weariness of all his life...and of all other lives that must aspire and suffer to make up one such life as his'" (p. 214).

Lives like Everett's are often sacrificed in the process. Everett is also a forest child who desires admission to the garden but is denied entrance. He appears more like the Teuton or barbarian, hammering at the gates of Rome, than like "the shepherd-boys who sang in the Vale of Tempe," the description usually applied to Adriance (p. 209). Even Everett's name is of Germanic origin while Adriance's is associated with the brilliant blue of the Adriatic Sea. In spite of his exclusion from the garden, Everett retains a certain innocence of spirit and selflessness which allow him to do the genuine thing, not just "the right thing, but the opportune, graceful, exquisite thing" (p. 211). Closed out of the troll garden, Everett does not lose his essential humanity and, consequently, is not destroyed by the demands of art.

Katharine is yet another forest child but one whose entry to the garden is fraught with ills and destines her for destruction. The struggle to achieve success has left her "thoroughly sophisticated and a trifle hard," unable to feel at home with her family and "both sad and cynical" (p. 204). Her pursuit of art has resulted in a physical demise and a longing to grasp again the goblin fruits. Like Thea Kronborg, Katharine's personal sacrifice is great, and she learns to wear a mask to hide her true feelings. Beneath the mask Katharine has cared too much, not just for Adriance but for art itself. Only in death can "the madness of art [be] over for Katharine" (p. 217).

Although Katharine could approach her impending death with bitterness stemming from unrequited love, she instead confronts death with Stoic resignation like that of Brutus, whose farewell to Cassius becomes Katharine's farewell to Everett. The courage with which Katharine accepts her destiny is, in part, supported by the mythic allusions which surround her. The reader first sees Katharine alone in a phaeton, dressed in white, the reins lying loosely in her hands. The scene is not unusual until examined in light of subsequent descriptions. Everett later meets Katharine in her studio, admittedly a copy of Adriance's, and she appears as a goddess in her own

72

temple. In the *Scribner's* version of the story (January, 1903), Cather had included a detailed description of this room which well prepared the reader for the description of Katharine herself:

> In every detail Adriance's taste was so manifest that the room seemed to exhale his personality. The black-oak ceiling and floor, the dull red walls, the huge brick fireplace with a Wagnerian inscription on the tiles, the old Venetian lamp that hung under the copy of the Mona Lisa, the cast of the Parthenon frieze that ran about the room, the tall brass candlesticks with their sacerdotal candles, were all exactly as Adriance would have had them.[8]

Cather did not include this passage in the reprinting of "'A Death in the Desert'" in either *The Troll Garden* or *Youth and the Bright Medusa*. Most likely she considered it superfluous, striking out those excesses of detail which she believed unnecessary to the well-wrought story. Yet, this passage is one of the first indications of the sacredness which surrounds Katharine. Her name means "pure," and, like the goddess of the original Parthenon, she stands very tall and virginal, the "long, loose folds of her white gown" draping around her. Her skin is "transparently white, and cold to the touch," not unlike Phidias' ivory-veneered, marble Athena. Her head is "well shaped and proudly poised," disdaining sympathy and commanding respect. She is a goddess, but one who is "older, sadder, softer" (pp. 204-205). Katharine's chief charm is her eyes, which Everett describes as possessing "a warm, life-giving quality like sunlight...." The original text further describes them as "generous, fearless eyes which glowed with sympathy and good cheer for all living things."[9] Athena, too, was known for the brightness and radiance of her eyes, earning her the epithet of *glaukopis*, which may also have referred to her eyes' grey or green color. But it is the "courage in her eyes like the clear light of a star" (p. 216) that equates Katharine with Athena and brings Everett to her house daily like a worshiper in a Panathenaic procession under a blistering summer sun.

Katharine is in complete control in her private temple where Everett comes again and again, a devout worshiper. Like Athena, though, she is

---

8.   James Woodress, ed., "Table of Revisions," in *The Troll Garden* (Lincoln: Univ. of Nebraska Press, 1983), p. 150.

9.   Woodress, ed., "Table of Revisions," in *The Troll Garden*, p. 151.

stirred only by her attachment to one man, her Odysseus, who wanders the earth and, according to the earliest version of the story, even has slept in a grotto like Calypso's where George Sand once shut up Chopin and gave him only goat's milk to drink.[10] As a goddess impervious to love, Athena was hardly a vicious virago who demanded awe and respect without inspiring love. She did show deep and abiding affection for Odysseus but did not respond to or solicit such devotion from other mortal men. With the kindness and aloofness of a goddess, Katharine also rejects Everett's overture of love; she does so with the "infinite loyalty and tenderness" (p. 216) of Athena-Parthenos who protected her warriors while rejecting them as lovers. Everett understands the rejection of his suit, for he has, since his early acquaintance with Katharine, known that they were from two very different planes of life, he the earthly and she the ethereal. In the *Scribner's* edition, Cather described this distinction in mythic terms:

> He told himself that he had in common with this woman only the baser uses of life. That sixth sense, the passion for perfect expression, and the lustre of her achievement were like a rosy mist veiling her, such as the goddesses of the elder days wrapped about themselves when they vanished from the arms of men.[11]

Indeed, Everett cannot hold Katharine, for she dedicates her love to only one hero.

Katharine's particular interest in the happenings of New York also includes an inquiry about her companion virgin-goddess: "Does the chaste Diana on the Garden Theatre still keep her vestal vows through all the exasperating changes of weather?" (p. 206). The pointed remark is in keeping with Katharine's Athena-like pose, for, unlike the protectress of Athens, Diana (Artemis) did not always exhibit impeccable character when men made sexual advances. Katharine has apparently kept to her vows in spite of the "exasperating changes of weather" within her social circle.[12]

---

10. Woodress, ed., "Table of Revisions," in *The Troll Garden*, p. 159.

11. Woodress, ed., "Table of Revisions," in *The Troll Garden*, p. 155.

12. Sharon O'Brien offers an alternative reading of this comment, suggesting that, unlike Katharine who has abandoned her art for Adriance's, the goddess Diana "reminds us that only the woman who resists the goblin men's blandishments retains autonomy and creative power" [*Willa Cather: The Emerging Voice*, p. 276].

74

Moreover, Cather includes Katharine in the ranks of other warrior-maidens who meet their enemies in mortal combat. Katharine remarks that in the past she was expected to sing Brünnhilde, a role in Wagner's *Die Walküre*. With Valkyrie-like vehemence, Katharine confronts her death. Never does she lose her regalness nor does she regret anything about her life. "On the whole I am not ashamed of it. I have fought a good fight," she tells Everett (p. 215). So it was that Brünnhilde, influenced by love and without regret, resolved to disobey Wotan, although she would be stripped of her divinity and condemned to a deep sleep. The courage with which Katharine meets death only confirms Everett's general impression of her: "There had always been a little of the imperatrix about her and her pose...revived all his old impressions of her unattachedness, of how absolutely and valiantly she stood alone" (p. 205). Reflecting the strength of her surname, Gaylord, Katharine meets death with a lordly mien, but the gaiety she attempts to muster is only a disguise for the agony she suffers, not just as a forgotten lover but also as a diminished artist.

The admirable qualities of Katharine do not place her outside the role of woman as victim, though. Woven within the texture of the tale are references to *Proserpine*, a cantata which, some years before, had made Adriance famous. Katharine, caught up and ravished by the art that created the "Spring Song" of *Proserpine*, has devoted herself in silent admiration to Adriance's genius. The joy of the "Spring Song" corresponds to Adriance's early career and to the youthful days he spent with Katharine. But, like Proserpina, she has descended into the depths with him as his music matured and assumed an autumnal tone, a serenity that comes after the fulfillment of summer. During a pounding rainstorm in Florence, Katharine and Adriance had clung together in their recognition of "that awful, vague, universal pain, that cold fear of life and death and God and hope..." (p. 214). Both have experienced a disintegration of self, a descent into the Underworld, into the desert where Death awaits. Adriance escapes his death through art; but, as Richard Giannone suggests, Katharine's song cannot rescue her, for it is "a Winter Song lamenting a singer's final hour...."[13] Hers is Proserpina's song of

---

13.   Giannone, p. 41.

the dying seasons. Appropriately, Katharine dies in the summer, the time that the Kore goes underground while the Greek fields are bare and unproductive.

Yet, in fulfilling the birth-death imagery associated with Proserpina, Katharine need not relinquish her stature as a warrior goddess fighting against death. For, as C. Kerenyi explains in his study of the Earth Mother cults of Eleusis, the Kore and corn-maiden for the Athenians was none other than Athena herself: "Another Great Goddess, the archaic cult image of Athena Nike in her temple on the Athens Akropolis, held a pomegranate in her right hand, in her left a helmet: the simple explanation of this is the somber Persephone-like aspect of the goddess...."[14] Katharine embodies the traits of two classical goddesses, one the courageous protectress, Athena, and the other the sacrificial victim, Proserpina, giving up her joy so that life may go on for those remaining on earth. In writing "'A Death in the Desert,'" Cather thus clarifies the Roman/Teuton or troll/forest child mythic structure of *The Troll Garden* and also introduces her theme of the interplay of life and death in the guise of the classical goddesses, the primitive Earth Mothers who will appear in Cather's later frontier novels.

"'A Death in the Desert'" also reinforces Cather's abiding concern for women who fail to maintain identity as artists. Perhaps Cather realized that her own potential as a writer had not yet been realized, but that she should wither in the desert like Katharine Gaylord, finding no outlet for her creative voice, was unacceptable. Cather makes clear in "'A Death in the Desert'" that Katharine's error was not in loving, but in loving the wrong thing – the artist rather than art itself. Katharine Gaylord's recognition of this comes too late. Bitterness, but not guilt, gnaws at her soul: "That ironical smile, worn like a mask through so many years, had gradually changed even the lines of her face completely, and when she looked in the mirror she saw not herself, but the scathing critic, the amused observer and satirist of herself" (p. 214). Closed out of the garden by her own misguided affections, Katharine finds herself alone, unfulfilled by, but still desirous of, the troll garden's fruits. In

---

14.   C. Kerenyi, *Eleusis: Archetypal Image of Mother and Daughter*, trans. Ralph Manheim (New York: Pantheon Books, 1967), pp. 137-138.

this story, Cather once again confirms that, even for women of heroic endurance, the male mythos subverts their triumphs. The choice between Dionysus (the passions) and Apollo (the purity of art) is not a viable one. In either case, "No matter when or how love did befall,/ 'Tis Loneliness that loves [them] best of all" ("L'Envoi," *AT*, p. 51).

The last of the stories in *The Troll Garden* which presents a female protagonist is "A Wagner Matinee," and here Cather pictures an aspiring artist and forest child who has been prevented for thirty years from entering the troll garden. Although direct mention of classical mythology is absent from this story, Cather interweaves music and myth to describe a woman whose personal sacrifice gives her heroic dimensions.

After Clark, the narrator of "A Wagner Matinee," unexpectedly receives a letter informing him that his Aunt Georgiana will arrive shortly, the reader begins to piece together the details of the martyrdom of a woman who gave up the ideals of art for a homestead in Red Willow County, Nebraska. Clark, however, has a "reverential affection" for his aunt and views her pathetic figure in heroic terms: "As for myself, I saw my aunt's misshapen figure with that feeling of awe and respect with which we hold explorers who have left their ears and fingers north of Franz-Joseph-Land, or their health somewhere along the Upper Congo" (p. 236). The respect Clark bears for his aunt stems from his memories of this woman, who carried the Muse with her into a hostile world and made it possible for him to reach beyond the cowshed and plowed furrows to the finer and more beautiful things in life. It was Aunt Georgiana who heard him "recite Latin declensions and conjugations," and "her old text-book on mythology was the first that ever came into [his] empty hands" (p. 237). Although she had long suppressed her passion for music to the daily necessities of farm life, Aunt Georgiana had taught Clark his scales on a little parlor organ, warning him not to love his music too well or it might be taken from him. Georgiana, whose name echoes Vergil's *Georgics*, becomes symbolic of the pioneer spirit for Clark.

However, Cather's deliberate use of Georgiana's name is ironic. Georgiana hardly reflects the Vergilian beauty and dignity of a rural life, a dedication to a love of the land, or a virtuous struggle with the forces of nature. Georgiana does not emerge from the cornfields with a pious dedication to the virtues of rural life, as Vergil describes it. Instead, her life is filled with worry about old Maggie's weakling calf and a freshly opened kit of mackerel that may spoil. Cather substitutes the rustic simplicity of the *Georgics* with a "tall, unpainted house, with weather-curled boards; naked as a tower, the crooked-backed ash seedlings where the dishcloths hung to dry; the gaunt, molting turkeys picking up refuse about the kitchen door" (p. 242).

Aunt Georgiana found no world of romance in her marriage and life on the plains. Only the old scores of operas among her music remind her of the rare and beautiful things she had lost in being barred from the troll garden. Like Euryanthe, whose song Clark had struggled to play as a child, Georgiana has been deceived by romance.[15] Also like Euryanthe, though, she has a second chance at life after her exile into a hostile world. Georgiana's revival comes at a performance of Wagner's *Tannhaüser*. As the orchestra begins to play, Aunt Georgiana is, for the first time in thirty years, thrust into the troll garden and feels again the yearnings for art. Clark describes the scene as a "wind-tossed forest of fiddle necks and bows," each bow moving like "a conjurer's stick" (p. 239). The magic of the overture enthralls Aunt Georgiana, but in what Richard Giannone calls the "seductive spell of the Venusberg motif,"[16] the conflict of what is and what might have been clutches at Georgiana. Clark, too, when he hears "the frenzy of the Venusberg theme and its ripping of strings," is overcome by "an overwhelming sense of the waste and wear we are so powerless to combat" (p. 239). The desires of Venus are those of Red Willow County, a grasping for the material, an effort to satisfy a lust for land, position, and success. For Aunt Georgiana, the Venusberg motif reminds her of her youthful yearning for physical love, which led only to a frontier burying ground where "hope has lain down with hope and dream with dream, and renouncing, slept" (p. 241).

---

15.   In the romantic opera *Euryanthe* by Carl Maria von Weber, Euryanthe is deceived by a friend who reveals Euryanthe's family secret to the jealous Count Lysiart. When Lysiart makes public that secret, Euryanthe's fiance deserts her, abandoning her in a forest where she collapses in despair. When the treachery and lies are finally exposed, Euryanthe revives from her supposed death due to grief, and the lovers are reunited. [*Phaidon Book of the Opera: A Survey of 780 Operas from 1597*, trans. Catherine Atthill, and others (Oxford: Phaidon Press Limited, 1979), pp. 146-147.]

16.   Giannone, p.43.

The music of Wagner awakens her briefly from her slumber; her sacred yearnings for art have never really died, as Clark realizes, in spite of the soul's excruciating and interminable suffering.

The concert ends, and Aunt Georgiana cries out to hold the magic spell a little longer. Her protests are in vain, though, for like other women protagonists in *The Troll Garden*, pure and high art scores no victory over mundane realities. Dionysus is victorious over Apollo. Flavia Hamilton falls victim to a love of a false art and fame; Caroline Noble succumbs to a desire for security and contentment; Katharine Gaylord is vanquished by her own passion and death itself. Aunt Georgiana follows in their footsteps. Her attempt to enter the troll garden is thwarted by the demands of a world hostile to art, a world of which she has chosen to be a part and from which there is no escape. Each of these women has the potential to create and, given a different set of circumstances and a nature less subject to passion, might have become an Alexandra Bergson or a Thea Kronborg. In *The Troll Garden*, then, Cather explores a conflict central to her later works – the struggle of the artist against the demands of the world.

Although stories of women grasping for the goblin fruits dominate *The Troll Garden*, Cather does not exclude men from this struggle. She is, however, less likely to describe their plight in mythic terms. In "The Sculptor's Funeral," death conquers Harvey Merrick as it did Katharine Gaylord, and the lawyer Jim Laird, another individual of artistic sensibilities, drowns his unhappiness in liquor, just as Aunt Georgiana suppressed hers in farm work and quiet resignation. Paul of "Paul's Case" is another Flavia Hamilton, unable to distinguish true from false art and subsequently destroyed by the goblin fruits he tries to possess.

Only in "The Marriage of Phaedra" does Cather toy with mythic allusions. Although the sale of a painting which depicts Phaedra's first encounter with her stepson is the subject of this very Jamesian story, the subject of the painting itself seems to have little connection to the events of the story. To liken Sir Hugh Treffinger to Theseus and Lady Ellen to Phaedra would only be justifiable in that both marriages were filled with unhappiness. But Lady Ellen exhibits none of Phaedra's sense of guilt and settles the problems of her own marriage, not by suicide, but by vengefully selling the painting into which her husband had poured his greatest efforts. Nor is Sir Hugh an Hippolytus, for his devotion to purity in art does not, like Hippolytus, prevent him from pursuing a woman with "the air of a man who could storm his way through anything to get what he wanted" (p. 224). "The Marriage of Phaedra" does not utilize mythic allusions as essential for understanding the theme of the artist's all-consuming passion for art, a passion which can replace even the commitment to one's spouse and can make marriage "a mutual misunderstanding" (p. 224). Cather had visited the studio of Burne-Jones in 1902 and based much of the detail of "The Marriage of Phaedra" on her observations there. Burne-Jones did not, however, create a work depicting the fatal triangle of Theseus, Phaedra, and Hippolytus. He had used parts of the Theseus legend as subjects for at least three works,[17] but Cather apparently selected the title for Treffinger's painting purely from her own classical reading and to suit the focus of her story.

The allusion to this particular painting indicates Cather's skill at manipulating details of classical myth, often to release her female protagonists from the restrictions placed upon them by the myths of a patriarchal society. Such changes are usually subtle and brief, as in the case of Lady Ellen. In selling the painting, she asserts a strength of will more characteristic of Theseus than Phaedra, a defiance of the societal norm that difficulties in a marriage should remain hidden from the public eye. Lady Ellen does not shrink away and end her unhappy life; rather, she profits from an unhappy marriage, exhibiting the power and independence of spirit that heroic figures would display in Cather's later novels. One would be only partially justified in claiming that Cather's title is not integrated with the story and does not make a significant contribution to fulfilling its purpose. In the larger scheme, this apparently "misfit" reference typifies what James Woodress describes as Cather's use of allusion: "...she never uses a one-for-one correspondence between a myth or allegory and her fiction but

---

17.   Among the Burne-Jones' paintings based on the myths of Theseus are *Theseus and Ariadne* (ca. 1862), *Theseus and the Minotaur in the Labyrinth* (1861), and *Phyllis and Demophoon* (1870). [*Burne-Jones*, introd. John Christian (London: Arts Council of Great Britain, 1975), pp. 29, 37, 47.]

introduces her indirect references briefly and then moves on."[18] A close study of *The Troll Garden* thus belies an early review by Bessie de Bois that it is "a collection of freak stories that are either lurid, hysterical or unwholesome...."[19] In fact, these stories provide the seed both structurally and thematically for Cather's growing use of mythic allusions.

Less than a year after the publication of *The Troll Garden*, Willa Cather's life and work took on an entirely new dimension as she moved to New York and began a career at *McClure's Magazine*. With most of her energies devoted to her new responsibilities, Cather produced little of note between the years 1906 and 1908. Of greatest importance in shaping the direction of her art was not her work at *McClure's* but was her acquaintance with Mrs. James T. Fields and Sarah Orne Jewett. The atmosphere Cather found at 148 Charles Street, Boston, was one she had long sought, not the artificiality of a literary world geared to selling magazines, but a sanctuary where the values of the past, mementos of great writers, and the greatest thoughts of western culture still survived. Her friendship with Sarah Orne Jewett particularly provided the impetus for Cather's decision in 1912 to devote all her energies to writing. Many of the stories prior to her acquaintance with Jewett are imitative and merit Jewett's criticism that they do not "proceed from a quiet center" or are not "an organic development" from Cather's own fiber.[20] In these stories, Cather strays from the references to classical literature which had bolstered some of her earlier work. Although she frequently alludes to myth, these references are more embellishment than essential ingredients.

In "The Profile" (June, 1907), for instance, Cather prefaces the story with a discussion about the proper place in art for the grotesque or the maimed. The discussion centers on a young German's work *Circe's Swine*, in which the enchantress is surrounded by a variety of freakish creatures, half

---

18.   James Woodress, *Willa Cather: A Literary Life* (Lincoln: Univ. of Nebraska Press, 1987), p. 361.

19.   Bessie de Bois, rev. of *The Troll Garden*, by Willa Cather, *Bookman*, 5 Aug. 1905, p. 612.

20.   E. K. Brown, *Willa Cather: A Critical Biography* (1953; rpt. New York: Avon Books, 1980), p. 110.

animal and half human. The classical myth sets the stage for the exploration of Aaron Dunlap's theory that love might act as an enchantment, lessening or removing his wife's hurt over a hideous scar which mars her face. But, Cather makes no effort to pursue the classical subject further and abandons the Circe comparison for a violent scene in which the enraged wife tries to destroy her rival, much in the same way that Medea set out to destroy Glauce. The sorcery of desiring perfect beauty and the devastating consequences of that desire are evident in the inclusion of a direct allusion to Circe and in the analogy to Medea, but the importance of the story lies more in its parallel to Hawthorne's "The Birthmark" than in its classical allusions. The romantic tradition is evident, too, by the parallels the story suggests to Coleridge's "Cristabel." Susan Rosowski argues that, like Coleridge's work, "The Profile" focuses on the power of love to reconcile "beauty coupled with ugliness, joy with pain...."[21]

Thus, the brief mention of a painting of a classical subject serves in this story much as did the painting in "The Marriage of Phaedra." The reader is prepared for a plot in which unsightly appearances are repaired by love. Instead, the leading female character again deviates from her expected role, not healing wounds but inflicting more hurt. Readers glimpse once more a woman seeking vengeance against an order which would define her by the most traditional of female traits – physical beauty.

Similarly, "The Namesake," also published in 1907, makes a single reference to *The Aeneid* and another to "the sad one of the Destinies who, as the Greeks believed, watched from birth over those marked for a violent or untimely death" (p. 146). "The Namesake" is in keeping with the themes Cather had begun to explore in *April Twilights* when she was so influenced by the work of Housman. The story does not, however, integrate images of past cultures with the artistically barren present, a technique which some of her earlier works like "Jack-a-Boy" and "Eric Hermannson's Soul" had illustrated. In Lyon Hartwell's discovery of familial and spiritual roots in his ancestor's copy of *The Aeneid*, Cather is wrestling with her own feelings toward her

---

21.   Susan J. Rosowski, *The Voyage Perilous: Willa Cather's Romanticism* (Lincoln: Univ. of Nebraska Press, 1986), p. 212.

82

Virginian heritage and has little room to explore ties to a classical world whose values might have been slipping from her in the hectic environs of the *McClure's* office. Miss Jewett's observation was correct that these stories and others of the period "had the defects inseparable from creative work done in a hurry, when one was tired, and seeking relief from exacting work of another sort."[22]

The same indiscriminate use of classical references appears in "The Willing Muse" and "Eleanor's House," both stories imitative of James and set either in Europe or among the sophisticates of New York. Kenneth Gray, the genuine artist of "The Willing Muse," comes from Olympia, Ohio, where he had "naturally found himself in a place of official sanctity" (p. 116). His godliness, though, is subdued in an unfortunate marriage to Bertha Torrence, a carbon copy of Flavia Hamilton, who worships art as a commercial venture and drains her husband's creative genius in the process. In "Eleanor's House," Cather describes her characters' love as Olympian but makes no attempt to equate either Harold or Eleanor with a specific deity. Neither of these stories achieves the quality of the best of *The Troll Garden*, and the mythic references often seem forced or unrelated to the structure of the stories themselves.

What had happened to that firm grasp of classical studies which Cather had displayed in her work, first as a student of Classics and later as a teacher of Latin? Perhaps the daily grind of meeting deadlines and filling pages had lessened Cather's easy familiarity with classical ideas. In April, 1908, however, Cather set out with Isabelle McClung for a long Mediterranean vacation, an excursion which would renew her acquaintance with the classical world and stimulate again her mythic consciousness.

One can only imagine the inspiration which Cather must have found in visits to Rome, Naples, and Salerno and in spending a week in the Apennines, all sites which had been prominent in the works of authors from Caesar and Horace to Vergil and Ovid. Although few written records exist of this journey, Cather did write to her former high school principal, Mrs. Goudy, remarking that "she had seen in the Naples museum the wonderful

22. Brown, pp. 110-111.

head of Caesar that had illustrated the high-school text of Caesars' commentaries she had read under Mr. Goudy."[23] So memorable had been her studies of classical literature that seeing the relics of the ancient world must have sparked her imagination. Like Thea Kronborg, who chose a print of the Naples bust of Caesar as the sole decoration for the walls of her room, Cather would turn to the ancient world again as a means of "decorating" her stories, a process which was most useful artistically and most satisfying to her personally. Bernice Slote agrees that Cather's work shows a clear shift in emphasis at this time:

> At some point around 1908...Willa Cather seems to have made a deliberate effort to use primary experience in a mythical or allusive structure. In the dissembling of myth (and myth fragmented, changed, slanting into other forms) one may both extend and mask his original material.[24]

This Cather did, for many of the stories and novels after 1908 show deliberate use of classical myth, though rarely do they correspond in every detail to the ancient versions of those myths.

In the first poem she published after her trip to Italy, Cather returned to the theme of civilization's decay as she had earlier expressed it in *April Twilights*. The melancholic strain which mourned the disappearance of Apollo and a golden age is, however, no longer evident. In "The Palatine (In the 'Dark Ages')," Cather's tone is less one of regret than one of acceptance of the passing of a glorious civilization. The Roman world, like the troll garden, has decayed both from internal corruption and external invasion. But, a certain tranquillity exists in the poppies that grow on Caesar's banquet seat, the cattle that browse on palace floors, and the fire-flies that gleam where the Caesar's gold once shone. In accepting the demise of one culture, Cather seems to have reconciled herself to the cyclical nature of all life. Although in her poem the "Rhineland orchard and Danube fen/ Fatten their

---

23. James Woodress, *Willa Cather: Her Life and Art* (1970; rpt. Lincoln: Univ. of Nebraska Press, 1982), p. 39.

24. Bernice Slote, ed., *The Kingdom of Art: Willa Cather's First Principles and Critical Statements 1893-1896* (Lincoln: Univ. of Nebraska Press, 1966), p. 103.

84

roots on Caesar's men," young Saxon boys still go on climbing their hills, oblivious to Rome's fall and not hurting their heads "that the world is sad."[25]

This recognition and acceptance of the larger patterns of human experience lend to Cather's work yet another mythic dimension. Reconciliation to the birth-death-rebirth cycle brings to stories like "The Joy of Nelly Deane" (1911) more than echoes of Housman's theme that those who die a sad but early death have somehow escaped life's greatest despair and disillusionment. Nelly Deane, the prototype for Lucy Gayheart, is a sprite-like girl whose "unquenchable joy" (p. 56) makes her a favorite of all the townspeople of Riverbend. Her natural talent as a singer and her beauty earn her the role of Queen Esther in the Baptist Church Christmas play, although her vivaciousness and spirit often make her an object of concern and a topic of discussion at the church's sewing circles. Nelly believes she loves and is loved by Guy Franklin, a traveling salesman, who comes to the frontier town like one of Caesar's merchants into Gaul, offering to the forest children the rare goblin fruits, "those things which effeminate the mind" (p. 60). Eventually abandoned by Franklin, Nelly concedes to marry the dark and moody Scott Spinny, whose hardware business has made him wealthy. Nelly's fullness of life does not conform to the traditional values and expectations of a small town, but eventually she submits, joins the church, marries Spinny, and dies after the birth of her second child.

The conclusion of "The Joy of Nelly Deane" couples a sense of loss with an acknowledgment of the on-goingness of life and the inevitable return of Nelly's joy in succeeding generations. "The Joy of Nelly Deane" well exemplifies Cather's growing skill at slanting myth to achieve multiple meanings in her work and to reflect her own ambivalence toward the events she describes.

Hovering over Nelly throughout her youth are three old women – Mrs. Dow, Mrs. Freeze, and Mrs. Spinny – whose guardianship becomes central to the mythic structure of the story. They are certainly the Greek fates, the Moirai, whose functions were to determine each individual's portion in life.

---

25. Willa Cather, *April Twilights and Other Poems* (New York: Alfred A. Knopf, 1923), pp. 47-48.

In this capacity, the three "guardians" conjure up for the reader dark visions of impending doom and premature death. These women do hover over Nelly with an attentiveness almost akin to vulture-like preying upon one who would dare to escape their grasp. Susan Rosowski interprets their roles as sinister ones and further argues that the fate which Mrs. Dow, Mrs. Freeze, and Mrs. Spinny spin for Nelly, is engulfment in a female culture where her spirit will be subdued by immersion into traditional female roles.[26]

Indeed, the details of the story lend some support to this view. The narrator, upon her return to Riverbend after Nelly's death, is distraught to learn that Nelly's death "needn't have been," but Mrs. Dow discourages that way of thinking: "'We musn't look at it that way, dear,' she said tremulously and a little sternly; 'we musn't let ourselves.'" Mrs. Dow's subsequent comment seems hollow and offers little comfort: "'We must just feel that our Lord wanted her *then*, and took her to Himself'" (p. 66). Mrs. Dow maintains her image as a fatalistic power as she sits in her familiar but aged parlor, not looking "greatly changed," her body still exhibiting "its old activity" (p. 65). And, although the "contented ticking of the clock" gives to the narrator "a great sense of comfort and completeness" (p. 65), Mrs. Dow seems outside of time. Death is an integral part of her life; she even is "haunted by thoughts of shipwreck and suffering upon wintry seas," a comment which indicates that Cather might have been recalling the three witches of *Macbeth* (I.iii.) as she composed her tale. Mrs. Dow also chronicles the whereabouts of Nelly's daughter, Margaret, as if each minute of the girl's life is known to her. Like her counterparts, Mrs. Dow is vitalized by the opportunity to "watch over" Margaret; Mrs. Spinny is "like a young woman with her first" (p. 66). A subtle sense of foreboding, of inevitable entrapment, envelops Margaret and even hovers over Nelly's son in the final scene of the story. The pride the three old women feel in the boy is a pride of possession, perhaps of their age-old power to shape destiny.

Yet, these women also appear kindly, not like the dark Fates of later literature, the blind Furies of Milton's *Lycidas* or the cruel Fates of Landor's "Orpheus and Eurydice." Cather draws the figures in their original roles, as

---

26. Rosowski, p. 221.

well, as birth-spirits who determine what each child's lot in life is to be. In this case, the Fates retain the function which their Latin name, Parcae, implies. The verb *parere* means to bring forth as in childbirth, and from her reading of Ovid and Vergil, Cather surely knew that the Fates could allot largess as well as death to the new-born. Mrs. Spinny is Clotho, the spinner, whose personal interest in Nelly as a prospective bride for her son causes her to smile softly at Nelly's beauty and to care for her with motherly pride. Mrs. Dow, the Lachesis figure, is equally attentive, chronicling for the reader each lot in life as it is doled out to Nelly. She, like the others, is always looking for good influences for Nelly, trying to "endow" the girl with the best qualities without altering her enthusiasm for life. The least evident of the three "Dear old ladies," as Cather calls them (p. 57), is Mrs. Freeze, the figure of Atropos, whose Greek name indicates her inflexibility and inability to turn from the given course of life. Although Cather does not describe in detail Mrs. Freeze's attentiveness to Nelly, she is silently present throughout the story. She is present at Nelly's triumph in *Queen Esther* on the very night that the narrator feels "a sense of imminent change and danger" (p. 61). She is present at Nelly's baptism when Nelly rises from the water and goes up into the arms of "those three dear guardians" (p. 63). And, in the final scenes, Mrs Freeze is one of the three white heads that bend over Nelly's baby. That death is part of the continuum of life is the message Cather makes clear through the ironical and dual nature of her characters. Whether in Riverbend or in far-off Rome, the narrator discovers that life is as if "it was all arranged, written out like a story..." (p. 64).

In such arrangement lies a cyclical pattern of death and recovery, a pattern which denies the power of neither the Moirai nor the Parcae. Nelly's vitality wanes, but the joy of life does not disappear forever with her death. Nelly assumes some traits of the mythic Persephone, whose story best illustrates Cather's point. Cather describes Nelly as possessing the maidenly beauty of Persephone, as "pink and eager" with "yellow-brown eyes, which dilated so easily and sparkled with a kind of golden effervescence" (pp. 60, 56). She is the darling of the high school youths, who send all the way to Denver for her flowers. Her dressing room is bedecked with floral tributes from the townspeople as well and becomes another meadow of Enna, the legendary site of Persephone's abduction by Hades. In fact, the dark figure of Scott Spinny awaits glumly outside the door of the baptistry dressing room on the very night of the performance. Even Nelly's bedroom has a virginal purity about it with its white sash curtains, a white counterpane, and a white fur rug. It was "a warm, gay little room flooded all day long with sunlight from east and south windows that had climbing roses all about them in summer" – the perfect bower for a goddess of springtime (p. 60). Surrounding Nelly is a quality which makes her divine. The narrator describes the sensation Nelly's person evokes to those around her: "I felt as I did when I got up early on picnic mornings in summer, and saw the dawn come up in a breathless sky above the river meadows and make all the corn fields golden" (p. 61). Nelly, then, becomes another Kore, scattering the seeds of life about her.

Set against Nelly's brightness and vitality is the somber aspect of Scott Spinny who, like Hades, has long lain in wait to seize Persephone:

> There was something grim and saturnine about his powerful body and bearded face and his strong, cold hands. I wondered what perverse fate had driven him for eight years to dog the footsteps of a girl whose charm was due to qualities naturally distasteful to him. (p. 62)

Scott is "a prosperous hardware merchant and notoriously penurious" (p. 58), guarding his wealth as jealously as did Hades, whose dominion included all wealth dug from under the earth. With his taciturn nature and domineering ways, Scott offends the two capable doctors of Riverbend and is thus indirectly responsible for his wife's death since he summons only an inexperienced young physician to her bedside. Scott's dark demeanor makes him hostile to youth but desirous of having as his own the "little grasshopper" whose ways enchant him.

The imagery of the story points to the death of Nelly who, like Persephone, is drawn into an unhappy marriage where death awaits. Her death, however, is only a winter's stay from summer's fruitfulness. Nelly's daughter Margaret is an equally beautiful child, filled with the same joy for life that characterized Nelly. Admittedly, Cather's ending can be regarded as a sentimental one with the three old women, like the Magi, bending over Nelly's baby in a church decorated for Christmas. The child, so unlike its father, is a Christ-child figure with a "golden fuzz on his head" and "so warm and tingling with...the flush of new beginnings, of the new morning and the new rose" (p. 68). The intermingling of Christian and pagan mythologies did not appear to bother Cather, as long as those allusions fulfilled her purpose. In "The Joy of Nelly Deane" both mythologies well support a belief in birth, death, and rebirth as a pattern of real life. But accepting this order of things does not deny the poignancy of sorrow and loss that is equally a part of life, as Cather would demonstrate in *O Pioneers!* and *My Antonia*. In these novels the vegetation myth of Persephone is reenacted on the Nebraska plains where Nature can be both threatening and beneficent. Cather's incorporation of myth in her later works would not differ greatly from that in "The Joy of Nelly Deane," where dual meanings exist as myth is disassembled.

In fact, Nebraska provides the background for one of the last stories Cather completed before her resignation from *McClure's Magazine* in the spring of 1912. In "The Bohemian Girl," Willa Cather shows for the first time her ability to work with the scenes of her girlhood in an appreciative manner with a ready acceptance of both those who have made the land habitable and those who must escape from the land to which they can never truly belong. The story indicates Cather's own reconciliation with Nebraska, from which she had been absent for many years but about which she was beginning to write more objectively.

In developing "The Bohemian Girl," Cather returns to the theme of a lost Arcadia, now an unnatural garden which no longer appeals to those with creative genius and the spark of life. Only a few sensitive natures like Nils Ericson's and Clara Vavrika's can still appreciate the spell of that "great, silent country," the splendor that "seemed to transcend human life and human fate" (p. 34). For the others, the land is something to work, to take from, and has no aesthetic significance. These land owners are not the heroic caretakers of the frontier but are the spoilers of the delights in the troll garden. Nils had, at a young age, left this world, which was hostile to his temperament, and later returns to find his older brothers, caught up in their dull routine, stolid, insensitive, and unyielding. Nils is made from another mold. His "brown face and neck and strong back," his reddish-brown hair and eyebrows, and his "teasing, not unkindly smile" set him apart (p. 3). He arrives carrying only a small valise and having a flute case tucked under one arm. Nils is a self-exiled Pan who has returned in search of his Syrinx. Like Pan he prefers the short-cuts through pastures, and he first glimpses the Bohemian girl from his blind "behind a thicket of wild plum bushes" (p. 6). With "rather kindly mockery" he reacquaints himself with his family (p. 3) but shows genuine affection for those other sensitive creatures in this inimical environment, particularly for his gentle younger brother Eric and his orphaned cousin Hilda.

In his pursuit of Clara Vavrika, now the wife of his older and sullen brother Olaf, Nils exercises all his charm. He stands like a lithe god before the heavy Teutonic features of Olaf whose "head was large and square, like a block of wood" (p. 19). Clara is of the forest children, as is Nils, and assumes classically mythic dimensions, as well. Clara is often associated with moonlight, tearing about the country on horseback at night, and keeping her tryst with Nils "under the great, golden, tender midsummer moon" (p. 34). Clara's parallel to Diana, cold-hearted moon goddess, is enhanced by her selfishness and her pride, for which Mrs. Ericson criticizes her. Having been raised in a Bohemian community where emotions were easily expressed and enjoyment of life was one's goal, Clara has become bitter in marriage and has suppressed expression of love for all but her father. She, like Diana, is aloof, often "cold as an icicle," and defiant (p. 27). Nils recognizes that she is a wild thing that cannot be tamed and that only by escaping from her stifling marriage can she learn again to love life. The vindictiveness with which Clara first responds to Nils' overtures of love typify that of a woman striving to fulfill the role of the goddess who is impervious to love:

> "Let me go, Nils Ericson!" she cried. "I hate you more than any of them. You were created to torture me, the whole tribe of you – to make me suffer in every possible way." (p. 24)

Even when in her father's garden, Clara tries to maintain the Artemisian mask by which she has avoided the hurt associated with love. She sits frigidly beneath the cherry tree, drawing her white muslin skirts tightly about her.

But, the fun-loving nature of her father Joe and the delightful music from Nils' flute batter away at Clara's defenses. She is no match for revelry which recalls lost youth and happiness. Joe Vavrika is a Bohemian Bacchus, the patron of a delightful tavern, who cherishes his wines as if they were children and playfully encourages Nils to make his sweetheart his wife. In his private garden "between two buildings... inclosed by a high board fence as tight as a partition" (p. 21), Joe Vavrika keeps a last remnant of Arcadia where simple pleasures are the daily fare. This cheerful place hardly stands as a bastion against the real world, though, for already it is "off-limits" to the Ericson clan and to other farmers because Joe "'was taking money that other people had worked hard for in the fields'" (p. 19). The grasping materialism of the world outside will eventually destroy "'the one jolly house in this country for a boy to go to,'" as Nils describes it (p. 19).

Yet, in the environs of the Vavrika tavern Clara's resistance to Nils decays. She laughs easily in the late afternoon sun, and fire returns to her gypsy eyes. She responds passionately to the enjoyment her aged father gets from swallowing the last drops of a special wine, and she cries out in an appeal to unknown powers that she might grow old in the same way. Clara responds with equal fervor to the music of Nils' flute, an instrument mythically related to regeneration because of its association with the sensual earth deity, Pan. Clara's final seduction is also reminiscent of a mythic encounter. Just as Pan once seduced Selene (the ancient moon goddess) in the depths of the woods,[27] Nils psychologically rapes Clara at the base of a straw stack in a reaped field flooded with moonlight. The sensuousness of the scene is overwhelming: "The senses were too feeble to take it in, and every time one looked up at the sky one felt unequal to it, as if one were sitting deaf under the waves of a great river of melody" (p. 34). But, Clara is not deaf to her Pan's melody, and, like a Diana entranced by Endymion, she succumbs. When Nils kisses her, she feels something lash out from him "like a knife out of a sheath...[She] felt everything slipping away from her ..." (p. 36). The phallic symbolism is undisguised in Nils' role as the impulsive and amorous Pan who conquers Clara. Her reaction typifies that of one who has felt again the impulses of a primitive nature, unrestricted by conventional morality and societal expectations. Clara panics, the verb itself conjuring up

---

27.   Virgil, *Eclogues, Georgics, Aeneid I-VI*, I, trans. H. Rushton Fairclough (New York: G. P. Putnam's Sons, 1929), p. 183. ["Twas with gift of such snowy wool, if we may trust the tale, that Pan, Arcadia's god, charmed and beguiled thee, O Moon, calling thee to the depths of the woods; nor didst thou scorn his call."]

images of Pan's frightening and unexpected appearance, much like Nils' sudden re-entry into her life. Her "love of life" and "capacity for delight" do, however, vanquish her fears as she and Nils leave behind the "resinous smell of sunflowers and ironweed" in search of a new Arcadia (pp. 35, 6).

In their flight, reminiscent of Madeline and Porphyro's in Keats' "The Eve of St. Agnes," the young lovers follow the romantic tradition of turning their backs on the forces which would thwart both their love and their spirits. Unlike Nelly Deane, who is "tamed" in marriage and whose vitality withers, Clara Vavrika escapes from the confinement of a culture which is principally matriarchal. But, as in "The Joy of Nelly Deane," Cather's attitude toward this culture is ambiguous. Cather admires the very thing Nils admires, the aging frontier women who, as mothers of their race, have retained their youthful love of life. They become heroic figures, the earth goddesses of earlier civilizations:

> There were fat, rosy old women who looked hot in their best black dresses; spare, alert old women with brown, dark-veined hands; and several of almost heroic frame, not less massive than old Mrs. Ericson herself....Mrs. Oleson, who had twelve big grandchildren, could still show two braids of yellow hair as thick as her own wrists. Among all these grandmothers there were more brown heads than white. They all had a pleased, prosperous air, as if they were more than satisfied with themselves and with life. (p. 29)

At Olaf's barn dance, Nils admires them from afar and thinks "of the Herculean labors those fifteen pairs of hands had performed..." (p. 29). Yet, they have retained an enthusiasm for living which keeps them delighted, applauding, and keeping time with their feet as Joe and Clara Vavrika whirl across the floor in a sprightly Bohemian dance. Such matriarchs have brought order to life on the prairies.

Mrs. Ericson also is a matriarch; she is head in her own household and in the eight households of her married sons and their thirty-one children. Her strength is that of a renewed heroic age, but an age in which matriarchal powers of earth mothers like Gaea and Rhea have not yet been supplanted by the Olympian patriarchy. Her interest in her children is genuine, and she is proud of their successes. Yet, she is often curt, reluctant to express her affection, and is continually on the alert for individuals or circumstances which might disrupt the ordered existence over which she rules. She worries

about Clara's ineffectualness as a wife and homemaker; she worries that
Eric's gentleness may make him unfit for rugged farm life; she worries that
Nils' "roving blood" and generous nature will cause him never to be
successful. The severity of her comments and her grim appearance are
expressions of the responsibilities she has shouldered in raising a large family
on the limited income of her preacher-husband, who liked everybody and
made little mark in the world. Mrs. Ericson is a self-reliant woman, capable
of waging war, like mother Gaea, against any who threaten her family, but
such strength does not necessarily cause her to lack maternal tenderness. For
instance, her unemotional reunion with Nils is tempered by her abrupt
comment that he has grown better looking. She is, indeed, keenly observant
of her children, conscious of their weaknesses, and ready to chastize them for
their indiscretions. Mrs. Ericson and the women of her generation come to
represent what Evelyn Helmick considers the female principle necessary for
the development of a successful society.[28]

In that protective watchfulness over her children, though, lurks a
threat, especially for those with temperaments like Clara's or with sensitive
natures like Eric's. Nils recognized the loss of self, which would necessarily
accompany his remaining on the farm under his mother's watchful eye, and
he escaped. Clara's fate would likely have been that of Nelly Deane had she
remained. Her "guardian" deity is also a woman, a matriarchal power which
can both nourish and stifle. Perhaps in Clara's escape, Cather reflects her
own ambivalent feelings toward the Nebraska landscape which both inspired
her creativity and, in its awesomeness, threatened erasure of her identity. For
some, the power of the earth mother is too great, as it was for Eric. In Mrs.
Ericson's tender demonstration of love for her prodigal son lies entrapment,
too: "Her fingers twined themselves in his soft, pale hair. His tears splashed
down on the boards; happiness filled his heart" (p. 51). Order is not
disrupted; Mrs. Ericson's net holds Eric fast. Such an ending is in keeping
with the nature of the mythic associations upon which Cather was drawing.
She saw much to admire in the civilizing influence of a female culture, but

---

28.   Evelyn Thomas Helmick, "The Broken World: Medievalism in *A Lost Lady*,"
Renascence, 28 (Autumn 1975), 46.

also much to fear. For Cather, the greatest fear lay in a woman's inability to break away from the expected female role, to rebel against Gaea, while also combating the Dionysian powers which would bar her from the temple of art, from worship of Apollo.

"The Bohemian Girl" marks a turning point in Cather's career and in her direction as a writer. She had long drawn upon classical and mythic allusions to support the details and themes of her work, but most references had pointed to a loss of a golden age, to the absence of Apollo, to the disappearance of Arcadia, or to the decline of civilization. Cather now coupled the pensive mood of *April Twilights* with a renewed interest in the frontier world, which for her assumed mythic dimensions as a link to older cultures and heroic ideals. How Cather would come to view those ideals would become evident in her working, and reworking, of classical myth.

CHAPTER V
ALEXANDER TO ALEXANDRA:
THE APOTHEOSIS OF THE EPIC HERO

Cather's final break from *McClure's* in the spring of 1912 signaled a shift in her career from writing short literary pieces to writing novels. This shift in genre was accompanied by a shift in theme and in illustration of that theme in mythic terms. Whereas *The Troll Garden* stories frequently pointed to cultural decay through increasing materialism and unresponsiveness to fundamental human desires, Cather's first novels concentrate on the efforts of heroic individuals to reestablish a golden age of gods, conquerors, and seekers of permanent values. Never denying the cyclic pattern of civilization's triumph and eventual decay, Cather, nevertheless, admired the heroic endeavors of individuals who strove to create "a monument more lasting than bronze," as Horace would state it.[1] These few individuals – Bartley Alexander, Alexandra Bergson, Antonia Shimerda, and Thea Kronborg – exhibit savage strength and near deific stature. Especially in her first three novels of a western setting, the reader finds a reworking of the Vergilian epic tradition in which the opening of the Nebraskan frontier becomes for Cather another heroic age.

Cather's first novel, *Alexander's Bridge*, was completed by the fall of 1911, prior to her beginning "The Bohemian Girl," but the two pieces when

---

1.   Horace, "Liber III: Carmen xxx," in *Carminum Libri IV*, ed. T.E. Page (New York: Macmillan and Co., 1964), p. 101. [Exegi monumentum aere perennius]

considered in conjunction with one another point to the thematic concerns of this first period of Cather's novels. "The Bohemian Girl" provided the setting in which Cather could examine the ascendancy of culture in a pattern similar to that of the ancient world, wherein exiles carved out a new civilization in a dramatic struggle against a hostile environment. In *Alexander's Bridge*, however, Cather began to fashion the heroic character required for achieving victory in this struggle. Although Cather was later deeply critical of her first novel as an imitation of the Jamesian style and a clumsy attempt to work with the cosmopolitan scenes which had impressed her in her first journey abroad, reviewers were quick to recognize that in Bartley Alexander's character Cather had captured "the salient features of personality both mental and physical."[2] These "salient features" are those of a conqueror, a mythic hero, whose passion to create something that will endure becomes the dominant trait of heroes of Cather's frontier novels.

Bartley Alexander's name alone calls forth numerous associations with figures from both history and myth. Although Cather's selection of the name has been attributed to her acquaintance with Ibsen's "The Master Builder," to her reviewing of James' *The Other House*, and even to her early association with the philosopher and educator Hartley B. Alexander,[3] the classical parallels to Bartley Alexander were surely foremost in her mind. Bartley's tall and powerful figure is that of a Theseus or a Jason:

> When Alexander reached the library door, he switched on the lights and stood six feet and more in the archway, glowing with strength and cordiality and rugged, blond good looks.... Under his tumbled sandy hair his head seemed as hard and powerful as a catapult, and his shoulders looked strong enough in themselves to support a span of any one of his ten bridges that cut the air above as many rivers.[4]

2.   Rev. of *Alexander's Bridge*, by Willa Cather, *New York Times*, 12 May 1912, p. 295. The *Athenaeum* review (31 Aug. 1912) praises the novel as chiefly a psychological study, and *Outlook* (8 June 1912) judges it "brilliant in its reflections of character and life...."

3.   Mildred Bennett, "How Willa Cather Chose Her Names," *Names*, 19 (1962), 32; Bernice Slote, Introd., *Alexander's Bridge* (1912; rpt. Lincoln: Univ. of Nebraska Press, 1977), p. xvii; L. V. Jacks, "The Classics and Willa Cather," *Prairie Schooner*, 35 (1961), 292.

4.   Willa Cather, *Alexander's Bridge*, introd. Bernice Slote (1912; rpt. Lincoln: Univ. of Nebraska Press, 1977), p. 9. Subsequent references to this work will be cited parenthetically in the text by page number.

In keeping with the heroic tradition, Bartley had come from obscure beginnings and was raised in the West, the setting ideal for fostering traits of independence and resolve. His "rugged, blond good looks" recall Alexander of Macedon, who became a "tamer of rivers" (p. 9) in his own right by bridging the Danube and the Indus in innovative ways. Bartley Alexander has the potential to be a world conqueror, for he belongs to "the people who make the play," not to the mere onlookers (p. 138). Like Alexander the Great, he finds that success brings not the expected freedom and power but only the "power that [is] in itself another kind of restraint" (p. 38). His determination to forge ahead, not to become a cautious "*Nestor de pontibus*" (p. 38), he finds thwarted by industrial unrest and strikes, just as Alexander faced the mutinous refusal of his troops to press on to the River Ocean. Bartley has a "powerfully equipped nature" (p. 13) which serves him in building the cantilever Moorlock Bridge, his Promethean attempt to create something enduring and good.

Yet, the classical myth upon which Cather draws most heavily in writing *Alexander's Bridge* is that of Paris, called Alexandros in the *Iliad*, and the fatal triangle of his relationship with Helen and the nymph Oenone. According to myth, the river nymph Oenone wed Paris (Alexandros) when he still served as a shepherd, was as yet unaware of his royal heritage, and had not even considered going to Greece to meet Helen. Blinded by her passion for the beautiful prince, Oenone paid no heed to the prophecies of the destruction Helen would bring to Paris' life. After Paris deserts her for Helen, Oenone remains steadfast in her love but is consumed by a vengeful jealousy. When Paris, mortally wounded by Philoctetes' arrow, comes to Oenone and reminds her of her promise to heal him, she refuses him aid. Too late, Oenone repents of her rash vengeance and, filled with remorse, hurries to the bedside of Paris. All she can do is grieve over his body.

Cather's acquaintance with this myth undoubtedly came from her study of Homer as well as from at least one of two extant literary accounts, namely Ovid's *Heroides*.[5] Yet, as was often the case, Cather altered the

5.   Howard Jacobson, *Ovid's Heroides* (Princeton: Princeton Univ. Press, 1974), p. 176. Jacobson cites Quintus Smyranaeus' account as the only other surviving literary treatment of the Paris and Oenone myth.

98

details of the myth to suit her purposes, even interchanging the qualities associated with Oenone and Helen. Winifred Alexander, Bartley's wife, becomes the Oenone figure, but of a regal rather than nymph-like appearance. Lucius Wilson first observes Winifred from afar, noting that she was "a person of distinction" who "carried her beautiful head proudly, and moved with ease and certainty" (p. 3). He liked "the suggestion of stormy possibilities in the proud curve of her lip and nostril" (p. 7). Winifred's pride is like that of Ovid's Oenone, whose letter to Paris begins with a statement of pride in herself as a nymph, in spite of having lowered herself to her husband's level:

> Not yet so great was thou, when I, a Nymph, sprung from a great river, was content with thee for a husband. Thou, who are now a son of Priam (let respect be paid to truth), was *then but* a slave: I, a Nymph, condescended to wed a slave.[6]

Although Bartley was scarcely "a slave" when Winifred accepted his offer of marriage, his humble western origins were not comparable to "the costly privileges and fine space" (p. 3) which characterized Winifred's way of life. Bartley admits to himself that "The obligations imposed by his wife's fortune and position were sometimes distracting to a man who followed his profession..." (p. 37). Such queenly aspect and wealth, however, would be more appropriately associated with Helen than with Oenone, who later in her letter to Paris admits to having exaggerated her social status. In attributing such regal splendor to her Oenone figure, Cather again displays a slanting of myth to elevate female protagonists to positions of power, making them less susceptible to victimization and male dominance. From the outset, the reader recognizes Winifred's quiet strength which moves her beyond the callous independence of Lady Ellen Treffinger in "The Marriage of Phaedra" and in the direction of the stoic endurance of Alexandra Bergson.

In other ways, though, Winifred fulfills the role of Oenone. She possesses the same potential for violent and jealous anger that Oenone demonstrated in refusing to treat the wounded Paris. When courting Winifred, Bartley had introduced the subject of his youthful affair abroad,

---

6.   Henry T. Riley, trans., "Epistle V: Oenone to Paris," in *The Heroides or Epistles of the Heroines, The Amours, Art of Love, Remedy of Love, and Minor Works of Ovid*, by Ovid (London: George Bell and Sons, 1887), p. 42.

and Winifred's response revealed a nymph-like impulsiveness which lay latent beneath her reserve:

> "You see, one can't be jealous about things in general; but about particular, definite, personal things,"–here she had thrown her hands up to his shoulders with a quick, impulsive gesture–"oh, about those I should be very jealous. I should torture myself–I couldn't help it." (p. 29)

Yet Winifred's occasion to display such jealousy never arises. In keeping with Ovid's portrayal of Oenone, Winifred is not a seer, as some versions of the myth would have her be. She neither foresees nor suspects her husband's infidelity. She remains throughout the novel a dignified lady and devoted wife, the very role Ovid casts for Oenone in naming her a "matrona."

In her decision to marry Bartley, Winifred is again similar to Oenone. Just as Oenone chose to ignore both the prophecy of destruction associated with Paris' birth and Cassandra's ravings about the "Grecian heifer" that would ruin her,[7] Winifred chose the stormy life which marriage with Bartley promised:

> "Oh, I faced that long ago, when you were on your first bridge, up at old Allway. I knew then that your paths were not to be paths of peace, but I decided that I wanted to follow them." (p. 71)

Such "high confidence and fearless pride" (p. 71), as Professor Lucius Wilson calls it, remain with Winifred even after Bartley's death. She, like Oenone, is destined to lose, and with that loss, her hardness surfaces. As Professor Wilson remarks, "More, even, than the rest of us she didn't choose her destiny. She underwent it. And it has left her chilled" (p. 137). This aloofness and hardness, of which even Bartley had accused her, does not diminish Winifred's love for her husband. Like Oenone, whose hardness prevented her from ministering to Paris' wounds but whose love drove her to grieve at Paris' deathbed, Winifred walks quietly and alone behind Bartley's stretcher and alone washes and dresses his body for burial. In drawing upon the ancient myth for fashioning the character of Winifred, Cather, therefore, intertwined the regality of a Helen with the role of Oenone as betrayed wife.

---

7. Riley, trans., pp. 47-48.

Hilda Burgoyne consequently assumes the role of Helen. Even her name, which means "maid of battle," stands in direct contrast to Winifred's name, meaning "pure and white." Hilda is the maid of the battle which Bartley wages against himself, and she recalls Helen as the cause of the devastating war between Greece and Troy. Like Helen, Hilda exudes an aura of mystery and power of enchantment that keeps an admiring group of men constantly attentive but always distant from her. This aloofness keeps Hilda Burgoyne uninvolved with the human conditions of marriage and childbearing, thereby equating her with Artemis who is "known for her purity and austerity," as Kenneth Atchity writes in his study of Homer's *Iliad*. He goes on to point out that "Helen has even been considered a moon goddess, in another association with Artemis."[8] Cather draws upon the Artemisian image in *Alexander's Bridge* and describes Hilda in terms of the moon myth, a myth which appears repeatedly throughout her works.

Hilda is associated with shades of yellow and gold, the colors which Cather links with love and sexuality, the distinguishing traits of Helen herself. At the same time, Hilda fits many of the epithets which Oenone, in her outraged letter to Paris, uses to describe Helen. Like Helen, Hilda is a foreigner, Irish by birth, and according to rumor she is also a "dira paelex," and a "turpis amica," a remorseless and shameless mistress.[9] Yet her nature is more that of a nymph, like Oenone. Hilda's sprightliness, sparkling laughter, and excitability attract the attention of men like Bartley and bring instantaneous applause from audiences when she steps on stage: "Whatever she wore, people felt the charm of her active, girlish body with its slender hips and quick, eager shoulders" (p. 42). The sense of life which Hilda kindles in Bartley is like that which Helen rekindles in Paris when he is whisked from the battlefield by Aphrodite, his duel with Menelaus having reached no satisfying conclusion. Paris admits that the passion he then feels is even stronger than when he first took Helen to his bed (*Iliad* III.442-446).

---

8.   Kenneth John Atchity, *Homer's "Iliad": The Shield of Memory* (Carbondale: Southern Illinois Univ. Press, 1978), pp. 22-23.

9.   Ovid, *Heroides*, ed. Arthur Palmer (Hildesheim, Germany: Georg Olms Verlagsbuchhandlung, 1967), p. 27.

Similarly, Bartley finds his renewed interest in Hilda overwhelming and inescapable.

Bartley's passion is, in part, explained in that Hilda represents something more than mortal. Her appearance as the moon goddess is accentuated by repeated images of golden light. Cather once more freely combines images from more than one mythic figure into a single female personality. She avoids the stereotype of Hilda as merely a temptress, responsible for Bartley's tragedy, and suggests that Hilda is a chaste goddess, as well. At the theater Bartley is captivated by Hilda singing "The Rising of the Moon" while she wreathes primroses for her donkey in an almost pagan celebration of life's simple pleasures. Even as he walks about London, obsessed with the memory of Hilda, yellow light pours through the trees and the laburnums drip gold over garden walls (pp. 35-36). Hilda herself dresses in canary-colored slippers and a primrose gown whose "yellow train glide[s] down the long floor" (p. 45), just as did the long-trailing gowns of the women of Ilium. Bartley expresses the hope that she will wear a yellow gown in her next stage part, for the color only heightens his attraction to her immortal beauty. The wine Hilda shares with Bartley is a "dry yellow Rhone wine," and the candles shed a yellow light upon their dining table (pp. 52-54). Her "slender yellow figure in front of him" (p. 58) finally snaps the tense control Bartley holds over himself and leads him to profess his love again.

By equating her Helen figure with Artemis or Diana, Cather employs another classical myth to support the theme of *Alexander's Bridge*. Bartley Alexander becomes an Endymion, desiring the most bewitching of the goddesses, the source of life's vitality. In seeking Diana (Hilda), he grasps for all the youth and energy she symbolically represents; this could be his escape from the "dead calm of middle life" (p. 38). But such a relationship is impossible, for, as in the ancient myth, Endymion is barred from sharing eternity with his moon goddess. Intimations of immortality surround Hilda. Like Diana, she "doesn't take up with anybody" (p. 26); she remains aloof and uninvolved with precarious love relationships. Even Bartley recognizes that Hilda is different from other women, incapable of entering into an alliance with a man she does not love. Rather, he claims, "[Y]ou can love as queens did, in the old time" (p. 111). The kind of love Hilda expresses is devoted and unwavering, directed forever to only one man, the love of which legends are made. She does not, in fact, marry one of her many admirers, as she professes she will do. Like Diana, she remains faithful to her Endymion, and the novel closes with Hilda saying softly, "...nothing can happen to one after Bartley" (p. 138). Although Cather assures the reader that Bartley does, and Hilda will, one day join "the ultimate repository of mortality" (p. 33), what Hilda represents as the moon goddess cannot die. Hilda becomes the spokesperson for the ongoingness of life itself. This all mortals, even those of heroic stature, seek:

> "Life seems the strongest and most indestructible thing in the world. Do you really believe that all those people rushing about down there, going to good dinners and clubs and theatres, will be dead some day, and not care about anything? I don't believe it, and I know I shan't die, ever! You see, I feel too – too powerful!"   (p. 95)

Alexander's Bridge, then, becomes much more than a story of a love triangle and the flaw in man's nature. By utilizing images from ancient myths, Cather introduces a concern about the passage of time and the individual's efforts to defeat it. This heroic struggle underlies the four novels of Cather's early period. Bartley Alexander is the first figure who strives to defeat time, to create through his bridge building, as did Helen of Troy through her weaving, an object which will survive himself. Kenneth Atchity considers this creative drive fundamental to the Homeric epic from which Cather drew in writing *Alexander's Bridge*:

> ...[I]n the *Iliad*...creativity is connected with mortality, the individual's need to create an artifact that outlasts him – a need directly parallel to the hero's need to overcome death and to influence the future by heroic acts. The two needs, artistic and active, are complementary.[10]

A similar need will drive Godfrey St. Peter to complete his history of the Spanish explorers, will compel Alexandra Bergson to establish a productive farm out of a potential wasteland, and will challenge Thea Kronborg to sing Sieglinde and Isolde as they have never been sung before.

Coupled with this epic desire to create, however, is Bartley Alexander's passion for regaining his own youth, the weak spot which

---

10.   Atchity, pp. 24-25.

Professor Wilson felt would someday produce too much strain and bring Bartley crashing down like his bridge. His desire to feel again the consciousness that was Life itself (p. 39) and his desire to be really free lead Bartley back to Hilda, whose goddess image offers him a taste of immortality. What Bartley fails to recognize is that his is an Orphic quest, doomed from the outset. Indeed, the youth he seeks is "the most dangerous of companions" (p. 41), for the memory of this second self deludes him into believing in its existence while it denies him access to that very existence. Like Orpheus, his desire is great, but his love for a lost self, not his love for a lost Eurydice, drives him onward.

Blind passion for "the impetuousness, the intense excitement, the increasing expectancy of youth" (p. 77) compels Bartley to return to Hilda who, in her Artemisian role, represents these dimensions of life. Hilda's presence brings the past side by side with the present, just as Aphrodite's presence in the guise of the old Spartan nurse spurred Helen to rejoin Paris in the bedchamber as she had on the night of her abduction some ten years earlier (*Iliad* III.385-394). Bartley sees Hilda much as Paris saw Helen in this scene from the *Iliad*. His love harkens back to an initial meeting with his Helen, and the progress of years seems to stop in the presence of renewed passion. Having reminisced together about the beggar who wished them happy love in a tone "vibrating with pity for their youth and despair at the terribleness of life" (p. 55), Hilda and Bartley stand entranced before an open window:

> For a long time neither Hilda nor Bartley spoke. They stood close together, looking out into the wan, watery sky, breathing always more quickly and lightly, and it seemed as if all the clocks in the world had stopped. Suddenly he moved the clenched hand he held behind him and dropped it violently at his side. He felt a tremor run through the slender yellow figure in front of him. (p. 58)

Bartley, a man who is "never introspective" and is merely a "response to stimuli" (pp. 7-8), succumbs to a renewed sense of self which only the presence of Hilda can stir from his memory. Bartley falls victim to self-delusion in that moment, for, as Cather well knew, youth once spent was irrecoverable. Bartley is one of the first of Cather's characters to suffer from what Howard Mumford Jones calls "the Dionysian fascination, the Bacchic appeal, the illusion of youth, which create in him a new and overwhelming feeling of self, sensed in a series of mystical insights superior to his normal self and eventually controlling it."[11] This desire does not discriminate by gender, as revealed by both Marian Forrester's final dinner party and Professor St. Peter's isolated reveries.

Hilda then serves the same role as Helen in the ancient myth. She sparks desire by resurrecting the past and brings confusion into the established order of Bartley's life. Just as Oenone served as a reminder to Paris of the past of which he wished to be free, so Winifred comes to represent the ordered existence under which Bartley feels his vital force fading and dying. Yet, Bartley admits that "whenever he was deeply stirred" he turned to Winifred, "the woman who had made his life, gratified his pride, given direction to his tastes and habits" (pp. 114-115). Bartley becomes like his Homeric counterpart, torn by the contradictory elements of his nature and unable to resolve that conflict. In the last moments of his life he thinks of Winifred, as the injured Paris thought of Oenone. But, in his pocket Bartley carries a letter to Winifred, presumably admitting his love for Hilda. Similarly, Paris cried out to Helen at the very instant of his death.[12]

Bartley is right when he assesses his situation as that of Actaeon's: "The little boy drank of the prettiest brook in the forest and he became a stag" (p. 102). The vengeance of Diana destroyed Actaeon, and Bartley, having glimpsed the beauty of immortal youth, likewise faces destruction.

---

11.   Howard Mumford Jones, *The Bright Medusa* (Urbana: The Univ. of Illinois Press, 1952), pp. 22-23.

12.   This incident is recounted by William Morris in Book III of "The Earthly Paradise," a poem with which Cather was probably acquainted, for as early as 1896, she had identified Morris as one of the few English poets worthy of being considered for the laureateship (see "The Passing Show," *Nebraska State Journal*, 19 Jan. 1896, p. 9). Morris' poem, however, is less likely to have been Cather's source for *Alexander's Bridge* than are the ancient texts themselves or even Lempriere's rendering of those myths, which Morris' daughter contends provided the basis for her father's poem "The Death of Paris." "The Death of Paris" by William Morris deals little with the psychological turmoil of Paris and concentrates instead on Oenone's grief, anger, and love. Yet, in *Alexander's Bridge*, Cather focuses on the struggles of the Homeric hero, drawing little upon the pre-Raphaelite interpretation of the myth and utilizing more fully the Homeric and Ovidian versions of the tale. [Cf. William Morris, "The Death of Paris," in *The Collected Works of William Morris*, introd. May Morris (New York: Russell and Russell, 1966),V, xxii and 4-21.]

Bartley comes to realize that only two things lie awake under the moon – death and love (p. 118). Even on the morning of his death, the sun rises through "pale golden ripples of cloud," and a "fresh yellow light" vibrates through the forest (p. 119). For Bartley, the enticement still exists to defeat mortality by allying the past to the present and by creating for the future. The dream of doing so is the source of heroic action, but the inability to reconcile desire with possibility can only result in tragedy. Bartley's drowning beneath the yellow foam of the rushing river only emphasizes the crucial relationship between past and present, a relationship which underscores the Ovidian account of the Oenone-Paris-Helen triangle. Just as Paris could not finally choose between Oenone and Helen, so Bartley cannot choose between a calm, ordered life, as represented by Winifred, and the freedom of youth, as represented by Hilda. He fails to wed the past to the present, to reconcile himself to the advance of time. His efforts to do so, however, are heroic and his reputation remains untarnished: "Fortune, which had smiled upon him consistently all his life, did not desert him in the end" (p. 131).

Bernice Slote is surely justified in her observation that the "texture of myth is allusive in *Alexander's Bridge*, but its power seems deliberately invoked, in Willa Cather's true language."[13] The novel draws heavily upon both the epic tradition and the myth of Alexandros, a hero of the Trojan War but a man who, like Bartley Alexander, wrestled unsuccessfully to unite a divided spirit. In spite of their ambition, both men find their lives shaped by other forces. These forces are female, forerunners of the matriarchal figures, who succeed in establishing order in Cather's next three novels.

Neither Winifred nor Hilda forced Bartley to any specific action, but in setting before him two quite different and irreconcilable alternatives, they direct the course of his life. The mythic personages upon which Cather draws to characterize these two women are those whose clashes often rocked Olympus. The eternal confrontation between Aphrodite (freedom, both sexual and social) and Athena/Hera/Artemis (restraint and order) dimmed by comparison the petty wars of men, wherein the male deities found their triumphs. So is the case in *Alexander's Bridge*. Although Cather recognizes

13.   Slote, Introd., *Alexander's Bridge*, p. xviii.

that men are the builders and shapers of the physical world, she attributes to women the subtle but progressive power of shaping civilization. Significantly, Winifred and Hilda survive Bartley. Bartley Alexander dies in his prime, like Alexander of Macedon, having failed to create something "more lasting than bronze." But, Bartley's efforts to establish order in his personal life by reuniting a divided spirit are those of a hero. The bridge he attempts to build would have spanned more than a river; it would have connected the past to the future. Cather would leave that monumental task to the heroic figures of her next novels.

The classical values for which Willa Cather was searching she discovered through a long visit to Nebraska and the Southwest in the spring of 1912. Cather, who had been somewhat astounded by the popularity of *Alexander's Bridge*, did not feel she had yet "come into her own" as a writer and found the stimuli for her next novel in the open plains of the West and the pioneers' efforts to tame them. In a 1921 interview, Cather recalled her response to the land and the epic struggle which had tamed it:

> "I knew every farm, every tree, every field in the region around my home and they all called out to me. My deepest feelings were rooted in this country because one's strongest emotions and one's most vivid mental pictures are acquired before one is fifteen. I had searched for books telling about the beauty of the country I loved, its romance, the heroism and strength and courage of its people that had been plowed into the very furrows of its soil and I did not find them. And so I wrote *O Pioneers!*."[14]

In the ancient Indian settlements of New Mexico Cather found the record of an admirable culture which had become victim to the cycle of civilization's rise and fall. She also discovered the vitality of the Mexican people and reacquainted herself with the Bohemian settlements on the Divide. These experiences affirmed Cather's feeling for the past and renewed her interest in and sympathy for both the people and the land they inhabited.

In writing *O Pioneers!*, Cather returned to the Vergilian epic tradition, finding in her pioneers the heroic traits of old and a dedication to building a

---

14.   Willa Cather, as quoted by Eva Mahoney, *Sunday World-Herald*, Omaha, 27 Nov. 1921, in Mildred Bennett, *The World of Willa Cather*, rev. ed. (Lincoln: Univ. of Nebraska Press, 1961), p. 139.

culture which would preserve the values of the past while meeting the demands of the present. *O Pioneers!* was destined to succeed in those areas where *Alexander's Bridge* had failed because Cather could now explore the heroic dimensions of human character in a setting worthy of them, in a true frontier. The novel explores concerns which Cather had introduced in her first novel, and, as in *Alexander's Bridge*, Cather found her expression for these ideas in terms of classical myth.

The most apparent reference to classical myth comes in Cather's choice of a name for her main character. Alexandra Bergson's name is the feminine form of the great conqueror's name and calls forth not only a "whole body of associations" but also "some habitual emotional values" for the author, a fact which Bernice Slote contends is typical of any writer who uses myth "organically" as Willa Cather did.[15] Indeed, Alexandra is a strong woman, a defender of her family and her land, as her name implies. Her physical appearance alone is impressive; her stature is such that "no man on the Divide could have carried [her] very far."[16] The impression she makes is enhanced by a certain military aggressiveness which she displays even as a young girl. Early in the novel when a "little drummer" compliments Alexandra on her beautiful hair, she "stab[s] him with a glance of Amazonian fierceness," subjecting him to her scorn and making him wish he were more of a man (p. 8). She wears her man's ulster coat like "a young soldier" (p. 6), and in her opposition to those who would not love the land, she sustains her image as an ancient woman warrior. Alexandra dominates her brothers Lou and Oscar, keeps aloof from sexual relationships, and assumes an almost asexual role.

She is clearly feminine, though, with a shining mass of reddish-yellow hair much like the helmet of hair which defines the goddess-like beauty of Margie in "The Treasure of Far Island." She plaits her hair into "two thick braids" (p. 7), the symbols of matriarchal authority and fertility for which Nils Ericson admired the old Norse women in "The Bohemian Girl." Yet,

15.   Bernice Slote, ed., *The Kingdom of Art: Willa Cather's First Principles and Critical Statements 1893-1896* (Lincoln: Univ. of Nebraska Press, 1966), p. 97.
16.   Willa Cather, *O Pioneers!* (Boston: Houghton Mifflin Co., 1913) p. 206. All further references to this novel will be cited within the text by page number.

throughout the novel, Alexandra hides this symbol of her sexuality beneath a variety of veils, sun-bonnets, and scarves. When she does appear outdoors and bare-headed, she also finds herself in emotionally vulnerable situations.[17] Like an Amazon queen, Alexandra must deny the traditionally passive feminine roles expected of her in order to meet the challenges of an untamed land. Like the mythic race of women warriors, Alexandra cannot afford to think of herself as a sensual woman. From the age of twelve when John Bergson had begun to rely upon her good judgment and resourcefulness, Alexandra had assumed the male role of the one "to whom he could entrust the future of his family and the possibilities of his hard-won land" (p. 24).

Yet, curiously enough, in exercising a characteristically masculine strong will and rational judgment, Alexandra becomes one with her land, which responds to her nurturing rather than submits to her strength. Sixteen years after John Bergson's death, Alexandra looks over a land which has been protected by her maternal watchfulness and now yields to the plow in all its regenerative power:

> There are few scenes more gratifying than a spring plowing in that country, where the furrows of a single field often lie a mile in length, and the brown earth, with such a strong, clean smell, and such a power of growth and fertility in it, yields itself eagerly to the plow; rolls away from the shear, not even dimming the brightness of the metal, with a soft, deep sigh of happiness. (p. 76)

The earth's fecundity has responded to the same maternal attentiveness that Alexandra showed in arranging to rescue her little brother's kitten and to wrap Emil closely against the cold. Alexandra's quintessential characteristic harkens back to myths older than those of Amazonian conquerors. In her oneness with the land and its fertility, Alexandra becomes an Earth Mother.

---

17. Alexandra wears no covering on her head when Carl announces that he is leaving, and she is emotionally shaken by the announcement (pp. 48-51). She also stands in the garden bare-headed, shading her eyes with her hand, when Carl unexpectedly returns from the East (pp. 105-106). Alexandra uncovers her head in a touching scene with Marie in the Shabata's orchard (p. 135). In both instances in which Alexandra talks at length with Carl, first in the flower garden and again at the close of the novel in the fields at sunset, Cather makes no mention of Alexandra wearing a scarf or hat (p. 115ff. and p. 300ff.). Significantly, Carl dreamily remembers Alexandra as a milkmaid, "her skirts pinned up, her head bare..." (p. 126).

In the capacity of an earth goddess, Alexandra nurtures the soil, planting wheat rather than corn and revitalizing the soil's fertility with alfalfa crops. The land flourishes under her attentiveness and responds with increased productivity. She, in turn, is responsive to the land's needs, unlike Oscar, whose insistence on routine, and Lou, whose flightiness, make them users of the land but not part of it. Alexandra in appearance as well as action suggests Demeter as described in classical literature. Her thick braids encircle her head like the chaplet of corn worn by Demeter, and the fringe of curls which escapes from her braids is the color of the corn's tassels. Like some *alma mater*, Alexandra is frequently found in the garden, surrounded by the earth's abundance. So she appears on the evening when Carl tells her that his family is leaving:

> She was standing lost in thought, leaning upon her pitchfork, her sunbonnet lying beside her on the ground. The dry garden patch smelled of drying vines and was strewn with yellow seed-cucumbers and pumkins and citrons. At one end, next the rhubarb, grew feathery asparagus, with red berries.... She was standing perfectly still, with that serious ease so characteristic of her. Her thick, reddish braids, twisted about her head, fairly burned in the sunlight. (pp. 48-49)

The divine benignity and the hushed atmosphere of the scene serve to reinforce the image of Alexandra as an earth mother. Even as Alexandra reaches middle age, she retains a kind of immortal beauty:

> Her figure is fuller, and she has more color.... But she still has the same calmness and deliberation of manner, the same clear eyes, and she still wears her hair in two braids wound round her head.... But where her collar falls away from her neck, or where her sleeves are pushed back from her wrist, the skin is of such smoothness and whiteness as none but Swedish women ever possess; skin with the freshness of snow itself. (pp. 87-88)

Alexandra's unchanging relation with the land also places her among the primitive earth goddesses. She is not, however, a Gaea, goddess of a wild and chaotic earth untouched by humankind. Nor is she like Rhea, the goddess of an earth teeming with animals but untilled. Alexandra is a Demeter, who represents "the fertile earth as cultivated by the farmer" and is the symbol of "justifiable earthly desires."[18] Alexandra's success comes, then, not from dominating the land as a conqueror but from loving it as a patron deity.

Alexandra succeeds where Bartley Alexander failed. Whereas Bartley was unable to reconcile the opposing forces of order and unrestrained passion in order to create that which would endure, Alexandra splits her world into two realms. Carol Pearson and Katharine Pope in *The Female Hero in American and British Literature* describe these realms as the Dionysian – "chaotic, dynamic, sensual" – and the Apollonian – "ordered, static, cerebral."[19] By choosing the latter as the direction for her life, the protagonist of *O Pioneers!* represses the passionate world of Dionysus and, thus, only confronts the dilemma of Bartley Alexander through her dreams. Alexandra can maintain her asexual role, not by denying all passion, but simply by focusing it on something impersonal. For Alexandra that is the land. As a creator-artist she gives herself completely to it, much in the same way that Willa Cather believed a writer must "[give] himself absolutely to his material" if he wishes to achieve "anything noble, anything enduring."[20]

Yet, when Alexandra's energies are most drained, she is haunted by a dream whose sexual implications are undeniable. The dream comes to Alexandra on those few idle Sunday mornings when her defense against male superiority is weakened by sheer physical exhaustion:

> Sometimes, as she lay thus luxuriously idle, her eyes closed, she used to have an illusion of being lifted up bodily and carried lightly by some one very strong. It was a man, certainly, who carried her, but he was like no man she knew; he was much larger and stronger and swifter, and he carried her as easily as if she were a sheaf of wheat. She never saw him, but, with eyes closed, she could feel that he was yellow like the sunlight, and there was the smell of ripe cornfields about him. She could feel him approach, bend over her and lift her, and then she could feel herself being carried swiftly off across the fields. (p. 206)

---

18.   Paul Diel, *Symbolism in Greek Mythology: Human Desire and Its Transformations,* trans. Vincent Stuart, Micheline Stuart, Rebecca Folkman (1966; rpt. Boulder, CO: Shambhala Publications, 1980), p. 99.

19.   Carol Pearson and Katharine Pope, *The Female Hero in American and British Literature* (New York: R. R. Bowker Co., 1981), p. 155.

20.   Willa Cather, "Miss Jewett," in *Not Under Forty* (New York: Alfred A. Knopf, 1936), pp. 79-80.

Alexandra is angry with herself after indulging in this fantasy, for the dream acknowledges a sexual need that she has suppressed in working the land. The dream challenges the scenario of Amazonian autonomy that Alexandra lives in her waking hours, and yet Alexandra feels no fear of this dream phantom who "As she grew older...more often came to her when she was tired than when she was fresh and strong" (pp. 206-207). Like Demeter who, wearied by searching for Persephone, was unable to resist the advances of her brother Poseidon, Alexandra succumbs in her dream to this god, who is both guardian and lover. From his appearance this apparently beneficent god could be an Adonis or Apollo himself, glowing with the life-giving power of the sun, a force with which Alexandra is associated when she is described as looking like a double sunflower (p. 88). Clearly, the dream figure is a vegetation god who embodies the very powers upon which Alexandra must rely to sustain herself and her family. As a harvest god, this strong being of Alexandra's dream has been variously identified as Gilgamesh at the spring corn festival, the corn-god of the Canaanite myth of Aquat, the First Man of the Pawnee fertility rite, and Eros of the corn.[21] The commonality underlying all these myths, though, is the earth god's abduction and ravishment of the earth goddess, resulting in the establishment of a patriarchal power over the earth. Alexandra's reaction to her dream reflects her role as an earth goddess since Demeter, in addition to being a kind and nourishing mother, was the first goddess to represent women in their fight to retain power against Olympian, masculine forces. Cather, too, had long been fighting to establish herself in a profession dominated by men, and, in Alexandra's symbolic rejection of the vegetation god, one can see Cather's own reluctance to conform to traditional women's roles, a tendency she had shown since cutting her hair short and wearing four-in-hand ties during her university days. Like Alexandra Bergson, Cather had disregarded stereotypical roles and found support and comfort in the friendship of women like Isabelle McClung, Zoe Akins, and Edith Lewis. Such relationships, whether or not sexual, sustained Cather in her creative endeavors, much as the homoerotic friendships of ancient Greek heroes sustained them in times of personal crisis.

---

21.   J. Russell Reaver, "Mythic Motivation in Willa Cather's *O Pioneers!*," *Western Folklore*, 27 (Jan. 1968), pp. 20-23.

Alexandra similarly seeks escape from the part she is expected to play in her dream. Awaking from her reverie, she purifies herself in a ritualistic manner reminiscent of ancient fertility rites:

> After such a reverie she would rise hastily, angry with herself, and go down to the bath-house that was partitioned off the kitchen shed. There she would stand in a tin tub and prosecute her bath with vigor, finishing it by pouring buckets of cold well-water over her gleaming white body.....(p. 206)

The punishing nature of this act may represent her rejection of the corn-god, but it hardly shows what Maynard Fox calls "a revulsion against the idea of physical contact with a man."[22] Alexandra is indeed angry with herself, but she certainly is not revolted by the dream. The soothing feeling which comes in her dream, the draining of "all her bodily weariness" (p. 207), indicates a powerful sexuality which she must conceal during her waking life. Alexandra is not, after all, asexual, just as Demeter is not. Indeed, Demeter resented the sexual union forced upon her by Poseidon, a union which diverted her from the arduous task of finding her daughter. But, Demeter also enjoyed the attentions of the mortal Iasion with whom she made love in a thrice-plowed field.

So is the case with Alexandra. On an unconscious level, in the mythos of her dream, Alexandra reacts not so much to an individual desire as to a desire as old as the race itself, to the impulse for sexual union. Only on waking does Alexandra realize that the passionate energy she feels, if shared as in her dream, would drain the resources she needs to live out her commitment to taming the land. The purgation by water which she executes becomes Alexandra's "dying to passion" as she comes to realize that death and love are the only things under the moon – a fact Bartley Alexander, too, had unhappily discovered. Only after Alexandra comes to accept the erotic urge as a part of waking existence will she be able to assume all the dimensions of a classical epic hero, in addition to her roles as Earth Mother and female conqueror.

---

22.   Maynard Fox, "Symbolic Representation in Willa Cather's *O Pioneers!*," *Western American Literature*, 9 (1974), 196.

But, it is in her relationship to the land that Alexandra begins to assume the proportions of epic hero. As patron goddess of a civilization based on agriculture, Alexandra establishes the regulation of a civilized life, a function attributed to Demeter in the Greek world and celebrated in her festival of Thesmophoria. Even during the first three difficult farming years after her father's death, Alexandra resists the demands of her brothers to abandon the high land on the Divide, land which Lou says "wasn't never meant to grow nothing on..."(p. 58). Alexandra's determination to bring order out of disorder, to carve civilization out of a land plagued by drought, chinch-bugs, and coyotes, is a fundamentally heroic trait. She resists the violence and destructiveness associated with her brothers' masculine approach to establishing order and instead insists on awaiting the fruition of the land that "Some day...will be worth more than all we can ever raise on it" (p. 58). Sue Rosowski describes Alexandra's position as synthesizing "the traditional pioneer qualities of expansive movement with the traditional pioneer female ones of stability...."[23] These are the qualities of the female figure of the classical epic, as well. Alexandra is a Penelope, maintaining a realm while Odysseus "moves on"; she is a Lavinia, offering the stability of family life in Aeneas' world dominated by war. Alexandra is the peacemaker like the hero of the Frithyoh Saga, a story she knows by heart. She is the civilizing force, entrancing Emil, Carl, and Oscar as she reads from *The Swiss Family Robinson*, another account of carving civilization out of wilderness. In Alexandra, Cather therefore expands the role of woman in the classical epics, making her at once both the masculine explorer-conqueror and the feminine peacemaker-civilizer. The Old World myth proves inadequate in developing a New World "epic." Cather is not reluctant to Americanize her classical echoes and, in some instances, as in *My Antonia*, even to personalize them. She does not bind her female characters by the limits of literary tradition.

Alexandra, though, maintains a matriarchal, Demetrian role throughout the novel. Each Sunday she sits at the head of her family's table, surrounded by the emblems of her prosperity and mindful of the needs of her

---

23.   Susan Rosowski, "Willa Cather's Pioneer Women," in *Where the West Begins*, ed. Arthur R. Huseboe and William Geyer (Sioux Falls, SD: Center for Western Studies Press, 1978), pp. 141-142.

many nieces and nephews. Like a patron goddess, she provides not only sustenance for the next generation but also the gifts of civilization, such as a piano for Milly. The regulation of life she brings to her home reflects the orderliness she has established on the farm itself:

> When you go out of the house into the flower garden, there you feel again the order and fine arrangement manifest all over the great farm; in the fencing and hedging, in the windbreaks and sheds, in the symmetrical pasture ponds, planted with scrub willows to give shade to the cattle in fly-time. There is even a white row of beehives in the orchard, under the walnut trees. (p. 84)

Willa Cather surely selected the detail of a "white row of beehives" as the classical prototype of human society, as a gynecocratic system. The bee had long been associated with Demeter, the earth and its fruitfulness, and the thriftiness of the keepers of the hive. These are the aspects explored by Vergil in his *Georgics*, Book IV. Cather was equally well acquainted with the epic simile Vergil used in Book I of *The Aeneid* when Aeneas marvels at the building and orderly advance of another woman's realm:

> Eagerly the Tyrians press on, some to build walls, to rear the citadel, and roll up stones by hand; some to choose the site for a dwelling and enclose it with a furrow...Even as bees in early summer, amid flowery fields, ply their task in sunshine, when they lead forth the full-grown young of their race... all aglow is the work and the fragrant honey is sweet with thyme. [24]

Like Dido, Alexandra directs the building of a new civilization, imposing an orderliness through her maternal presence. She is the "pure mother bee," the form in which Demeter was sometimes worshiped, and neither Alexandra nor the primitive Earth Mother submits to a superior, powerful male. Instead, Alexandra identifies with the land, merging with its spirit and bringing fertility to it. The pleasure Alexandra finds in the animals also places her among the great goddesses of earth to whom domesticated animals, as well as wild creatures like "the swamp birds–goose, duck, and

24.   H. Rushton Fairclough, trans., "Aeneid I-VI," in *Virgil: Eclogues, Georgics, Aeneid I-VI*, eds. T. E. Page, E. Capps, and W. H. D. Rouse (New York: G. P. Putnam's Sons, 1929), I, 271.

heron – the nocturnal owl and the dove," were sacred.[25] Appropriately, Alexandra remembers the wild duck she and Emil had watched as "a kind of enchanted bird that did not know age or change" (p. 205).

In her close ties to the soil, though, Alexandra most resembles a mythic earth mother. She remembers as "peculiarly happy" those days when "she was close to the flat, fallow world about her, and felt, as it were, in her own body the joyous germination in the soil" (p. 204). She yearns for union with the land, and it responds to her presence:

> For the first time, perhaps, since the land emerged from the waters of geologic ages, a human face was set toward it with love and yearning. It seemed beautiful to her, rich and strong and glorious. Her eyes drank in the breadth of it, until her tears blinded her. Then the Genius of the Divide, the great, free spirit which breathes across it, must have bent lower than it ever bent to a human will before. (p. 65)

The land appeals to Alexandra as a living creature with a personality. As a student of the Classics, Cather was surely aware of the ancient concept of a land spirit, a "Genius," and accordingly she used the term to describe Alexandra's closeness to the land. Alexandra responds to the Genius of the Divide as she will not allow herself to respond to the figure of male sexuality in her dream, for in alliance with the land she can retain independence. She need not submit to this Genius since it is a protective spirit, not a threatening one.

The "garden" Alexandra establishes seems a cross between Eden and primordial innocence and happiness as John H. Randall, III, proposes in *The Landscape and The Looking Glass*.[26] In so transforming the land, Alexandra steps into another classical role, becoming the shepherdess in a new Vale of Tempe. Indeed, the mood and atmosphere of a Golden Age prevail in much of the novel; but, as indicated by her poetry and *The Troll Garden* stories, Cather was well aware that loss and tragedy would eventually disrupt such a world, and a tragedy does occur in *O Pioneers!*. The inclusion of the Emil-

---

25. Erich Neumann, *The Great Mother: An Analysis of the Archetype*, trans. Ralph Manheim, 2nd ed. (Princeton: Princeton Univ. Press, 1963), p. 275.

26. John H. Randall, III, *The Landscape and The Looking Glass* (Boston: Houghton Mifflin Co., 1960), p. 75.

Marie romance in Alexandra's story may, at first, seem disruptive to the established mood. But, in bringing together these two stories, which were conceived of and written independently of one another, Cather may well have recognized that the pastoral tradition encompassed both stories. Susan Rosowski argues that Cather had in mind the Vergilian pastoral mode and especially the *Eclogues* when revising her stories for the novel. This seems likely since, as Rosowski points out, more parallels do exist than simply those between characters in the ancient poems and Cather's novel.[27] Just as she continued to do with the epic tradition in this novel, Cather also Americanized the pastoral tradition, and her young lovers' plight is only rudimentally that of Corydon and Alexis. The pastoral mode, then, works hand-in-hand with the epic tradition in *O Pioneers!* as the second parable of the novel emerges.

The love of Emil and Marie is that parable. Their love blossoms in and eventually shatters the newly created Arcadia. Undeniably, the passion of the two young lovers does destroy them, but this same passion only strengthens Alexandra's epic heroism. One of the novel's early scenes depicts young Alexandra carrying her lantern alone "deeper and deeper into that dark country" (p. 18). The picture recalls Demeter wandering at night about the countryside of Greece, searching for her lost daughter, her way lighted only by a torch. Like Demeter, who is unafraid of challenging the powers of Death, Alexandra faces the future fearlessly after Emil's death, never giving in to Thanatos, as Sister Peter Damian Charles suggests in her extensive study of love and death in *O Pioneers!*[28] Rather, Alexandra accepts her part in the birth-death-rebirth cycle which underscores so much of classical mythology as well as the epic tradition. She recovers from her personal loss, not regaining a lost paradise, but accepting a world where death and life

---

27.   Susan J. Rosowski, *The Voyage Perilous: Willa Cather's Romanticism* (Lincoln: Univ. of Nebraska Press, 1986), p. 46ff. Besides citing the *Eclogues* as a model for structuring the novel by "bringing together apparently disparate subjects," Rosowski cites the threat of land dispossession, the harmony in nature, the shepherd's wooing of his love, and "the tragic rhythm" of the novel as reflections of Vergil's pastoral poems. She also suggests more specific parallels in character: Ivar to Silenus, Amedee to Daphnis, Marie to Amaryllis, and so forth.

28.   Sister Peter Damian Charles, "Love and Death in Willa Cather's *O Pioneers!*," *College Language Association Journal*, 9 (Dec. 1965), 141-142.

coexist. In her poem "Prairie Spring," which acts as a preface to *O Pioneers!*, Cather clearly had in mind such a thematic concern, for, in the poem, Youth with "Its fierce necessity,/ Its sharp desire" is joined with "the lips of silence" and "the earthy dusk."

Cather also portrays this vitality of youth and its inevitable loss through mythic allusions in *O Pioneers!*. In her appearance and personality, Marie suggests not only Alexis of Vergil's Second Eclogue but also the goddess of spring, Persephone. The seasonal cycle of the novel even follows the pattern of Persephone's return to earth and subsequent descent to the Underworld. Cather was aware of the Demeter and Persephone myth, having had exposure to it either through the Homeric Hymns or the Latin version in Ovid's *Metamorphoses*. Marie is spontaneously and naturally affectionate. Her yellow-brown eyes are "the color of sunflower honey" and reflect points of light "like the sparks from a forge" (pp. 135-136). In these eyes, "like the Colorado mineral called tiger eye" (p. 11), lies an animal vitality. Marie is at least twice linked to cats, once as a child entertaining an admiring throng of farmers while she played with Emil's kitten and again as a married woman whose large yellow cat suns itself on the doorstep. Yellow is the dominant color associated with Marie – as it was with Hilda Burgoyne – an indication of passionate temperament. Marie is stimulated by nature itself and rejoices in the flowers and life-giving rains that come with summer. When Emil arrives to cut the grass in the orchard, Marie flits about, her sensibilities heightened by the earth's beauty:

> "Don't let me disturb you, Emil. I'm going to pick cherries. Isn't everything beautiful after the rain?...Just smell the wild roses! They are always so spicy after a rain. We never had so many of them in here before. I suppose it's the wet season. Will you have to cut them, too?" (p. 150)

Marie's response to the wild rose mirrors the delight of Persephone upon spying the lovely narcissus, especially created as a snare for her. Like the ancient goddess of springtime, Marie is frequently associated with flower gardens. Wild roses flame along her fence rows; geraniums and fuchsias fill her window sills even in winter. The clearest association of Marie with Persephone is in the poppies which trim her hat and invite a comparison of her round and rich-colored face to a red poppy (p. 79). The poppy was the flower of Persephone, for its deep color was like the spark of youth, while its soporific effects equated it with the regions of the dead over which Persephone came to rule.

In her relationship with Alexandra, too, Marie fulfills the role of Persephone. Alexandra confesses that Marie is more than a neighbor for her; she is "really a companion, some one I can talk to quite frankly," she remarks (p. 130). Alexandra takes pride in Marie's openness, her genuine enthusiasm for life, and her daughter-like attentiveness. Marie sits at the feet of Alexandra in the orchard, much as Persephone must have sat at the feet of "Demeter of the beautiful hair"[29] as she is called in the Homeric Hymn. In the orchard scene Cather shows Alexandra in a motherly role, head uncovered, listening to the chatter of the young girl. An almost religious atmosphere prevails:

> Alexandra took off her shade-hat and threw it on the ground. Marie picked it up and played with the white ribbons, twisting them about her brown fingers as she talked. They made a pretty picture in the strong sunlight, the leafy pattern surrounding them like a net; the Swedish woman so white and gold, kindly and amused, but armored in calm, and the alert brown one, her full lips parted, points of yellow light dancing in her eyes as she laughed and chattered. (p. 135)

Alexandra is quietly indulgent of the child-like eagerness of Marie, the very trait which in the ancient version of the story attracted the attention of Hades.

In many ways, Frank Shabata fills the role of Hades. He is dark and moody, "'jealous about everything, his farm and his horses and his pretty wife'" (p. 120). As Cather describes, Frank could easily be the brother of Zeus: "He was burned a dull red down to his neckband, and there was a heavy three-days' stubble on his face. Even in his agitation he was handsome, but he looked a rash and violent man" (pp. 139-140). Although Marie had freely gone with Frank, her father viewed the incident as an abduction and accepted the marriage only "because there was nothing else to do..." (p. 146). So did Zeus accept the marriage of his daughter to his own brother. But,

---

29. Mark P. O. Morford and Robert J. Lenardon, "The Homeric Hymn to Demeter, No. 2," in *Mythology* (New York: David McKay Co., 1971), p. 199.

Marie's marriage to Frank is in many ways a marriage of death. Although he is not cruel in his treatment of Marie, Frank is difficult to live with, often working himself into a rage and offending his neighbors as a result. Marie's efforts to be thoughtfully attentive to his needs go unacknowledged and her spirit withers. She becomes "like a white night-moth out of the fields":

> The years seemed to stretch before her like the land; spring, summer, autumn, winter, spring; always the same patient fields, the patient little trees, the patient lives; always the same yearning, the same pulling at the chain – until the instinct to live had torn itself and bled and weakened for the last time, until the chain secured a dead woman, who might cautiously be released. (p. 248)

Marie's marriage, like Persephone's, is an encounter with death, has no happy ending, and remains childless. Cather even describes Marie as a shade from Tartarus: "She seemed like a troubled spirit, like some shadow out of the earth..." (p. 232). Just as Hades' character is an enemy to youthful vitality, Frank's sullenness eats away at Marie's carefree nature.

Frank's domination of his wife merely re-enacts the Olympian command over the female world, a fact Alexandra clearly resents. When Frank rudely ignores her suggestion that he mend his neighbors' fence, Alexandra resolutely walks away, fully aware of Marie's subjugation. Marie is not an Alexandra, capable of challenging patriarchal law, and Alexandra continues to exhibit protectiveness toward her. Alexandra claims that Marie is "too young and pretty for this sort of life" (p. 121), but she is powerless to change life for the young girl, just as Demeter stood powerless before the Fates and Zeus' claim that "It's no disgrace to marry Jove's own brother,/ For all he needs is your good will, my dear."[30] But like Demeter, Alexandra is not very successful in her attempts to extend good will to Frank:

> "Frank's not a bad neighbor, but to get on with him you've got to make a fuss over him and act as if you thought he was a very important person all the time, and different from other people. I find it hard to keep that up from one year's end to another." (p. 120)

---

30.   Horace Gregory, trans., *The Metamorphoses*, by Ovid (New York: New American Library, 1958), p. 155.

Alexandra's Demetrian concern for Marie is obvious. She harbors bitterness toward what seems Frank's sexual aggression against Marie. Along with old Mr. Tovesky, Alexandra still views Marie's elopement as a theft and Marie as a victim. The relationship between Alexandra and Marie is, then, much like that of Demeter and Persephone. In Marie, Alexandra finds an extension of a sexual self, as well, but a self which she has unconsciously denied. They stand in relation to one another as lovers of the spirit, much as Willa Cather described her own relationship with Isabelle McClung. Marie greets Alexandra in a display of genuine affection, "throwing her arms about Alexandra" (p. 134), just as Persephone alights from Hermes' chariot, "throwing her arms about (Demeter's) neck in an embrace."[31] The bond between these women is an unusually strong one, for it is based on the woman's challenge of the patriarchy and resentment of the role of woman as victim.

Particularly in the winter when she is forced to stay indoors, Marie feels victimized by an emptiness akin to that Persephone felt when living beneath the earth with her husband:

> She seemed to feel the weight of all the snow that lay down there. The branches had become so hard that they wounded your hand if you but tried to break a twig. And yet, down under the frozen crusts, at the roots of the trees, the secret of life was still safe, warm as the blood in one's heart; and the spring would come again! Oh, it would come again! (p. 202)

Her ache to return to springtime is Persephone's. Like the Kore of the Homeric Hymn, Marie must suppress her love for life during the long winter season and must cling to the promise of life renewed. Sister Peter Damian Charles concludes that in utilizing the seasonal motif in her novel, Cather returns to the ancient sources. She plants the seeds for the love-death conflict in the first two parts of the book and allows them to germinate in the short chapters of "Winter Memories."[32] So the ancients planted the wheat in the fall, watched over the winter growth, and harvested in the spring. The celebration of Demeter's beneficence was a summer festival of harvest when

---

31. Morford and Lenardon, p. 207.
32. Sister Charles, p. 146.

the grain was hidden underground, stored away to await the Kore's return in autumn. By following this seasonal cycle, Cather arranges Marie's descent to the Underworld in mid-summer when the grain stands ripe under a hot afternoon sun (p. 257). Significantly, Alexandra's reawakening to life comes in the fall following Marie's and Emil's deaths, the time at which, in the ancient world, Persephone reappeared on earth and the land became productive. Alexandra discovers her part in the fertility cycle of birth, death, and rebirth and describes her feelings to old Ivar:

> "After you once get cold clear through, the feeling of rain on you is sweet. It seems to bring back feelings you had when you were a baby. It carries you back into the dark, before you were born; you can't see things, but they come to you, somehow, and you know them and aren't afraid of them." (p. 281)

In *O Pioneers!*, Alexandra struggles to overcome both the loss of her "daughter" and the loss of her "son." Emil embodies the admirable traits of Youth which Cather cites in "Prairie Spring"–"insupportable sweetness," "fierce necessity," and "sharp desire." As Carl Linstrum says, "...he was the best there was..." (p. 305). In appearance Emil, too, assumes a mythic posture. Like a graceful Adonis, he rhythmically swings his scythe with "that long, even stroke that few American boys ever learn" (p. 151). He is "a splendid figure of a boy, tall and straight as a young pine tree, with a handsome head, and stormy gray eyes, deeply set under a serious brow" (p. 77).

In his relationship to Alexandra, though, Emil fulfills another role in connection with Venus. He becomes not her beloved Adonis but her son Cupid. Emil always shared a special relationship with his older sister, first as a small boy who hid his face in her skirts when he was teased and later as a young man to whom she gives "a whole chance" to do "whatever he wants to" (p. 117). Alexandra demonstrates a mother's pride in Emil, who is so full of promise, sensitive in spirit, and responsive to her needs. Together they spend days "which she loved to look back on" (p. 204) and moments of "warm, friendly silence, full of perfect understanding..." (p. 238). They even share a love for the same wild creatures and for the flowers, particularly the roses which Emil saves from the swath of his scythe. Alexandra delights in the charming ways he develops at college, and, at the church supper, she watches

122

with pride "while the French girls [flutter] about him in their white dresses and ribbons..." (p. 217). Her protectiveness is also a possessiveness, manifesting itself in Alexandra's reaction to Emil's love for Marie, a love reminiscent of Cupid's love for Psyche.

Although Alexandra comes to admit that "she had omitted no opportunity of throwing Marie and Emil together" (p. 284), she still views his affair with Marie as treachery and desertion. Just as Venus vented her anger on Psyche rather than on her son when she discovered their love, Alexandra is vexed at Marie. After the young lovers die, Alexandra blames Marie bitterly and feels the girl has betrayed her trust. After all, she claims, Marie was a married woman while "Emil was a good boy, and only bad boys ran after married women" (p. 284). Alexandra, like Venus, absolves her son of responsibility for the affair. Blinded by motherly affection for Emil, Alexandra finds it easy to forget her Cupid's teasing ways and "strikingly exotic figure" (p. 212). Although Alexandra's relationship to Emil hardly has the incestuous overtones of Venus' to Cupid as described by Apuleius in the ancient text,[33] the love she feels toward Emil is as strong as that she feels for Marie. Alexandra's distress at their betrayal of her is two-fold: the distress of Venus losing her son to Psyche and the distress of Demeter losing her daughter to Hades. Moreover, Emil has so long been the sole object of his sister's affection that he is perplexed by the suggestion that she might love Carl, and he reacts by laughing and dismissing the idea with a shrug.

Throughout the novel Cather builds images of love and death in preparation for the climactic scene of "The White Mulberry Tree" in which she weaves together allusions from two classical myths. Forebodings of death surround Emil. On first meeting Marie he is mowing in the cemetery, swinging his scythe through the long grasses. Although the scene suggests the Grim Reaper, the second appearance of Emil in Marie's orchard, scythe in hand, points to an older myth. Each scene is charged with intense but suppressed passion, and the sickle emerges as a fertility symbol from the

33.   John F. Makowski, "Persephone, Psyche, and the Mother-Maiden Archetype," *The Classical Outlook*, 62 (March-April 1985), 77. Makowski quotes Apuleius' lines "osculis hiantibus filium diu ac pressule saviata" as the evidence of incestuous love between Venus and Cupid.

myth of Cronus and Gaea, whose attack upon Uranus both fructified the earth and produced a race of death-bearing monsters. Cather portrays Emil's association with love and death even more acutely at the Confirmation ceremony following Amedee's funeral:

> He was at that height of excitement from which everything is foreshortened, from which life seems short and simple, death very near, and the soul seems to soar like an eagle.... The heart, when it is too much alive, aches for the brown earth, and ecstasy has no fear of death. (p. 257)

Emil, then, comes to Marie in the orchard as Cupid came to Psyche, keen in his desire but enveloped by the presence of death. Emil also had shared the first kiss with his lover under the cover of darkness at the church fair and was surprised at its naturalness (pp. 224-225). Marie responded to that kiss as Psyche did after she had outgrown her anxiety about her "demon lover" and could freely share her love. In his commitment to Marie, Emil also outgrows the temerity of a youthful Cupid and becomes a mature lover for his Psyche. Alexandra, although unaware of Emil's love for Marie, notes this change in his character in the same tones of regret that Venus might have used: "He is a man now, sure enough. I have no boy left" (p. 215).

The tragic scene in the orchard also echoes the myth of Cupid and Psyche. Marie lies alone in the orchard, dreaming of her lover's arrival, a dream which, like Psyche's, is fulfilled. Marie meets her death in a search for happiness, but the "look of ineffable content" on her face (p. 269) confirms that the allegory of the ancient myth is borne out: the soul's pursuit of divine love is satisfied only in eternal union. Psyche is said to represent "the human soul, which is purified by passions and misfortunes and thus prepared for the enjoyment of true and pure happiness."[34] So is the case with Marie. Cather makes reference to the myth by her final description of the lovers:

> Above Marie and Emil, two white butterflies from Frank's alfalfa-field were fluttering in and out among the interlacing shadows; diving and soaring, now close together, now far apart; and in the long grass by the fence the last wild roses of the year opened their pink hearts to die. (p. 270)

---

[34]   William Smith, "Psyche," *A Smaller Classical Dictionary* (New York: Harper and Brothers, 1882), p. 323.

For the Greeks, the soul of man was winged and assumed the shape of the butterfly, and in their art, Psyche became the butterfly maiden whose soul joined Cupid's in flight to Olympus. Furthermore, Cather concludes her novel as Apuleius concludes the myth of Cupid and Psyche. Just as Venus works through her anger and accepts her daughter-in-law, Alexandra puts aside the hurt she feels and comes to terms with the inevitable – the death of the two persons most dear to her.

However, the Cupid and Psyche myth does not alone provide details for "The White Mulberry Tree" section of the novel. As the title indicates, Cather borrowed from the myth of Pyramus and Thisbe, as well, and this myth provides a significant thematic basis for this portion of the novel. Although Cather departs markedly from the Ovidian account of the myth in changing suicide to murder, a similar atmosphere of innocence prevails in both tales. The orchard is bathed in an almost unearthly light:

> When he reached the orchard the sun was hanging low over the wheatfield. Long fingers of light reached through the apple branches as through a net; the orchard was riddled and shot with gold; light was the reality, the trees were merely interferences that reflected and refracted light. (p. 258)

Marie lies under the white mulberry tree much as Thisbe must have awaited her lover. Even Marie's name evokes the purity of the Virgin; in hearing the variant form of her name in "The Ave Maria," Emil had been spurred to rush to her. In other details, like Marie's resting in her lover's arms after death, Cather follows Ovid's narrative. She does, however, more realistically explain the change in the mulberries' color. Rather than having Emil's [Pyramus'] blood spurt upward from his body to stain the fruit, the fruit falls during the night and is covered with the dark stain of the lovers' blood.

Although at least one critic has suggested further parallels to the myths of Endymion or Baucis and Philemon,[35] Cather's blatant use of the mulberry tree assures that the myth of young love, which ends abruptly and disastrously, was in her mind when writing *O Pioneers!*. Even while incorporating the Greek myth into her story "The White Mulberry Tree," Cather was profoundly influenced by other versions of the tale, particularly

---

[35] David Stouck, *Willa Cather's Imagination* (Lincoln: Univ. of Nebraska Press, 1975), p. 31.

as they had appeared in the works of Shakespeare and Keats. Emil and Marie are frontier versions of Romeo and Juliet, led by their passion to disregard the censure of their families and finding happiness only in death. Shakespeare accentuates the pathos of his star-crossed lovers' situation by creating a series of unlucky mishaps, but Cather presents more mature lovers who move steadily toward a union, the tragic consequences of which they are fully capable of understanding.

Susan Rosowski suggests that Cather also turned to Keats's "The Eve of St. Agnes" for her characterizations, particularly since Emil and Marie display "passionate individuality" more in keeping with Porphyro and Madeline than with "Ovid's stylized figures."[36] Similarities do, indeed, exist between Cather's novel and Keats' poem, especially the dream-like unreality in the orchard. The close reader recalls the dream state from which Madeline is awakened by her lover and their escape, not into death, but "into the storm." The murders of Emil and Marie also recall the story of Paolo and Francesca, a tale which Cather knew well and from which she had quoted in "'Death in the Desert.'" In other aspects, the orchard scene suggests an even older account of lovers cast out of the Edenic garden for their sin, especially because of the idyllic nature of the Shabata orchard. Cather was apt to combine Biblical and classical images with little concern over what could be their antithetical elements.

Cather's wide-ranging literary background must be acknowledged, and her story of a fatal love serves as an excellent example of her bringing together materials from two or more literary traditions, without sacrificing the integrity of her work. No single mythic source seems adequate to explain the complexity of emotion and range of character in *O Pioneers!*. The Emil-Marie story is drawn from myths whose universality of theme is undeniable, but their story assumes a truth unique to itself in Alexandra's reaction to the young lovers' deaths.

By combining descendant myths with images of innocence from the Pyramus-Thisbe myth and images of a more mature love from the Cupid-Psyche myth, Cather more readily supports Alexandra's (and, perhaps, the

---

36.   Rosowski, *The Voyage Perilous*, p. 54.

126

reader's) reactions to the deaths of Marie and Emil. Both censure and sympathy are present, for Alexandra is one whose "blind side" was human relationships, and "Her personal life, her own realization of herself, was almost a subconscious existence..." (p. 203). Alexandra's anger with Marie shows that, in spite of Demetrian-like resistance toward male superiority, she does not completely reject Carl's characterization of Marie as temptress:

> "There are women who spread ruin around them through no fault of theirs, just by being too beautiful, too full of life and love. They can't help it. People come to them as people go to a warm fire in winter." (p. 304)

In striving to understand the forces that destroyed Marie and Emil, Alexandra reassesses her life, which has "all been toward the end of making her proficient in what she had undertaken to do" (p. 203). Alexandra wonders if, in spite of her deep affection for Emil, Marie, and Carl, she has duly deserved Lou's criticism, "Alexandra ain't much like other women-folks" (p. 173). In diverting all her energies into the land had she failed to respond to an increasingly complex society that demanded she conform to a different role?

In Alexandra's reaction to her dream, she confronts these problems and apparently reconciles herself to the powers of love and death. The dream comes to her as she lies exhausted after exposing herself to a drenching rainstorm. For the first time, she clearly sees the figure in her dream and knows him. The corn-god of her earlier dream assumes new proportions. The love she is now ready to accept is that of a real companion, not a mythic or ideal being. Awakened to her own sexuality and admitting to its power in her own life, Alexandra can accept Carl without descending to a traditionally passive feminine role. She will forever be an earth goddess, as Carl realizes, but one who does not wish to be alienated from mortal life:

> "You belong to the land," Carl murmured, "as you have always said. Now more than ever."
>
> "Yes, now more than ever. You remember what you once said about the graveyard, and the old story writing itself over? Only it is we who write it, with the best we have." (p. 307)

Alexandra relives one of those "two or three human stories...[which] go on repeating themselves as fiercely as if they had never happened before..." (p. 119). In her role as Earth Mother, she relives the ancient fertility myth of loss and rebirth. In her role as epic hero, she makes a descent into the realm of death and emerges more fully cognizant of herself and her destiny. Alexandra succeeds in reconciling the forces which destroyed Bartley Alexander, namely order and passion. Cather closes her novel not with "the rosy tints of romanticism" as one critic calls it,[37] but with a pensive sadness. The battle Alexandra waged was a heroic one, but it left her tired and aware of the loneliness she had suffered. Her struggle was, perhaps, that of Cather herself, who had long resisted conforming to societal expectations for women and had found the emotional demands of art as draining as were the demands of the pioneering experience. In returning to the world of classical myth, Cather found a medium for wrestling with these concerns while illustrating, in the character of Alexandra Bergson, the heroic greatness of which human beings are capable.

37. Robert Edson Lee, *From West to East: Studies in the Literature of the American West* (Urbana: Univ. of Illinois Press, 1966), p. 135.

CHAPTER VI
THE MATRIARCHY REALIZED:
THE SONG OF THE LARK AND *MY ANTONIA*

Memories of her trip to the Southwest were still foremost in Willa Cather's mind when she began writing *The Song of the Lark* in 1913. If she had at last found her "home pasture" in writing *O Pioneers!*, in writing her next novel she found much more than an evocation of the heroic values of the pioneer age. In the ruins of the Cliff-Dwellers, Cather discovered a link to the past, not just a chronological link but an artistic one. Once Cather began writing *The Song of the Lark*, the work went quickly, in spite of numerous interruptions, and she finished the novel in a little less than a year. Cather found that this story about the struggle of a small-town girl of artistic sensibilities was, in many ways, her own story and she became very close to her heroine. Yet, the inspiration for the character of the successful and mature Thea Kronborg came from Cather's acquaintance with Olive Fremstad, the famed operatic soprano, in whom Cather recognized the same strength of purpose and creativity which she had admired in first-generation Nebraskan pioneers. In writing of Thea Kronborg, then, Cather employed some of the same mythic images that had served her in describing the epic heroism and matriarchal dignity of Alexandra Bergson. In *The Song of the Lark*, though, these allusions are coupled with others from classical myth which portray Thea as the Muse of her own art. For Thea, as for Cather, art becomes an enduring value, a stay against the onslaught of time.

130

Cather first turns to the Greek world in selecting the name of her principal character. Although Thea Kronborg's name may have its source in Ibsen's work, as Mildred Bennett suggests,[1] the imagery of the novel points to an earlier association of her name with Greek mythology. Like Theodosia's name in "Tommy, the Unsentimental," Thea Kronborg's echoes the Greek term *theoi* and those primitive powers over which human beings have no control. For Thea, the power beyond her control is not an external god of storms or earthquakes but an internal and undeniable force to which sacrifice must be offered – a sacrifice of self if necessary. Even her surname, Kronborg, with its Scandinavian origin, referring to both the crown (kron) and a walled city (borg), recalls an abode for kings, if not gods. For Cather the name also surely echoed the Titanic powers of Cronus (Kronos) in his battle against the familial forces that would wrest his kingdom from him. Thea, too, wages war against the stifling Philistinism of her small town, a battle she eventually recognizes as a battle against her family, as well:

> Thea felt that she had been betrayed... Thea had always taken it for granted that her sister and brothers recognized that she had special abilities and that they were proud of it. She had done them the honor, she told herself bitterly, to believe that...*they were of her kind*, and not of the Moonstone kind. Now they had all grown up and become persons... [and] were among the people whom she had always recognized as her natural enemies.[2]

Thea, unlike Cronus, is victorious in her battle against such forces and successfully defends the realm of artistic creation.

The most direct source for Thea's name, however, comes from the mythic Theia, who, according to Hesiod, was the daughter of Uranus and Gaea and the wife of Hyperion. As the mother of Helios (the sun), Eos (dawn), and Selene (the moon), Theia was considered by the ancients as the

---

[1] Mildred R. Bennett, "How Willa Cather Chose Her Names," *Names*, 19 (1962), 34. Bennett notes that prior to 1913 Willa Cather made "two prolonged vacations" to the home of her cousin Howard Gore and his Scandinavian wife Lillian. Together with Lillian, Cather read Ibsen, and Thea's name may have been drawn from the name he used in "Hedda Gabler."

[2] Willa Cather, *The Song of the Lark* (1915; rpt. Lincoln: Univ. of Nebraska Press, 1978), pp. 239-240. All further references to this work will be cited parenthetically in the text.

deity from whom all light proceeded. Cather draws heavily upon the concept of this mythic being, surrounding her characters, Thea in particular, with varying degrees of light, corresponding to the emotional intensity of the situation. The opening scenes of *The Song of the Lark* show Dr. Archie responding to the glorious starlight of a "flashing night" (p. 5), while feeling disgust with the petty concerns of foolish men like Rev. Peter Kronborg. Dr. Archie associates just such light with Thea who, crowned by her yellow braids, seems almost a goddess as she rocks her baby brother and the sunlight pours over her shoulders. Thea reacts with equal excitement to the beauty of a moonlit night. She stands on the trestle with only a rabbit to share her solitude and "lap[s] up the moonlight like cream" (p. 80).

Just as the light of expectancy and youth envelopes Thea in Moonstone, so do images of light surround her after her first immersion into the world of art. In Chicago, she steps from the concert hall into crowded, cold streets, but beyond all the bustle, "The sun was setting in a clear, windy sky, that flamed with red as if there were a great fire somewhere on the edge of the city" (p. 200). Her awakening to beauty is a moment of intense emotion reflected in the light of a sunset older than the human race. Thea responds to light and it emanates from her. In the early morning she awakens refreshed in that "sunny cave" of her own room where she dreamed of a world beyond Moonstone (p. 222). Thea's life is "full of light" (p. 297), like the goddess for whom she is named, and in her efforts to create a thing of beauty, she assumes mythic dimensions.

Like Alexandra Bergson, Thea fiercely commits herself to creating the enduring and the beautiful. Her determination in pursuing her goals is heroic, and Thea frequently identifies herself with historical militaristic leaders. At the Art Institute of Chicago she admires the statue of the Dying Gladiator, and "better than anything else she liked a great equestrian statue of an evil, cruel-looking general with an unpronounceable name" (p. 196). She stands puzzled before Venus di Milo and does not consider Apollo Belvedere Handsome. Such figures and what they represent have little to do with Thea's view of life as an epic struggle against her "natural enemies." A photograph of the Naples bust of Julius Caesar is her choice as the sole decoration for her rented room in Chicago, and the choice seems not so curious if one keeps in mind the titanic struggle Thea faces. She exhibits the same Amazonian fierceness toward succeeding in her career that Alexandra Bergson showed in defying men who prevent her from achieving her goals. For Cather, both struggles are a part of building civilization, and both women are epic heroes.

Thea also demonstrates a Dionysian passion for living. In childhood she showed a preference for Byron's "There was a sound of revelry" as opposed to "Maid of Athens," and, even then, yet unformulated desires drew her to Mexican town and to a delighted appreciation of life:

> There was an atmosphere of ease and friendly pleasure in the low, dimly lit room, and Thea could not help wondering whether the Mexicans had no jealousies or neighborly grudges as the people of Moonstone had. There was not constraint of any kind there to-night, but a kind of natural harmony about their movements, their greetings, their low conversations, their smiles. (p. 230)

The lights Thea sees in Johnny Tellamantez's eyes on this same evening are "like those moonlight makes on black, running water" and supposedly indicate one of his "spells" when madness descends upon him (p. 233). His madness, however, is Thea's. Both are "highly charged with the desire to live" (p. 224).

As in *Alexander's Bridge*, Cather describes this passion for life in relation to the moon myth. Significantly, Cather renames her hometown "Moonstone" in the novel, and moonflowers vine about the Tellamantez house where Thea drinks in the love of song. In her devotion to the purity of art Thea becomes a Diana, a moon goddess. The Mexican youth Silvo even worships at Thea's feet when she begins to sing. He lies looking at the moon "under the impression that he was still looking at Thea" (p. 232). On summer nights when the moon hangs full in the sky, Thea reveals her passion for living beyond the confines of a stubborn Colorado town. Then, as Dr. Archie oberves, the moon "was the great fact in the world" (p. 41). Thea pulsates with an excitement for life itself:

> She used to drag her mattress beside her low window and lie awake for a long while, vibrating with excitement, as a machine vibrates from speed. Life rushed in upon her through that

window – or so it seemed. In reality, of course, life rushes from within, not from without. There is no work of art so big or so beautiful that it was not once contained in some youthful body, like this one which lay on the floor in the moonlight, pulsing with ardor and anticipation. (p. 140)

Whereas Bartley Alexander never achieved the union of his desire with the order of civilization, Thea follows in the footsteps of Alexandra Bergson, directing her passion toward an impersonal object – her art – and thereby avoiding death, the consequence of unrestrained desire in human relationships. Thea would always have her Endymion in the perfection of song, but she finds that loving an intangible object is a process of continuous giving but receiving nothing in return.

In exploring the relationship between Thea's desires and the possibility of attaining them, Cather turned again to the myth of Orpheus and Eurydice.[3] Cather introduces the myth through the person of Herr Wunsch, a displaced but talented musician, who recognizes Thea's potential and first makes her aware of melodies other than those sung at the Methodist Church. Wunsch, whose name in German means "wish" or "desire," is himself an aging Orpheus who, having lost his Eurydice, finds his youthful dream resurfacing as he teaches Thea. Whether Wunsch's "Eurydice" was the lure of musical perfection or the Spanish alto whom he had heard as a youth, Wunsch lives the life of regret and self-torture that Orpheus did. Attracted to the splendor of art but unable to be constant to its ideal, his Orphic quest must end as Mrs. Kohler predicts: "He would drift on from new town to town, from catastrophe to catastrophe" (p. 97).

Thea, however, lives out a variant pattern of the myth, becoming a kind of female Orpheus. In receiving Wunsch's parting gift, the score of Gluck's *Orpheus*, Thea accepts the part of the mythic artist, which can only lead to perfection and the loss of self. When first scanning the pages of the opera, Thea frowns at the difficult passages and laughs disconcertedly. Well aware of the obstacles which lie before her in her pursuit of art, she believes

---

3.   James Woodress, *Willa Cather: Her Life and Art* (1970; rpt. Lincoln: Univ. of Nebraska Press, 1982), p. 168. Woodress considers the Orpheus myth as the principal "structural framework" for the narrative and argues that Wunsch lives out "the eternal story of the striving artist whose reach exceeds his grasp...."

these obstacles are enemies and must be treated as such. Orpheus waged just such a war against those forces which denied Eurydice's return and, overwhelmed by anger and failure, was ultimately destroyed by them. Wunsch recognizes that Thea must develop a more mature attitude, a willingness to compromise with "difficult things." Only then can she achieve the eternal union with the sublime, a union that Orpheus denied to himself.

Characteristically, Cather selects that version of the Orpheus myth which will best convey Thea's triumph over death. Cather chooses not the early operatic versions like Rossi's, which closely follow the myth as recorded by Ovid; instead, she selects Glück's opera *Orfeo ed Euridice* in which Eurydice, pitied by Eros and the other gods, is returned to life and marries Orpheus. For Glück, and for Willa Cather, it is not art that redeems life; it is desire (Eros). Thea's redemption comes after discovering that her relationship with Fred Ottenburg is founded on a lie about his marriage. Thea "break[s] through into the realities" (p. 357), as Fred says, and achieves that maturity toward approaching "difficult things" that Wunsch knew was necessary for achieving her goals as a singer. She survives her descent into hell, not by winning hell over to her grief, as did the mythic Orpheus, but by freeing herself from personal attachments which would divert her from her course. Even when he knows he has deceived her, Fred Ottenburg observes that Thea's courage and determination make her uniquely prepared to meet the challenges before her, both personal and professional: "She was right; she was not one of those who draw back. Some people get on by avoiding dangers, others by riding through them" (p. 342). Thea, impelled by her artistic desires, rides through her Orphic descent, not allowing Eros to intervene. The personal life, the Dionysian impulse which she had felt so strongly since childhood, she surrenders to Apollonian sublimity in art. In this, Orpheus had failed. But, by placing a woman in the role of Orpheus, Cather reconfirms the power of the matriarchy to establish the beautiful and enduring, just as Alexandra Bergson had done.

This success is achieved only by sacrificing personal needs. Thea must suppress her love for Fred Ottenburg as Alexandra did her love for Carl Linstrum. She must suffer the loss of her mother much as Alexandra endured the loss of Emil. As in Glück's opera, only Desire can help the artist to reconcile life to art. So Wunsch had made clear to the aspiring, young Thea: "Nothing is far and nothing is near, if one desires. The world is little, people are little, human life is little. There is only one big thing – desire. And before it, when it is big, all is little" (pp. 75-76).

But, Thea finds that her success is greatest only when memory is coupled with desire. She, therefore, becomes a Muse, the offspring of Mnemosyne (memory) and Zeus (desire). She can reconcile her childish desire "to go away forever" and "to stay forever" (pp. 139-140) only by turning to memories which sustain her commitment to art. Only after Thea finds meaning in "those old faces...long after they were hidden away under the earth" (p. 130) and only after she learns to go back to memories and to hold them in her heart, does she become the Muse of her art, inspiring others as well as herself. When she sings the role of Elizabeth, Thea instills within the scene the heartbreaking grief of her mother's death, but, as her accompanist Landry explains, the memory of this grief is more than personal: "It's full of the thing every plain creature finds out for himself, but that never gets written down. It's unconscious memory, maybe; inherited memory..." (p. 449). In assuming the role of Muse, Thea necessarily has no personal life, relying only on memory coupled with desire for inspiration. Like Cather, her greatness comes when she ceases to admire and begins to remember. Thea becomes a priestess of her art, drinking of the Pierian waters and vowing complete devotion to only one god.

Willa Cather had written as early as 1896 that "In the kingdom of art there is no God but one God, and his service is so exacting that there are few men born of women who are strong enough to take the vows."[4] Thea takes the vows and enters "into the inheritance that she herself had laid up, into the fullness of the faith she had kept before she knew its name or its meaning" (pp. 447-448). Like the Muses, Thea enters a vow of chastity, loving only her art, and, in doing so, finds that the service of gods is hard. Thea must devote all her energies to her art, and only in her performances can she live out for a brief time the passion she must deny. Thea must, then, involve both memory

---

4. Willa Cather, "The Passing Show," *Nebraska State Journal*, 1 March 1896, p. 9, in *The Kingdom of Art: Willa Cather's First Principles and Critical Statements 1893-1896*, ed. Bernice Slote (Lincoln: Univ. of Nebraska Press, 1966), p. 417.

and desire in singing her greatest roles, like that of Sieglinde. The subsequent perfection she achieves in her singing causes Johnny Tellamantez to uncover his head and to stand in mute adoration to a goddess of the arts (p. 479).

But, Thea is not the lark freely singing out its passion far above the earth. Patricia Yongue, in her article discussing Willa Cather's concept of the hero, argues that the Catheran hero must struggle "to reconcile his special aesthetic perception and impulses with his strictly human predicament."[5] Thea undergoes such a struggle before she emerges as Muse of Song. Striving to understand her relationship to human history, she discovers a link to the past in the Indian ruins of Panther Canyon. Here she experiences an awakening of both her spirit and her sexuality, an awakening that is attributable, in part, to a close relationship with the earth. As a girl growing up in Moonstone, Thea had felt an affinity for the land. She had reveled in the beauty of the earth that both stimulated her thoughts and nurtured her body:

> It was over flat lands like this, stretching out to drink the sun, that the larks sang – and one's heart sang there, too...She had the sense of going back to a friendly soil, whose friendship was somehow going to strengthen her; a naive, generous country that gave one its joyous force, its large-hearted, childlike power to love, just as it gave one its coarse, brilliant flowers. (p. 220)

The months Thea spends in Chicago studying music drain her of the vital energy she draws from this landscape, and she descends into a state of dispirited listlessness like that Persephone must have felt during her first stay in the realm of the dead.

In Part IV of *The Song of the Lark*, however, Thea experiences a transformation of self, a renewed acquaintance with the earth. Although hardly a primitive Earth Mother or even a Demetrian figure like Alexandra Bergson, Thea is nourished by the earth. In both her dreams of the canyon and in her early morning response to it, Thea senses "that peculiar sadness – a voice of the past, not very loud, that went on saying a few simple things to the solitude eternally" (p. 302). Removed from a society of patriarchal tradition,

---

5.   Patricia Lee Yongue, "Willa Cather on Heroes and Hero-Worship," *Neuphilologische Mitteilungen*, 79 (1977), 60.

Thea discovers within herself an intuitive understanding of the women who
spent their lives among the cliff-houses:

> She found herself trying to walk as they must have walked, with
> a feeling in her feet and knees and loins which she had never
> known before,—which must have come up to her out of the
> accustomed dust of that rocky trail. She could feel the weight
> of an Indian baby hanging to her back as she climbed. (p. 302)

The femaleness, which she felt must be suppressed in the pursuit of art, is
reawakened. The gladness she feels is the very aspect of her nature that she
had lost in her "enslaving desire to get on in the world" (p. 296):

> And now her power to think seemed converted into a power of
> sustained sensation. She could become a mere receptacle for
> heat, or become a color, like the bright lizards that darted
> about on hot stones outside her door; or she could become a
> continuous repetition of sound, like the cicadas. (p. 300)

In her renewed vitality and affinity with nature, Thea becomes part of the
primordial female order, undisturbed by male presence, an order which
Greek mythology associated with Demeter and Persephone.

In Panther Canyon, Thea realizes not only her physical involvement
with the earth but also her connection to the power of feminine creativity. In
examining the fragments of pottery she finds scattered about, Thea discovers
that she is bound "to a long chain of human endeavor" (p. 306), a chain that
brings the Indian women artisans closer to her. They, too, had been creators,
seeking "to make a sheath, a mould in which to imprison for a moment the
shining, elusive element which is life itself..." (p. 304). Their potsherds were
part of a female power of creation, apart from male control, that began with
primitive goddesses of nature. With this realization, Thea becomes even
more determined to challenge the patriarchal order. She has long been the
victim of this order, first held back by the expectations of her family and
hometown and then dominated by her tedious study with Mr. Bowers. No
longer bound by such limits, Thea finds personal strength in her ties to the
Indian earth mothers. The bath she takes every morning in the sunny pool at
the bottom of the canyon becomes a reenactment of an ancient rite and an
assertion of self: "Thea's bath came to have a ceremonial gravity. The
atmosphere of the canyon was ritualistic" (p. 304). Just as all the Cliff-

Dwellers' "customs and ceremonies and their religion went back to water," as Cather writes (p. 305), so Thea returns to the mythic life source. Her bath is not like Alexandra Bergson's, a purification from physical desires which would divert her from the creation of something lasting. Instead, Thea's bath is a rededication to creative powers, an immersion into the regenerative waters from which all life emerges.

Thea's bath, as a baptism of the spirit, is one more symbol of the mythic cycle of birth-death-rebirth through which Thea moves in the course of the novel. Cather was well aware of the importance of this cycle to classical mythology, for it arises in the establishment of the Olympian order; surfaces in numerous vegetation myths, like that of Persephone; and underlies the adventure of every epic hero. The Panther Canyon section of *The Song of the Lark* completes this mythic cycle by providing the setting for Thea's rebirth as an artist. In Part I, "Friends of Childhood," Thea is hampered by the environs of her first birth and is filled with indefinable longings. The "Song of the Lark" section takes her through a descent into worlds other than those of her origin, leaving her tired and frustrated. Even a visit home to the womb-like room where she had always awakened warm, secure, and eager for life no longer satisfies her yearnings:

> This would be her last summer in that room. Its services were over; its time was done. She rose and put her hand on the low ceiling. Two tears ran down her cheeks, as if they came from ice that melted slowly. She was not ready to leave her little shell. She was being pulled out too soon. (p. 238)

In Panther Canyon, though, Thea returns to the womb of all life, to nature itself, and is there reborn. Ellen Moers points out that the landscape of the canyon is clearly female, a setting ideal for the purpose of "solitary, feminine assertion"[6]:

> The canyon walls, for the first two hundred feet below the surface, were perpendicular cliffs, striped with ever-running strata of rock. From there on to the bottom the sides were less abrupt.... The effect was that of a gentler canyon within a wider one. The dead city lay at the point where the perpendicular outer wall ceased and the V-shaped inner gorge began. There a stratum of rock, softer than those above, had been hollowed out by the action of time until it was like a deep groove running along the sides of the canyon. (p. 297)

---

6. Ellen Moers, *Literary Woman* (Garden City, NY: Doubleday and Co., 1976), p. 259.

Here, "in this crack in the world," Thea identifies with the eternal feminine and its creative power, that "seed of sorrow, and of so much delight" (p. 305).

In taking up residence in her rock-house high on the cliff, Thea returns to a womb-like environment, reminiscent of her snug room in Moonstone. Both rooms have ceilings she can touch with her hand and both are periodically flooded with sunlight, the life-giving source. In this cave Thea is reborn as an artist, and the mythic parallel to the cave at Eleusis is striking. Through that cave Persephone both descended and returned to earth. Cather was surely aware of the Eleusinian rites which, in her time, were known almost exclusively through the Homeric "Hymn to Demeter." The Hymn was undoubtedly standard reading in her course in Greek lyric poetry. Thea is thus reborn, as was Persephone, and she drowses before her cliff-house, her mind and body full of contentment. In the flight of the eagle that she observes, Thea becomes a new and solitary individual, invigorated enough to fly above forces which would deny her achievement. She salutes the eagle in recognition of "Endeavor, achievement, desire, glorious striving of human art!" (p. 321).

These are the heroic qualities which Cather had found in the first generation of pioneers like Alexandra Bergson. But, again, Cather does not allow her heroine to assume these traits without a struggle against the sexual impulses that a closeness to the earth has awakened within her. Thea's joyous identification with and return to Mother Earth are tinged with a sorrow and confusion not unlike that Persephone exhibits when she stands silently before Demeter, torn between female and male lovers.[7] Fred Ottenburg poses such a problem for Thea. In her moments of lowest self-esteem, Thea had convinced herself that she wanted Fred for a sweetheart, but, after her experience in Panther Canyon, she struggles to maintain an equilibrium between her physical desires and her commitment to selfhood, the identity she achieves through art. Harsanyi had warned Thea that "Every artist makes himself born. It is very much harder than the other time and longer" (p. 175). Thea undergoes the pangs of this second birth in sorting out her feelings for

[7]   G. B. Stewart, "Mother, daughter, and the birth of the female artist," *Women's Studies*, 6, No. 2 (1979), 132.

Fred, and, only when she can freely give of herself without regard to masculine expectations, does Thea achieve a personal epiphany:

> When she kissed him she had not hidden her face on his shoulder, – she had risen a little on her toes, and stood straight and free....She became freer and stronger under impulses. When she rose to meet him like that, he felt her flash into everything that she had ever suggested to him, as if she filled out her own shadow. (p. 326)

As a consequence of her achieved individuation, Thea finds "Perfectly hideous!" Fred's offer of "a comfortable flat in Chicago, a summer camp up in the woods, musical evenings, and a family to bring up" (p. 317), an offer quite in keeping with a traditional male perspective. This is not to say, however, that Willa Cather rejected totally the role of the mother-woman. In fact, Elizabeth Sergeant recalled Cather once telling a friend of hers that she could conceive of nothing "more beautiful, if you had it in you, than to be the wife of a farmer and raise a big family in Nebraska."[8] But Thea, like Cather, has something more in her. To nurture the artist within, she must stand in defiance of the paternal society's expectations.

Thea's subsequent actions could be described in mythic terms. Although not openly hostile to sexual aggression by males, as Demeter and allied goddesses like Artemis and Hecate often are, Thea grows bitter after learning that Fred has deceived her. The nurturing and loving Thea then assumes Demeter's ancillary role as an awesome goddess demanding control over her daughter's and her own life. The offspring Thea protects is her own self, born anew in the Canyon, and this self emerges triumphant at the novel's close. The Thea whom Dr. Archie sees performing in New York is more than woman. She has an other-worldliness about her:

> ...[H]e seemed to be looking through an exalted calmness at a beautiful woman from far away, from another sort of life and feeling and understanding than his own, who had in her face something he had known long ago, much brightened and beautified. As a lad he used to believe that the faces of people who died were like that in the next world; the same faces, but shining with the light of a new understanding. (p. 412)

---

8.   Elizabeth Shepley Sergeant, *Willa Cather: A Memoir* (New York: J.B. Lippincott Co., 1953), p. 115.

Significantly, Cather titles this section of the novel simply "Kronborg" and gives Thea a singularity divorced from others' conceptions of her. No longer is she just the minister's talented daughter, Dr. Archie's spiritual ally, or even Tillie's dream heroine. She is an autonomous figure, regal in demeanor; she is a goddess armored against those forces which threaten her and her art.

Having come to a full understanding of her role as woman, Thea reassesses even the operatic parts she sings. She transforms Fricka from a nagging wife "into a mythical figure of strength." Grace Stewart further argues in her book *A New Mythos* that this performance indicates Thea's acceptance of the birth-death-rebirth cycle as a perpetual cycle for the woman artist:

> Understanding the sacrifices made by the Indian pottery makers, by her mother, and by herself as an artist helps her to transform the Wagnerian role of the hen-pecking bitch into a mythical figure of strength. Using matrifocal insights, she transmutes a patriarchal image of woman and gains nobility for herself, at least on stage. The sorrow and compassion she depicts there echo the sorrow and compassion dramatized in the myth of the lost Persephone.[9]

As she sings the role of Fricka, even Fred Ottenburg finds in Thea a nobility he had not previously observed: "She seemed to take on the look of immortal loveliness, the youth of the golden apples, the shining body and the shining mind" (p. 447). Thea becomes the personification of the eternal feminine, and the male characters of Cather's novel become worshipers at her shrine. Dr. Archie asks if he may still call her "Thea," and Johnny Tellamantez bows to her as she leaves the theater. Landry recognizes her ability as "a gift from the gods" (p. 448), and Harsanyi's eye follows Thea's figure about the stage "like a satellite," recognizing in her an achievement that is in no way common (p. 474). Like Sieglinde, Thea, the successful artist, is a goddess – "tall and shining like a Victory," filled with "hero-strength and hero-blood" (p. 475).

Thea emerges, therefore, as a mythic feminine force, having redirected her creative energies into art. In a total commitment to her muse, Thea loses a personal life, a fact which Dr. Archie brings to her attention:

---

9.   Grace Stewart, *A New Mythos: The Novel of the Artist as Heroine 1877-1977* (St. Albans, VT: Eden Press, 1979), pp. 68-69.

142

> "I'm afraid you don't have enough personal life, outside your
> work, Thea." The doctor looked at her anxiously.
> She smiled at him with her eyes half closed. "My dear doctor,
> I don't have any. Your work becomes your personal life. You
> are not much good until it does. It's like being woven into a big
> web. You can't pull away, because all your little tendrils are
> woven into the picture. It takes you up, and uses you, and spins
> you out; and that is your life. Not much else can happen to
> you." (pp. 455-456)

In using the image of the spider web, Cather may have consciously drawn
upon the myth of Arachne who, like Thea, dared to challenge the gods.
Although judged the superior artist, Arachne was subsequently punished and
changed into a monstrous creature. Thea realizes that she has become
insensitive to the needs of others, much as Alexandra Bergson failed to see
the emotional needs of Emil and Marie. When walking through the park with
Fred, Thea is both angry and troubled that he might consider her
unappreciative of the years of his attention and support. Whereas Thea
found art to be a substitute for a physical relationship, she failed to realize
that caring about her success was not a sufficient substitute for Fred. The
problem Cather poses here may be expressed in mythic terms as the struggle
between the two personalities of Demeter. As "Good" Mother, she creates
enduring beauty and exhibits loving concern; as "Terrible" Mother, she
withholds sustenance and displays indifference.[10] Thea's apparent ingratitude
and indifference are, however, merely masks for feelings which, although
necessarily suppressed, she has not forgotten. She aches to embrace the old
German couple who sit in front of her at Paderewski's recital and to ask
them how they have been able to keep their "intelligent enjoyment of the
music, and their friendliness with each other..." (p. 469).

In choosing to follow her muse, Thea is plagued by a sense of loss.
Even her marriage to Fred, which is mentioned only briefly in the Epilogue,
does little to dispel the tone of regret which colors the novel's conclusion.
Cather seems to arrange the marriage of these two friends much in the same
way that Alexandra and Carl come together in *O Pioneers!*. In both instances,
the strength of a matriarchal order is tinged with regret. Thea thus serves as
one further step in integrating the traits of a mythic goddess with those of an

---

10. Stewart, "Mother, daughter, and the birth of the female artist," p. 132.

Orpheus, a seeker of eternal beauty. Thea invokes only herself as Muse, becoming a goddess in her own right and challenging the Olympian order which would prevent her from doing "impossible things" (p. 243).

While Willa Cather's search for enduring order continued in her fiction, she found disruption in the order of her personal life. In the fall of 1915, Judge McClung died, and Cather knew that the house which had been her refuge for doing much of her writing was unlikely to remain so. A greater blow, however, was Isabelle McClung's announcement that within the year she would marry Jan Hambourg, a talented musician and long-time family friend. Elizabeth Sergeant writes that when Cather talked about Isabelle's impending marriage, she had a vacant expression and lacked her natural exuberance.[11] Cather must have viewed Isabelle's marriage as much more than the disruption of a fifteen-year-old friendship. Isabelle had served as an animating force for Cather's creative work, a voice of similar sympathies and interests, and Isabelle's entering into marriage became a kind of desertion for Cather. In the midst of this personal upheaval Cather apparently began to formulate the plans for her next novel in which memory would be a powerful force, perhaps carrying the author back to a simpler time of her childhood when her affections had been channeled into something more enduring than human relationships. In the spring of 1916 Cather tearfully and excitedly explained to Elizabeth Sergeant her intent to write about a childhood acquaintance whose name alone recalled a whole range of emotions. Work on this novel, *My Antonia*, seemed an antidote for Cather's personal problems, and after a very pleasant visit in Wyoming with her brother Roscoe and his family, she wrote that "Isabelle's marriage was still a hard blow to take and always would be, but the rest of the world was beginning to look as it used to."[12]

As *My Antonia* began to take shape, Cather apparently found some consolation in portraying a character whose strength and goodness placed

---

11.   Sergeant, p. 140. Sharon O'Brien also cites a letter to Dorothy Canfield in which Cather describes Isabelle's marriage as an overwhelming loss. O'Brien suggests that, along with Mrs Fields' death in the same year, Isabelle's marriage was a "direct blow" to Cather's creativity. [*Willa Cather: The Emerging Voice* (New York: Oxford Univ. Press, 1987), p. 239.]

12.   Woodress, p. 173.

her among those heroic figures that had haunted Cather since her first short stories. Antonia's memory evoked strong responses for Cather, and these responses led to an aura of myth in *My Antonia*. In her confrontation with human problems which "slid back into yesterday's seven thousand years," as Cather wrote in *Not Under Forty*,[13] Antonia assumes mythic dimensions and becomes the representative of a matriarchal order that protects civilization and ensures its survival.

Cather's debt to her classical studies is clear from the title page of *My Antonia*. A quote from Vergil's *Georgics* appears as an epigraph ("Optima dies ...prima fugit"), and echoes from Vergil are sprinkled throughout the novel. Subtle references to *The Aeneid* also exist, but the general tenor of *My Antonia* owes more to the mood of the *Georgics* than to the Roman epic. Cather does allude to the long drive to the Burden homestead as an epic journey over the pathless sea and relies upon an Homeric epithet to describe the prairie grass as "the colour of wine-stains."[14] Later scenes, like the idyllic picnic with the hired girls, show borrowings from Vergil's account of the Elysian Fields in *The Aeneid*, and even the image of the plow against the sun could remind the reader of Aeneas' vision of weapons glowing red in the sun's rays, arms that would serve to defeat the Latins (*Aeneid* Bk. VIII). As Cather was herself strongly influenced by the study of Vergil, so is Jim Burden. Against the backdrop of his reading *The Aeneid*, Jim matures and comes to recognize the sources of poetic inspiration. Antonia becomes much like Aeneas for him, bringing into a new world the values of an older culture.

Cather undoubtedly turns to the epic tradition for some details of *My Antonia*, but she differs markedly from that tradition in one important way. She replaces the story of the male adventurer, who founds a new civilization, with that of a female who embodies characteristics of Mother Earth. Paul Olson, in his discussion of the epic and Great Plains literature, suggests that the cultural losses of World War I so greatly affected Cather that in writing *My Antonia* she created an "epic displaced," showing that "the ancient epic,

---

13.   Willa Cather, *Not Under Forty* (New York: Alfred A. Knopf, 1936), p. v.

14.   Willa Cather, *My Antonia* (1918; rpt. Boston: Houghton Mifflin Co., 1954), p. 15. Subsequent references to this novel will be cited parenthetically in the text by page number only.

celebrating as it had the myth of military might, iron law, and male dominance, had run its course."[15] Although this theory has some merit, it does not take into account that prior even to the publication of *O Pioneers!* (1913), Cather had begun to explore the theme of woman's ascendancy as the stabilizing force for society. Whereas the classical epic depicted a hero of high social status waging war in an effort to found a new culture, in *My Antonia* Cather chose a woman of the lower classes whose triumph results from no great battle against human or divine forces. By reversing the emphasis of the traditional epic, Cather elevates women from their designated passive roles in a patriarchy to vital and creative forces that harken back to a pre-Olympian order.

Although Antonia does confront obstacles in her efforts to save her farm and to establish a home, a triumphant tone pervades the novel. Cather draws upon the mood of Vergil's *Georgics*, never denying the hard work that cultivating the land requires ("labor omnia vicit" – *Georgics* I.145), but celebrating that cultivation as a life which can, and must, withstand the onslaught of modernization and urbanization. Cather surely applauded Vergil's conclusion that values had become misplaced:

> For here are right and wrong inverted; so many wars overrun the world, so many are the shapes of sin; the plough meets not its honour due; our lands, robbed of the tillers, lie waste, and the crooked pruning-hooks are forged into stiff swords.[16]

By returning in *My Antonia* to rural and agrarian life as a defense against civilization's decay, Cather reflects both the beauty and artistry of the *Georgics* while emphasizing the fertility cults associated with Demeter, something Vergil does not do. Vergil does invoke Ceres, along with numerous other deities of earth, but the mystical powers of the fertility goddesses are not apparent in his poem which celebrates the joys of *rustica vita*. In her novel Cather does not rely upon the epic tradition of the hero's struggle for dominance over an enemy in a hostile environment. Antonia is

15.   Paul A. Olson, "The Epic and Great Plains Literature: Rolvaag, Cather, and Neihardt," *Prairie Schooner*, 55 (Spring/Summer 1981), 83-84.

16.   H. Rushton Fairclough, trans., "Georgics," by Vergil, in *Virgil: Eclogues, Georgics, Aeneid I-IV*, ed. T. E. Page, E. Capps and W. H. D. Rouse (New York: G. P. Putnam's Sons, 1929), p. 115.

not locked in a battle to tame the land. In keeping with the spirit of the *Georgics* and *O Pioneers!*, Antonia merges with the land, fashioning a garden out of the Nebraskan landscape. However, the sense of resignation and pensive sadness, which pervades the closing scenes of *O Pioneers!*, still exists in the final book of *My Antonia* as Jim Burden accepts the mature Antonia while regretting the loss of his childhood companion. Both Alexandra and Antonia endure hardship and emerge victorious, but Alexandra's battle is the exhaustive one of fighting the powerful enemy of masculine dominance in order to found a new Troy. Antonia triumphs as an Earth Mother who pays great Ceres her yearly rites, as Vergil commands in the *Georgics* (I.338-339), and, consequently, achieves heroic stature. Although Vergil's *Georgics* seem to have guided Cather in selecting the mood for *My Antonia*, she strayed from the ancient text when she began drawing moral meanings from it. In using Antonia as the safeguard of the old culture and the founding mother of a new civilization, Cather assigns her powers worthy of a Vergilian epic hero, but, of greater importance, she finds in Antonia a celebration of the eternal feminine.

Jim Burden claims that the story of Antonia is "pretty much all her name recalls to me" (Introd.), and in filtering that image through her narrator's memory, Cather has the ideal situation for imposing sympathetic, romantic, and even philosophic interpretations on actual events. It has been long accepted among Cather scholars that many of Jim Burden's experiences were Cather's own; nevertheless, the male narrator Cather employs provides a quite believable voice for her novel. Jim Burden, like Alexandra Bergson and perhaps like Cather herself, has suffered in his personal relationships. His wife is beautiful but remote, preferring to live her own life apart from a husband whose "quiet tastes irritate her" (Introd.). He fills the emotional void in his life with fond memories of Antonia, and, as David Stouck points out, although Jim's affection for Antonia is strong, he always enjoys her company more when other men are absent.[17] Such is the case even in his childhood when he and Antonia make trips to prairie-dog-town or lie on the chicken-

---

17. David Stouck, *Willa Cather's Imagination* (Lincoln: Univ. of Nebraska Press, 1975), p. 51.

house roof watching the storm brew. As a youth, Jim is happy resting with Antonia in the leafy nook along the riverbank. As an adult, Jim finds happiness visiting in Antonia's home, and significantly, her husband is away at the time of his arrival. But, Jim's love for Antonia is more than a jealous affection, and his role is not to become her lover. Jim is the singer of praises for a mythic *magna mater*. He is the instrument by which Cather works out her commitment to the female principle as the source of both society's stability and the artist's inspiration.

Jim wrestles with a wide range of emotions before he comes to accept Antonia as a goddess-woman. From his first meeting with Antonia, Jim is aware of her strength of character as she insists on his taking her ring, a token of her thanks but also the first symbol by which Jim is joined to Antonia in spirit (pp. 26-27). Antonia embodies all those traits which signal a challenge to Jim's control. She is four years older than he, vitally alive, eager to learn, and intelligent. Jim resents the superior tone she sometimes uses with him and considers her opinionated. The very traits which make Antonia interesting are those that make Jim fearful of her dominance. When Jim confronts and kills the rattlesnake at prairie-dog-town, he is more than the knight slaying his first dragon. Cather places the incident on a mythic level:

> As I turned him over, I began to feel proud of him, to have a kind of respect for his age and size. He seemed like the ancient, eldest Evil. Certainly his kind have left horrible unconscious memories in all warm-blooded life. (p. 47)

Jim becomes the slayer of the serpent, protecting his Edenic garden from the evil within. But, in keeping with the images from classical myth which abound in Cather's work, the event takes on an added dimension. The incident recalls Apollo's slaying of the Python, a monster whose lair was at Delphi, the "womb" of all Greece, and a monster who was sacred to Mother Earth (Gaea). The Homeric Hymn to Pythian Apollo emphasizes that Apollo's destruction of Python was in direct defiance of the earth goddesses who, up to that time, had ruled the world. Apollo instigates the transference of power from the matriarchy to patriarchy, from darkness to light. Jim kills his rattlesnake in the bright glare of an afternoon sun, adding to his self-respect and earning the admiration of Antonia. In his triumph over the snake, Jim re-

148

enacts Apollo's victory over the matriarchy, although Jim's triumph is destined to be only a temporary one. Jim observes that Antonia "liked me better from that time on, and she never took a supercilious air with me again" (p. 50). Even as a child, then, Jim places Antonia within the context of his own mythology, assigning to her a conventional role, which her actions will later deny.

After Mr. Shimerda's death, however, when Antonia must work in the fields, Jim "falls out of love" with her. She assumes a power and pride which are disagreeable to him, primarily because these traits make her "like a man" (p. 125) and are threats to his manhood. Blanche Gelfant, in her study of sex in *My Antonia*, concludes that Antonia becomes "an ultimately strange bisexual,"[18] a role which is not surprising if the dual nature of the mythic earth goddesses is considered. They possessed both a masculine awesomeness and a feminine nurturance, a blending of command and compassion. So Antonia appears, determined to "help make this land one good farm" and yet crying over the nice things she will miss at school (p. 123).

Jim's admiration for Antonia grows when she moves to town as a hired girl, but his attempt to develop a more intimate relationship with her is met with an indignant rebuff. Antonia cannot be a sexual creature for Jim, and, once again, Jim's projected image of her is shattered. He would have her conform to his expectations, including a passive receptivity to his attentions. Instead, she reprimands Jim for getting mixed up with the Swedish hired girls and threatens to scratch out Lena Lingard's eyes if "she's up to any of her nonsense" with him (p. 224). Antonia continues to exhibit the protectiveness of an older sister as well as the power of the matriarchy in her relations with Jim. Even Jim's thwarting Wick Cutter's attempt to rape Antonia becomes a service to a sacred image, a duty to keep inviolate the matriarchal order of things. Jim believes his grandmother and Antonia are to blame for exposing him to "all this disgustingness" (p. 250). His masculinity is not threatened so much by Wick Cutter's attack as by the feeling that he has stooped so low to serve. "I hated her almost as much as I hated Cutter," Jim remarks (p. 250),

18. Blanche H. Gelfant, "The Forgotten Reaping-Hook: Sex in *My Antonia*," *American Literature*, 43 (March 1971), 73.

but what he really hates is that Wick Cutter could have succeeded in possessing Antonia, a thing which Jim is unequivocably denied.

Jim must remain a worshiper at Antonia's shrine, a shrine to her innocence and virginity, which he alone has erected. He cannot, therefore, accept Antonia when she becomes Larry Donovan's lover. From Jim's point of view, Antonia's sexuality shatters her image as goddess and destroys the security of his childhood world, a world shaped by maternal presences. Only after he and Antonia are separated for several years does Jim forgive her for being less than he had envisioned, for being a woman. Yet, Jim then approaches Antonia with a new kind of respect as she steps from his old, conventional myth into a new mythic dimension. In her experience as a mother, Antonia assumes a deeper dignity and strength. She does not run to Jim as she might have in her youth. Instead, she stands like Demeter in the fields, awaiting patiently and lovingly the arrival of a devotee: "She stood still by her shocks, leaning on her pitchfork, watching me as I came. We met like the people in the old song, in silence, if not in tears" (p. 319). Antonia assures Jim that her happiness lies in providing well for her daughter and in living "where I know every stack and tree, and where all the ground is friendly" (p. 320). While sitting near Mr. Shimerda's grave, Jim finds himself pouring out the details of his life and his aspirations. With calm benignity Antonia assumes the role of confessor and Jim accepts not her, but the idea of her, as inseparable from himself:

> "Do you know, Antonia, since I've been away, I think of you more often than of anyone else in this part of the world. I'd have liked to have you for a sweetheart, or a wife, or my mother or my sister – anything a woman can be to a man. The idea of you is a part of my mind; you influence my likes and dislikes, all my tastes, hundreds of times when I don't realize it. You really are a part of me." (p. 321)

Antonia becomes a representative of the primordial female presence, which is a part of Jim's and every man's memory.

Cather describes Jim's mature acceptance of the goddess-woman's role in the order of things as a peaceful confrontation between two mythic powers:

> As we walked homeward across the fields, the sun dropped and lay like a great golden globe in the low west. While it hung there, the moon rose in the east, as big as a cart-wheel, pale silver and streaked with rose colour, thin as a bubble or a ghost-moon. For five, perhaps ten minutes, the two luminaries confronted each other across the level land, resting on opposite edges of the world. (pp. 321-322)

In classical myth, the sun is the masculine force (Apollo), and its appearance coincides with the establishment of the Olympian patriarchy. The moon, on the other hand, is the feminine power of the pre-Olympian matriarchy. Whether associated with Selene, Cynthia, or Artemis, the moon's presence harkens back to the mother of the universe. Cather brings both powers into Jim's view, confronting him with the ageless struggle for supremacy. As the sun sets, Jim feels "the old pull of the earth, the solemn magic that comes out of those fields by nightfall" (p. 332). In his wish to be a little boy again, Jim acknowledges the maternal powers which order all life. Antonia's hands are again "strong and warm and good" (p. 322), the nurturing hands of a kindly earth goddess. Through the imagination of Jim Burden, Cather successfully transforms a poor Bohemian girl into a mythic Earth Mother.

Elizabeth Sergeant believed that Cather intended for Antonia to be an integral part of the land and a maternal presence to which a youth like Jim Burden could only respond with love:

> Her role was so primeval, and so much woman's whether she plowed for her brother or cooked for Mrs. Harling in Black Hawk, that a detached lonely boy could think of her in the confused terms of a youthful projection of love and nature blended.[19]

Like Alexandra Bergson, Antonia possesses many attributes of an earth goddess but displays a warmth of personality that invites love rather than an "Amazonian fierceness" that commands respect. As a child Antonia shows a close affinity to the land as well as an animal vitality:

> The little girl was pretty, but An-tonia ...was still prettier. I remembered what the conductor had said about her eyes. They were big and warm and full of light, like the sun shining on brown pools in the wood. Her skin was brown, too, and in her cheeks she had a glow of rich, dark color. Her brown hair was curly and wild-looking. (p. 23)

---

19. Sergeant, p. 151.

The brown earthiness of the young Antonia anticipates the earth goddess image she projects in the last section of the book and represents the fecundity of the land itself. Even the little hole in which Antonia sleeps is "scooped out in the black earth" (p. 75) and anticipates the womb-like fruit cave in the closing pages of the novel.

Antonia also demonstrates an unrestrained love of life. As a girl, she shows an eagerness for learning the English names for things around her; as a young woman, she shows the same vitality when singing in the garden or hurrying off in an irresponsible manner to dance at the Vannis' tent. Her "wild-looking" hair reminds the reader of the female worshipers of Dionysus whose disheveled hair was an indication of their ecstatic celebration of life. Antonia's appearance is not that of the reserved Alexandra Bergson, whose blonde braids coil about her head like a helmet. Yet, both women embody a life-force of mythic proportions, the strength of the early earth goddesses. At fifteen Antonia works in the fields, her arms and throat "burned as brown as a sailor's," and her neck comes up strongly from her shoulders "like the bole of a tree out of the turf" (p. 122). Antonia, like the archetypal Great Mother, thus reflects the earth's fertility.

But to assume that Cather's classical background alone provided the basis for Antonia's portrait would be to deny the powerful, personal nature of this characterization for Willa Cather. Antonia was, after all, the fictional incarnation of the real Annie Sadilek, who in the "keenness and sensitiveness of her enjoyment, in her love of people and in her willingness to take pains," fascinated and inspired Cather.[20] Cather's view of Antonia is quite distinct from that which her narrator presents. It is not Cather, but Jim, who expects Antonia to behave in a more seemly manner when she moves into Black Hawk. Not Cather, but Jim, wants to keep Antonia removed from earthly stain and impervious to human weakness. Cather, on the other hand, celebrates the strength and vitality of this immigrant girl, elevating her above Jim Burden's stylized myths, which would not allow woman to sin and be redeemed or to be man-like and still be woman. Cather makes Antonia an

---

20.   Eleanor Hinman, "Willa Cather," *Lincoln Sunday Star*, 6 Nov. 1921, in *Willa Cather in Person: Interviews, Speeches and Letters*, ed. L. Brent Bohlke (Lincoln: Univ. of Nebraska Press, 1986), p. 44.

archetypal mother, but of a new race and time. She embodies the spirit of America's frontier expansion, integrating elements of both the classical, Old World matriarchy and the emergent, New World order.

This blending of two world views is most apparent in the memorable portrait of Antonia in the final book, "Cuzak's Boys." In her relationship with Larry Donovan, a kind of marriage of death and a death of innocence, Antonia had to leave the land she so loved to reside in a city, a locale in which she says she would never be happy: "I'd always be miserable in a city. I'd die of lonesomeness" (p. 320). Antonia, like her actual model Annie Sadilek, does not die of her loneliness but returns in the spring to the prairies. The reunion of Antonia is not with her familial mother alone but is with her symbolic mother, as well, with the earth itself. Antonia returns to the land, to plowing and harvesting; she becomes earth mother of the American mythos, not awaiting her devotees but actively contributing to the land's productivity. Even in bearing her child she fulfills the role of a New World Demeter, who sanctions the fertility of both the land and of woman:

> "That very night it happened. She got her cattle home, turned them into the corral, and went into the house, into her room behind the kitchen. There, without calling to anybody, without a groan, she lay down and bore her child." (p. 316)

Antonia's maternal instinct surfaces in her careful tending of both the land and her children. With the maternal affection of Demeter, Antonia vows to protect her daughter from masculine forces: "I'm going to see my little girl has a better chance than ever I had. I'm going to take care of that girl, Jim" (pp. 320-321). And, when her illegitimate daughter grows up and marries, Antonia reluctantly gives her up. "[A]t first I cried like I was putting her into her coffin," Antonia remarks (p. 355). Such grief is not just the grief of a Demeter relinquishing her daughter to marriage with the ruler of Hades, but is also the very real sadness of Annie Sadilek Pavelka as her oldest daughter married and left home.

In the final books of *My Antonia*, Antonia emerges as a "Venus genetrix...reincarnate," as George Whicher describes her.[21] She and her

---

21.   George F. Whicher, "In the American Grain," in *The Literature of the American People*, ed. Arthur H. Quinn (New York: Appleton-Century-Crofts, 1951), p. 908.

children display an animal vitality that ensures continuance of life. Antonia proudly exhibits her children "like a mother cat bringing in her kittens" (p. 332), and in her possessiveness of them, her antipathy toward death increases. Antonia becomes the great and good mother, further assuming the role of Demeter. From the fruit cellar, the cave which houses the products of the land's fertility, her children burst forth in "a veritable explosion of life" (p. 339). Antonia is, though, as much the goddess of the arts of cultivation as she is a Venus genetrix. She remarks, "I belong on a farm" (p. 343), and she has an almost paradisal garden to prove it. Her farm does not have the orderliness of Alexandra Bergson's but is lush with natural vegetation. The house is nearly buried in a forest of hollyhocks, and thorny locust hedges enclose the yard. A deep peacefulness envelops the orchard which is "full of sun, like a cup" and rich with the smell of ripe fruit (p. 341). Jim observes, "She had only to stand in the orchard, to put her hand on a little crab tree and look up at the apples, to make you feel the goodness of planting and tending and harvesting at last" (p. 353).

As Jim Burden reformulates "his myth" of Antonia, it comes to coincide with the author's. In the reality of her life, Annie Pavelka assumed an almost mythic dimension for Cather, who always recalled with delight her visits to the Pavelka farm where happy-faced children crowded around the kitchen table and she could look out on a productive garden and orchard.[22] The struggle which Annie had undergone in adjusting to a new country was worthy of epic celebration, in Cather's mind, but in fictionalizing that struggle, embellishment was hardly necessary, for Annie's life generated its own myth.

In creating her image of the archetypal mother in *My Antonia*, however, Cather makes little reference to the male presence. Cuzak is absent when Jim arrives at Antonia's farm, and she alone seems to be the creative force. Her marriage to Cuzak is an easy friendship, much like Alexandra Bergson's and Carl Linstrum's, and Cuzak's role as husband and procreator is subordinate to Antonia's. After returning from the fair at Wilber, Cuzak

---

22. Mildred R. Bennett, *The World of Willa Cather* (Lincoln: Univ. of Nebraska Press, 1961), pp. 50-52.

seems amused and surprised "that all these children should belong to him" (p. 359), and he accepts Antonia's ready affection much as if he were one of her children. To Cuzak, Antonia is a woman with a warm heart who makes life as good for him as she can. Antonia remains "a rich mine of life, like the founders of early races" (p. 353); she is the mythic matriarch – a Gaea or Rhea or Demeter–under whose control the earth continues to teem with life. Even Antonia's children take for granted that she is universally loved, and they think it surprising that Jim should make a point of saying, "She was a beautiful girl" (p. 345). Although pleased by Jim's admission that he was very much in love with their mother, Ambrosche and Anton are also embarrassed. To think of their mother as a sexual being apparently has never occurred to them.

Antonia's similarity to Demeter is enhanced by those details of the novel which point toward the seasonal myths of the ancient world. The novel begins and ends in the autumn, the season of memory and of the death necessary for rebirth. Antonia becomes symbolic of the cyclic nature of life, just as Demeter represented the cyclic pattern of life for the Greeks. Antonia was "a battered woman" when Jim visited her after a twenty-year absence, but she had retained and passed on to the next generation "the fire of life" and "inner glow" (p. 336) that assure renewal of life. Leo, the child Antonia says she loves best, is the epitome of this life-force. In appearance he is a carefree, rural deity of the classical world:

> He was a handsome one, this chap, fair-skinned and freckled, with red cheeks and a ruddy pelt as thick as a lamb's wool, growing down on his neck in little tufts....As he glanced at me, his face dimpled with a seizure of irrelevant merriment, and he shot up the windmill tower with a lightness that struck me as disdainful. (p. 330)

Like Arcadian Pan, Leo is filled with energy and displays "jealous, animal little love" toward Antonia (p. 352). Jim Burden notes that Leo, like his mother, gets hurt more than his siblings because he possesses "a keener power of enjoyment than other people" (p. 354). Leo is certainly faun-like and will pass on to the next generation his simple enjoyment of life.

In the number of her children–twelve–Antonia also represents the cycle of the seasons as celebrated in the worship of Demeter. By emphasizing that Leo has an Easter birthday, Cather joins seasonal imagery to the Christian myth of death and resurrection. Just as Cather had utilized the birth-death-rebirth cycle in writing *The Song of the Lark*, she alludes to this cycle by placing Antonia among mythic matriarchs who ensure survival of the race.

But, to view all the details of the final book of *My Antonia* as the re-creation of the Eleusinian fertility ritual is to overestimate both Cather's knowledge of the subject and the importance of this myth to the novel. Evelyn Helmick proposes just such a parallel in her article, "The Mysteries of Antonia." Helmick's claim that Cather "undoubtedly was familiar with the history of the Eleusinian mysteries"[23] from her reading of Greek lyric poetry is valid, but it is unlikely that from such reading Cather could have pieced together the details of a highly secretive ritual which even today is not fully understood. Cather surely had in mind the Great Mother cult of ancient Greece in describing Antonia in "Cuzak's Boys," for Jim does change spiritually as an ancient proselyte must have when initiated into the Mysteries of Eleusis. But, to equate Jim's first visit to Antonia with the Athenian celebration of the Lesser Mysteries and to parallel even the death of Jan's dog to the animal sacrifice of the Greater Mysteries is to assume Cather was more concerned with recounting the steps of an ancient rite than with portraying Jim's awakening to Antonia as a goddess-woman. Jan's whispered and sad tale of his dog's death is more than the *dromena* (dramatic reenactment) of the Eleusinian ritual. It reveals a child's need for empathy from a maternal figure who so well understands grief and loss. Nor is the children's tracing the outlines of fruit in their glass jars solely the *diekymena* (display of sacred objects) of the Greater Mysteries.[24] It is more simply the children's way of shyly communicating with a stranger, whose relationship to their mother calls for making him aware of her goodness. Although Helmick's in-depth comparison of the final chapter to the rites at Eleusis is

---

23.   Evelyn Helmick, "The Mysteries of Antonia," *The Midwest Quarterly*, 17 (Winter 1976), 185.

24.   Helmick, pp. 182-183. Helmick cites by the Greek designation each major step of the initiation process as it is now known and draws parallels with the events of Jim's visit to Antonia.

intriguing, Cather could not have drawn such parallels based solely on the reading of ancient texts. Many of the steps in the ritual that Helmick describes could only have been known after the 1930s, the period of extensive excavations at the site of Eleusis.

Nevertheless, Cather is deeply concerned with the return to a simpler time and to the enduring values of the primeval matriarchy. Jim experiences a return to origins when he comes upon the road he and Antonia had traveled together on their first night in Nebraska. After a disappointing day in Black Hawk, he has a "sense of coming home" and "of having found what a little circle man's experience is" (pp. 371-372). Jim does more than return physically to his beginnings; he returns philosophically to the values which pioneer mothers like Antonia embody–vitality, integrity, courage, and endurance. What Jim rediscovers is "the precious, incommunicable past" (p. 371), an affirmation of and identification with the eternal feminine.

In *My Antonia*, Cather also examines a mythic image of women other than that of nurturing Earth Mother. Lena Lingard celebrates erotic love rather than motherhood. Cather's descriptions of Lena place her among the more seductive figures from classical myth– Aphrodite, Eos, and Circe. Lena is no less a goddess-woman than is Antonia, but she is determined to get along independently from men. Yet, her appeal, as Jim Burden presents it, is purely to the senses, to immediate gratification.

Cather once again employs a form of the Greek name Helena in naming one of the most sensuous of the women in all her works. Lena is bathed in images of light, as her name implies, and stands in direct contrast to the brown earthiness of Antonia:

> Before I knew Lena I thought of her as something wild, that always lived on the prairie, because I had never seen her under a roof. Her yellow hair was burned to a ruddy thatch on her head; but her legs and arms, curiously enough, in spite of constant exposure to the sun, kept a miraculous whiteness which somehow made her seem more undressed than other girls who went scantily clad. (p. 165)

Not only is Lena another beauty like Helen of Troy, but, throughout the novel, she is also identified readily with her alter ego, Aphrodite. Her "deep violet eyes," "soft voice and easy, gentle ways" (p. 165) attract not only Jim but even married men like Ole Benson, who lost his head over Lena when she was still a child. Such were the effects of Aphrodite, "the Side-Glancer, who looks at us – and we are lost...."[25] Lena's mannerisms, too, recall Hesiod's description of Aphrodite in the *Theogony*: "...this is the portion allotted to her amongst men and undying gods, – the whisperings of maidens and smiles and deceits with sweet delight and graciousness."[26]

In other ways, too, Lena is clearly an incarnation of the mythic goddess of love. She is Homer's laughter-loving Aphrodite with "her mellow, easy laugh that was either very artless or very comprehending, one never quite knew which" (p. 266). Jim remarks that dancing with Lena "was like coming in with the tide" (p. 222), and the image of Aphrodite rising from the sea-foam on the Cytherean coast immediately comes to mind. Lena is also a dressmaker, an occupation suited to Aphrodite, who loved fine raiment and beautiful things. Among such things were the flowers, and, like Aphrodite Antheia (Aphrodite of the Flowers), Lena is often seen "carrying home a bunch of jonquils or a hyacinth plant" (p. 280). Just as Aphrodite represented the reproductive energy of the universe and showed a fondness for children, Lena likes children, but, along with her mythic counterpart, she rejects the responsibilities of marriage:

> "Well, it's mainly because I don't want a husband. Men are all right for friends, but as soon as you marry them they turn into cranky old fathers, even the wild ones. They begin to tell you what's sensible and what's foolish, and want you to stick at home all the time. I prefer to be foolish when I feel like it, and be accountable to nobody." (p. 291)

Lena, like the Aphrodite of Persuasion whom Sappho sometimes addresses, plies her wiles to ensure a life of freedom and fun. At the river picnic she mocks the sexually uninitiated Jim by slowly drawing her fingers through his hair on the pretense of removing the sand, and in her first visit to his room in

25. Geoffrey Grigson, *The Goddess of Love: The birth, triumph, death and return of Aphrodite* (London: Constable and Co., 1976), p. 95.

26. Hugh G. Evelyn-White, trans., "Theogony," by Hesiod, in *Hesiod: The Homeric Hymns and Homerica*, ed. T. E. Page and others (Cambridge: Harvard Univ. Press, 1936), p. 95.

Lincoln she turns a soft cheek to him and "whispers teasingly" in his ear (p. 270).

Lena also assumes the role of a goddess of the dawn, and Cather frequently describes her in auroral settings. Jim comments, "Lena was never so pretty as in the morning; she wakened fresh with the world every day..." (p.281). Even in his dream she is "flushed like the dawn, with a kind of luminous rosiness all about her" (p. 225). This relation to the dawn may, however, be a simple extension of Lena's Aphrodisian role, for, as a creatrix, Aphrodite, too, was associated with the sunlight. The goddess of love was as alluring by day as she was by night, as is evident in her seduction of Anchises. Yet, even in Anchises' case, Aphrodite's sexuality proved hostile, and he was ultimately blinded for boasting of his affair with the goddess.

Cather suggests that in Lena's sexuality a danger also awaits, but that danger is magnified by Jim Burden's imagination and his need to define Lena by his parameters, much as he attempted to do with Antonia. At the picnic for the hired girls, Lena intrudes on the shady bower in which Jim relaxes under the protective care of Demetrian Antonia. Bees hover above the blossoms of this bower but do not descend under the leaves where Jim and Antonia rest. (One is reminded that Demeter was often depicted in Greek mythology as the mother bee and these creatures were sacred to her.) But, the peaceful atmosphere changes when Lena arrives. Jim springs to his feet and runs up the bank, attracted by the sexual abandon which he believes Lena represents. Antonia recognizes the threat Lena poses to Jim's innocence, she roughly tousles Jim's hair, and she comments critically to Lena that her high-heeled slippers are inappropriate and too small (p. 240). For Jim, the danger Lena represents is the same the ancients recognized in Aphrodite Androphonos, Slayer of Men, and in their early identification of Aphrodite with Clotho, the spinner of destiny.

In Jim's recurring dream of Lena this affiliation of love with death becomes clear, much as it did in Alexandra Bergson's dream:

> One dream I dreamed a great many times, and it was always the same. I was in a harvest-field full of shocks, and I was lying against one of them. Lena Lingard came across the stubble barefoot, in a short skirt, with a curved reaping-hook in her hand, and she was flushed like the dawn, with a kind of luminous rosiness all about her. She sat down beside me, turned to me with a soft sigh and said, 'Now they are all gone, and I can kiss you as much as I like.' (pp. 225-226)

In this dream Lena approaches like the earth spirit Gaea, offering the sickle to Cronus, but the sickle is both a symbol of procreation and death. In reaching sexual maturity, Jim unconsciously acknowledges a death of self.

He believes that his dream becomes actuality when Lena comes to his room in Lincoln. She arrives while Jim is reading Vergil's *Georgics* and is caught up in the memories of his rural youth. Unlike in his dream, Lena is dressed in a close-fitting black suit and a blouse "of some soft, flimsy silk" (p. 266). Their meeting is somewhat furtive, and Lena seems to emerge from the dark hall as a temptress rather than as goddess of the dawn. Like Circe or Calypso, the classical enchantresses who succeeded in diverting Ulysses' mind from his return to Ithaca and to Penelope, Lena causes Jim to abandon his reveries of Antonia. Memory gives sway to desire, and Jim forgets the happiness he finds in memories of his youth. Lena tempts Jim into a dream of romance, but the dream, as his teacher Gaston Cleric recognizes, can only result in spent passion, not happiness. Cleric, whose name connotes celibacy, encourages Jim to redirect his passion into art, not to lose himself and his memories in fleeting physical pleasure. Throughout this section of the novel, Antonia is conspicuously absent; her name is only mentioned occasionally in conversations between Jim and Lena. Lena's presence, not the memory of Antonia, becomes reality for Jim and disturbs his serious study.

Yet, not so much Lena but Jim's inability to withdraw from her diverts him from his work. Like one obsessed by the very thing he fears, Jim accompanies Lena to the theater and breakfasts in her rooms. The Lena, whom the reader sees through Jim's eyes, is the classical temptress, but Cather evidently thought otherwise. Lena is one of Cather's independent women who carve out a place for themselves, a place where they will not always be "'under somebody's thumb'" (p. 292). Lena does not set out to trap Jim, like Aphrodite Androphonos, but sends him away with a "soft, slow, renunciatory kiss" (p. 293). She is no more intentionally a temptress to Jim than she had been to Ole Benson or Mr. Ordinsky, the Polish violin teacher. Lena's "Kindness of heart," as Mr. Ordinsky calls it (p. 286), is not subtle entrapment, and, although Jim insists that he understands and appreciates that fact, he still sees sexual allure beneath her quite stylish but modest velvet suit. The myth of temptation, which Jim spins for himself and relates to the reader, is challenged by Cather's admiration for Lena's success and determination. When Lena states, "I don't want a husband" and "I prefer to be...accountable to nobody" (p. 291), only Jim does not believe her. He cannot accept that his "temptress" intends to trap no one:

> Lena shifted her pillows and looked up at me in surprise. "Why, I'm not going to marry anybody. Didn't you know that?" "Nonsense, Lena. That's what girls say, but you know better. Every handsome girl like you marries, of course." (p. 290)

There is no room in Lena's plan for "of course," and what Jim actually resents is not that he has been tempted but that Lena has withstood the temptation of his own sexuality. When Lena gently mocks him with "Are you afraid I'll want you to marry me some day?", Jim confirms his plans to go away. Undeniably, Cather attributes to Lena the sun-lit beauty and persuasive ways of an Eos or Aphrodite, but Jim's myth of Lena is a conventional, masculine one, imposing upon her the danger of the classical temptress. Willa Cather has, however, counterpointed this classical image with a new myth of the beautiful woman who can live independently, releasing men rather than entrapping them. The real danger Lena represents for Jim is the same Fred Ottenburg posed for Thea Kronborg – sublimation of memory to desire.

For Willa Cather, only the alliance of memory and desire generates the force from which both art and civilization evolve. Ultimately, this is Cather's concern in *My Antonia*. Although Jim believes he discovers the true Muse of poetry in the sensuousness of girls like Lena, he, like Vergil, comes to realize that true poetical inspiration comes from the more enduring relationship between humankind and the land itself. Jim and Lena share a friendship but not the commonality of purpose which is necessary for achieving greatness either personally or collectively. As an Aphrodite figure, Lena offers a life defined by its immediacy. Antonia, on the other hand, offers the timeless values of the primeval matriarchs – home, family, productivity, and, finally, art. Jim becomes the first to bring the Muse into his country only when he comes to understand that Antonia and memories of her offer real human situations through which an artist can achieve transcendence. Just as the plow hieroglyphed against the sun is simultaneously very real and a symbol unbound by time or space, so does the real Antonia assume a universality: "She lent herself to immemorial human attitudes which we recognize by instinct as universal and true" (p. 353).

In leading Jim and the reader to this conclusion, Cather consciously employs allusions to classical myth, equating the pioneering experience with those early legends that defined the origins of civilization. The dominant figure is, of course, Antonia, who becomes both archetypal Earth Mother and Muse. In her triumph she becomes what James Woodress calls "the most heroic figure of them all, both the Madonna of the Wheat Fields and the embodiment of the American westering myth."[27] Antonia, like Alexandra Bergson and Thea Kronborg, is a seeker of permanent values, but, unlike them, she finds these values without loss of self. She maintains a matriarchal society where harmony and productivity abound. Through Antonia, then, Cather restructures her own world, establishing on the Nebraskan frontier the mythic golden age in which Mother Earth gave freely of her fruits and human beings were richly rewarded.

---

27. Woodress, pp. 179-180.

CHAPTER VII
THE DECAY OF THE HIPPOLYTEAN IDEAL

The publication of *My Antonia* in 1918 brought to a close the first great period of Willa Cather's work. In Antonia, Thea, and Alexandra, she had depicted women of great moral strength who confronted a world hostile to their aims and yet triumphed. These epic heroes and earth goddesses define a matriarchal stage of human progress, the civilizing of the western frontier. But, the matriarchal world to which Cather attributed the founding of civilization had passed out of existence by the beginning of World War I. In its stead had come an increasingly complex, mechanistic, and masculine-dominated society. The power of the dynamo, in the persons of men like Bartley Alexander, had created a new danger. Unleashed upon the world in a drive for commercial success, these men were, for Cather, the destroyers of time-honored values and the arts. In this falling away from perfection, the position of women was most precarious. Even if they were physically strong and psychologically stable, as were the heroines of Cather's early novels, the women of the post-war era would have to surmount new obstacles in a society no longer based on agrarian ideals. In her works of the next eight years, Cather depicts this struggle in terms of classical myth as the struggle of goddesses to maintain independence before the Olympian patriarchy. Whereas her frontier "goddesses" had ordered life by channeling their energies into the land, family, or art–things that posed no threat to maintaining identity–, the men who had "made the world safe for democracy" now ordered life. What Cather observes is that women must redirect their passions or be doomed to submission.

Although Cather's own life during this period had reached a plateau of stability – residence with Edith Lewis at 5 Bank Street, periodic visits to the West, and yearly excursions to Jaffrey – the effects of World War I weighed heavily upon her. Even before she heard of the death of a cousin, G. P. Cather, at the Battle of Cantigny in May of 1918, Cather had recognized the losses to her world that the War had brought. Youth with its "fierce necessity" and "sharp desire" had fallen victim. France, Cather's symbol of civilization and the beauty of the arts, lay devastated. In Cather's mind the fault for such ruin lay in human weakness, in greed and misdirected passion. Perhaps she envisioned her epic of the West ending with the same corruption that plagued the late Roman Empire. On an individual rather than universal scale, though, it was the personal desertion of the classical ideals which led to societal chaos. The desertion Cather had felt in Isabelle McClung's marriage was only heightened by the events going on around her in the years following World War I. Cather's works of this period depict characters governed by sensuality or succumbing to the powers of Aphrodite in the age-long struggle between passion and aesthetic ideals, as represented by Demeter and her virginal allies Athena and Artemis. Allusions to this mythic struggle between the Greek goddesses become central to the works of Cather's second major creative period.

While she was working on *My Antonia,* Cather continued to write some short fiction simply as a means of keeping a steady flow of income. Few stories of the period 1915-1920 are remarkable in either structure or content, but they do reveal Cather's continuing interest in both the world of art and the demanding world of business. Four of the tales concern the business world of New York and the hectic life from which Cather had gladly escaped when leaving *McClure's Magazine* in 1912. In each case Cather depicts a world whose values are far different from and less admirable than those of her Nebraska novels; modern society has lost concern, compassion, and commitment to ideals. In "Consequences" (1915), Cather portrays a young man of pleasure who is haunted by an alter ego and unexpectedly commits suicide. And, Percy Bixby, the conscientious bookkeeper of "The

Bookkeeper's Wife" (1916), resorts to embezzlement when he realizes that it is "very difficult for a woman with hair like his wife's to be shabby and to go without things."[1] In "Ardessa" (1918), Cather shows yet another effect of the workplace – complacency and misuse of power. Ardessa's overbearing nature and pride are no defense against the efficiency and modesty of a younger staff member.

The most vivid picture of humanitarianism gone awry, however, occurs in the 1919 story "Her Boss." Mr. Wanning, a highly successful lawyer, confronts alone the news of his impending death. His wife and daughters are too caught up in their rounds of social engagements even to consider that he might he seriously ill. His bohemian son and friends at the club are too immersed in their own careers or ailments to consider his predicament serious. Cather describes this callous lack of interest in terms of ancient luxuriousness. Mrs. Julia Wanning sits in a violet dressing gown like a Roman empress, touching up her coiffure, much as did her ancient counterpart Julia, whom Ovid immortalized in the *Ars Amatoria*.[2] Wanning notes that his daughter Roma looks as "the unrestrained beauties of later Rome must have looked":

> At costume balls and in living pictures she was always Semiramis, or Poppea, or Theodora. Barbaric accessories brought out something cruel and even rather brutal in her handsome face. The men who were attracted to her were somehow afraid of her. (p. 121)

---

1. Willa Cather, "The Bookkeeper's Wife," in *Uncle Valentine and Other Stories: Willa Cather's Uncollected Short Fiction 1915-1929*, ed. Benice Slote (Lincoln: Univ. of Nebraska Press, 1973) p. 95. Subsequent references to the story "Her Boss" from this collection will be cited in the text by page number.

2. The *Ars Amatoria* is Ovid's satiric poem on love, lovers' aims, and the customs of courting as practiced in Augustan Rome. The prevailing attitude toward love in Ovid's day was not much different from that of Roma and Florence Wanning who see courtship as a game with rules to follow and short-cuts to wealth and status available to those willing to resort to conniving or to "irregular" practices. The tone of *Ars Amatoria* challenged Augustus' efforts at moral reform, an attitude which Cather undoubtedly saw in her own society. Julia, daughter of Augustus, was banished from the Empire for her adulterous behavior, and Ovid's banishment at almost the same time raises speculation that the "carmen et error" for which he was punished was his knowing too much about Julia's escapades and recording these in his poem. [Graves Haydon Thompson, Introd., *Selections from the Ars Amatoria and Remedia Amoris of Ovid*, by Ovid (1952; rpt. Ann Arbor, MI: Edwards Brothers, Inc., 1958), pp. x-xi.]

Roma, together with her sister Florence, provides the model for Godfrey St. Peter's daughters who, with similar self-importance, fail to appreciate or understand their father's plight. Paul Wanning himself is like the Republican paterfamilias who, having long believed himself "very well done by" in both his possessions and his family, awakes one day to find "something sinister" about the rooms in which he lives (p. 125). The dying man's thoughts turn to an old friend who had chosen the freedom of the West to "all these years hustling about and getting ready to live..." (p. 129). Characteristically for Cather, the West is one bastion of admirable human values, a refuge from modernization. In his search for a simple enjoyment of life, Wanning turns to Annie Wooley, a young copyist in his office, whose bright eyes and girlish giggle recall a vitality of life missing in the elegant reserve of the women of his household. Wanning's musings are Cather's as he contemplates the brevity of life and the foolish efforts of human beings "to begin enterprises which they could follow for only a few years." Wanning notes, "All this material rubbish lasted.... But the human creature...had no chance – absolutely none" (p. 131). One recalls the same tone of regret in Cather's report as she first stood among the Roman ruins of Arles and thought of those Latin races who faced the setting sun. "Her Boss," therefore, becomes one of Cather's strongest statements against the powerful impersonalness and materialism which were eroding the very of American civilization and were forcing men like Paul Wanning to become a "money getter" rather than to remain the "mild contemplative youth he was in college" (p. 133). Even Paul Wanning's final effort to reward the kindly attentions of Annie is thwarted by the mean minds of his partner and grasping son. For Cather the world was fast becoming a decadent Rome where essential humanity and nobility lay crushed beneath the onslaught of barbaric greed and homage to false art.

Four other stories completed between 1916 and 1920 Cather collected into her second book of short stories, *Youth and the Bright Medusa*. When added to "Paul's Case," "A Wagner Matinee," "The Sculptor's Funeral," and "'A Death in the Desert,'" these newer works completed the picture of Cather's view of art and the artist. Serving as an addendum to *The Song of the*

Lark, these four stories expand upon the concept of art as presented in *The Troll Garden* and upon the relationship of the artist to material success and public acclaim. For these characters, the love of art is not the aesthetic ideal for which Thea Kronborg strove and for which Aunt Georgiana mourned. Rather the "bright Medusa" is the glitter of success, fame, and riches. Yet, Cather continues to portray aspiring artists as fearless and daring individuals, in the tradition of an Olive Fremstad or a Sarah Bernhardt. They are distinct from the common people and, like the forest children who hammered at the gates of the troll garden, they enter the garden of artistic delights, partake of the goblin fruits, and find only disappointment.

This time Cather uses the myth of Medusa to explain the hypnotic attraction of the arts for youth. But, Cather goes beyond the legend of a monster so terrifying in her ugliness that, ironically, she is seductively beautiful. Drawing upon her belief in the values of primeval matriarchy, Cather picks up the tale of Medusa at the beginning when the Gorgon was a beautiful young woman devoted to and associated with the earth goddesses. Ovid in *The Metamorphoses* retells the myth of Poseidon's rape of Medusa in Athena's temple, an act that caused the virgin goddess to curse Medusa for her vanity. As a skilled student of Greek, Cather must have recognized that Medusa's name meant "queen," an epithet of the earth mother, and that Poseidon's name (*posis das*) meant possessor of the earth.[3] In the myth itself lay expression of the conflict Cather observed in the post-war society. The matriarchy had fallen to a masculine possessor, and the demise of beauty was imminent.

In three of her four stories of aspiring artists, Cather places in women's paths an enemy which is male. In "Scandal" Kitty Ayrshire, whose name alone implies reaching for ethereal regions, finds her ambition balked by the repulsive Siegmund Stein who plots to be seen with her look-alike so that he might gain social prominence. In "A Gold Slipper," the same Kitty Ayrshire confronts Marshall McKann, a man whose view of the singer is that

3.   Hazel E. Barnes, "The Look of the Gorgon," in *The Meddling Gods: Four Essays on Classical Themes* (Lincoln: Univ. of Nebraska Press, 1974), p. 8.

she "was too much talked about, too much advertised; always being thrust in an American's face as if she were something to be proud of."[4] Even after spending an evening talking with Kitty alone, McKann maintains his dislike for her "professional personality" and a "natural distrust" of her variety of people (pp. 138-139). Siegmund Stein is attracted to her beauty, but McKann reacts differently. He does not want to use her beauty for his own gain; rather he blames such charm for the world's frivolity:

> "You are all," he went on steadily, watching her with indulgence, "fed on hectic emotions. You are pampered. You don't help to carry the burdens of the world. You are self indulgent and appetent." (p. 140)

The comment surely reflects a growing sentiment among those men who in 1917 were engaged in "the war to end all war." Yet, Kitty stands her ground in this primitive conflict of wills and of the sexes and retorts with Medusan fierceness:

> "Your morality seems to me the compromise of cowardice, apologetic and sneaking. When righteousness becomes alive and burning, you hate it as much as you do beauty. You want a little of each in your life, perhaps – adulterated, sterilized, with the sting taken out. It's true enough they are both fearsome things when they get loose in the world; they don't often." (p. 143)

Righteousness and beauty – two of the traits Cather associated with the matriarchy. And, like Poseidon, who strove to possess these traits by dominating their possessors, McKann never relents in his obstinacy but still keeps Kitty's gold slipper in his lock-box as a suggestion of life and youth.

The earliest of Cather's stories new to *Youth and the Bright Medusa* is "The Diamond Mine" (1916), and here she extends her study of *The Song of the Lark* to show a woman whose artistic sensibilities are preyed upon by a male-dominated and materialistic society. The prima donna Cressida Garnet is associated with images of success, this time in the form of jewels. She appeals to "the acquisitive instinct in men" and has "as many suitors as

---

4.   Willa Cather, "A Gold Slipper," in *Youth and the Bright Medusa* (1920; rpt. New York: Random House, 1975), p. 125. Subsequent references to this story or to others from the collection will be cited parenthetically in the text by page number.

Penelope" in the intervals between her marriages (pp. 81, 88). Like Kitty
Ayrshire, the beautiful Cressida is victimized by men, who feed on her
generosity, as well as by her grasping sisters. Even her son Horace, who like
his Roman namesake enjoys a casual life, lends his mother support in
exchange for her signature on a check. Cressida puts her struggling composer
husband Bouchalka on his feet, only to be deceived by him; she gratifies her
last husband by investing heavily and unwisely in his financial schemes. Like
Medusa, Cressida Garnet and Kitty Ayrshire, when set upon by male forces,
find their spiritual ambitions thwarted.

They become the terrifying Gorgons, stagnating beneath
unsympathetic forces and assuming hardened appearances, their only means
of defending selfhood. In a reversal of mythic roles, Marshall McKann, in "A
Gold Slipper," sees his reflection in Kitty Ayrshire's eye, as if she (the
Medusan figure and not Perseus) were "holding a mirror before him" (p.
129). The image McKann sees of himself is inexpressive: "Not a rock face,
exactly, but a kind of pressed-brick-and-cement face, a 'business' face upon
which years and feelings had made no mark..." (p. 129). Cather describes
Kitty with all the traits of the hideous Medusa. She wears "a reviling,
shrieking green [gown] which would have made a fright of any woman who
had not inextinguishable beauty..." (p. 127). Green is the color ancient
authors, like Ovid, attribute to the serpent-hair of Medusa (*Metamorphoses*,
Bk. IV). Moreover, the train of Kitty's gown loops about her ankles "like a
serpent's tail, turning up its gold lining as if it were squirming over on its
back" (p. 127). She smiles "bewitchingly" upon her audiences but accepts her
lot, as did Medusa, knowing that she is a victim of "ineradicable prejudices"
(p. 144). Kitty meets McKann's criticism with a cool manner, not taking his
dislike of artists as a personal affront. Out of necessity she has hardened
herself and become stone-like in order to survive in a mercenary society. In
"A Gold Slipper" Cather again chooses to disregard some details of the
classical myth while preserving its fundamental theme and applying that
theme to a contemporary problem.

Cressida Garnet in "The Diamond Mine" also becomes hardened in
her struggle for recognition as an artist and in her dealings with a succession
of disappointing husbands. Although she does not have the petrifying, cold

glance of Kitty Ayrshire, Cresida wears fluttering scarves, coiling about her head like lavender serpents, and she stands alone on deck, surrounded by immobile hillocks of other passengers who are huddled beneath quilts and shawls. She is "a strong, solitary figure on the white deck, the smoke-like scarf twisting and climbing and falling back upon itself in the light over her head" (p. 83). Cressida realizes that her plight is Medusa's – an inability to share herself with other people:

> "Somehow, my relations with people always become business relations in the end. I suppose it's because...I've not very much that's personal to give people. I've had too much else." (p. 79)

Cressida could be the sister of Thea Kronborg, who also sacrifices human relationships in her pursuit of art; but, unlike Thea who establishes a lasting relationship with Fred Ottenburg, Cressida succumbs to the merciless demands of a patriarchal system. By 1920, Cather had come to believe that even the most resolute women of artistic sensibilities would find their dreams thwarted by a mercantile, masculine society. The allure of beauty that had entranced their fore-mothers continued to shine brightly but, in the pursuit of the ideal, these women would become Gorgons, losing an essential humanity in their efforts to repulse new Poseidons, new possessors of mother earth.

In only one of the stories which she compiled for *Youth and the Bright Medusa* does Cather show a woman openly defiant of the masculine force which would inhibit her career goals. However, in "Coming, Aphrodite!" the reader does not feel compassion for Eden Bower as he or she did for Kitty Ayrshire or Cressida Garnet. Eden's motives are purely selfish, and, instead, her lover Don Hedger holds the ideals which earn Cather's and the reader's respect. The irony of the story lies in the conclusion. Eden Bower, too, becomes a Medusa, but not from defending against the onslaught of commercialism and the devaluation of art. Instead, her lover, whose artistic goals she rejects, becomes the defender of the purity of art. Cather obviously considered the message of "Coming, Aphrodite!" of great importance, for she chose to place this story first in her collection. By the time of this story's publication (August, 1920), Cather certainly knew that the hopes she had placed in pioneer and matriarchal values would not be realized in the Jazz Age. "Coming, Aphrodite!" introduces, then, a new theme which would dominate Cather's subsequent works like *A Lost Lady* and *My Mortal Enemy*. Marilyn Arnold in *Willa Cather's Short Fiction* defines Cather's subject as "the primeval drive that brings Eden and Hedger together in the first place," the human passion that somehow shapes the whole of civilization's progress from self-realization to the principles of art.[5] Aphrodite had succeeded as the moving force in the westering epic, and neither man nor woman was immune to her power. The realization undoubtedly became, in part, a reason for Cather's now famous statement, "The world broke in two in 1922 or thereabouts...."[6]

In acknowledging the materialism of the current day, however, Cather did not disavow the importance of the earlier stage of "epic" expansionism. Nor did she repudiate the order which frontier women brought to that expansion. Individual women with the strengths of Alexandra Bergson and Antonia Shimerda still existed, but in the second-stage of settlement, their roles were dimmed by a new generation's ambitions. The pioneers' children, no longer faced with the immediate challenge of taming the land, were turning instead to taking from it, to reaping a profit. Especially for some women, this shift in values led to a redefinition of self. Aware of the age-old roles of their sex as wives, mothers, and civilizers and yet not immune to ambition, passion, and greed, these women faced a puzzling dilemma. That dilemma was not new to twentieth-century America. It was older than recorded history, and Cather turned back to classical myth to describe it, back to a conflict between the ideals of Artemis and Aphrodite. She would address the problem in her next three novels, often with empathetic portrayal of her female characters, but in "Coming, Aphrodite!" she seemed not yet ready to accept a woman who would compromise the old ways for the new, and, perhaps, she never would.

In this most erotic of all her works, Cather introduces the mythic struggle between two goddesses, a struggle which she had toyed with in

---

5.   Marilyn Arnold, *Willa Cather's Short Fiction* (Athens: Ohio Univ. Press, 1984), p. 118.

6.   Willa Cather, *Not Under Forty* (New York: Alfred A. Knopf, 1936), p. v.

Alexander's Bridge and which would color much of the fiction in this middle period of her work. In naming her principal character, Cather focuses on the elemental and mythic forces which influence Hedger's life and draw him toward the devouring Medusa. Eden Bower serves as both Lilith and Eve, the Biblical prototypes of evil coupled with beauty. Moreover, in her primitive seductiveness, Eden arouses a mysterious passion in Hedger, much as Medusa did for Poseidon. Hedger, too, is associated with the sea, studying paradise fish at the Aquarium and living in a tank-like apartment. But, Eden's presence, like life-giving sunshine, penetrates the depths of his chamber. As she performs her daily exercise routine, she stands in "a pool of sunlight" like a Danae visited by Zeus' shower of gold:

> The soft flush of exercise and the gold of afternoon sun played over her flesh together, enveloped her in a luminous mist which, as she turned and twisted, made now an arm, now a shoulder, now a thigh, dissolve in pure light and instantly recover its outline with the next gesture. (p. 17)

In her unashamed nakedness, Eden Bower epitomizes the human race's early and close association with an undefiled earth.

Yet, she retains a certain remoteness that makes her voyeuristic neighbor both long for her and fear her, much as Jim Burden reacted to Lena Lingard. Cather pointedly associates Eden with Artemis, the intensely beautiful but regal goddess of chastity. Hedger's first impression is that "Her voice, like her figure inspired respect, – if one did not choose to call it admiration" (p. 13). When she berates Hedger for bathing his dog in the tub she must share with other residents of the apartment house, she waits for him in the hallway, "a flowing blue silk dressing gown [falling] away from her marble arms." She is "tall and positive" and is "fairly blazing with beauty and anger" (p. 14). Hedger feels he should bow low to her in supplication, for, like Actaeon, he believes he has intruded upon a goddess' privacy, but he is still defensive of his indiscretion:

> "Nobody has ever objected before. I always wash the tub, – and anyhow, he's cleaner than most people."
> "Cleaner than me?" her eyebrows went up, her white arms and neck and her fragrant person seemed to scream at him like a band of outraged nymphs. Something flashed through his mind about a man who was turned into a dog, or was pursued

by dogs, because he unwittingly intruded upon the bath of beauty. (pp. 14-15)

As Hedger's attraction to Eden increases, he worships her from afar and equates her with the moonlight that entranced Endymion, the beloved of Artemis. This first glimpse of Eden Bower colors his thoughts as he stands on the roof. The moon that May night is slender and girlish-looking to him and seems to be "playing with a whole company of silver stars" (p. 12), as Artemis played with her attendant nymphs or her virginal companions, The Pleiades. When the two young men in white flannels take Eden out to dinner, Hedger retreats into the Square where the moon beams fully in "regal glory" (p. 23). His thoughts, however, are murderous; he seeks jealous but righteous retribution against the Livingston boys for their presumptuous outrage against "his" deity. Eventually, though, Hedger's associating Eden with Artemis takes on a new sense of wonder. Having broken from Eden in a dispute over his ambitions for his work, Hedger lies alone on a sand dune and watches the moon rise up out of the sea. Again his thoughts turn to her, and he realizes that "there was no wonder in the world like the wonder of Eden Bower" (p. 55). This wonder is not what he has supposed it to be – an aesthetic delight in the purity of art. Hedger has deceived himself. What really enthralls him is the power of another goddess who is "older than art," namely Aphrodite.

Cather carefully weaves together images of Aphrodite and Artemis when describing Eden Bower, for she can thereby show the immemorial struggle between passion and chastity. Hedger at least temporarily succumbs to Aphrodite, to a young girl who dresses her splendid figure in lavender, arms herself with bunches of lilacs, and teases him with her "slowly curving upper lip and half-closed eyes..." (p. 7). Although his fingers twitch to draw Eden as she exercises in the sunlight, what unconsciously appeals to him is more than a study for drawing. He fails to understand "This thing whatever it was, [that] drank him up as ideas had sometimes done..." (p. 21). The power of Aphrodite rises "out of the remote past," striking him with the Helianthine fire which seems to pour over Eden's naked body:

He thought of that body as never having been clad, or as having worn the stuffs and dyes of all the centuries but his own.

> And for him she had no geographical associations; unless with
> Crete, or Alexandria, or Veronese's Venice. (p. 22)

She is the resurrected figure of the fertility serpent-goddess of Crete (a forerunner of Medusa), the merging of Isis with Aphrodite in post-Hellenic Alexandria, and the opulent beauty of Renaissance Italy. In whatever her guise, Eden Bower is the power of carnal love, "the immortal conception, the perennial theme" (p. 22).

Hedger is captivated by the sexuality of this modern goddess of love but overlooks those aspects of Aphrodite which make her favors dangerous and destructive. Eden is, indeed, the golden Aphrodite, who makes an enchanted spot of the "lake of gold" on the Turkish carpet where she ritualistically exercises. She wears "a disdainful, crafty smile" (p. 24) and has determined as a child that "she would be much admired by men and would have everything she wanted" (p. 29). Her disdain of common things is evident in the "defiant delight" (p. 24) with which she watches the white and silver pigeons soar skyward from the crowded and grimy city. (One is reminded that the dove, or pigeon, was sacred to Aphrodite.) Even in her ascension over the seashore in a balloon, Eden emulates Aphrodite rising from the sea, this time filling her arms with artificial roses and covering her shapely legs with black tights. Nevertheless, all eyes are focused on her and her wish is fulfilled: "She wanted to be admired and adored" (p. 40). Eden admits to herself the one essential maxim which she shared with the ancient goddess of love, an idea which fills her with potential danger: "... woman's chief adventure is man" (p. 47). In her developing relationship with Hedger, Eden never restrains her interest in other men whose attentions, like those of the Livingston boys, serve to make life pleasurable, or, like those of her capitalist friend Mr. Jones, ensure her trip to France and the advancement of her career. Like Aphrodite, Eden finds men's companionship a diversion or a means of achieving her own ends. She owes allegiance to no one, and, like the Olympian gods, is ruled only by Fate (p. 59).

Don Hedger becomes, then, the Hephaestus figure, devoted to Aphrodite but unloved by her. Hedger, whose name, if contrasted with Eden Bower's, connotes a tangled and impenetrable barrier as opposed to a flowery and bright haven, lives in a dingy and cheerless room, reminiscent of

Hephaestus' forge deep in the earth. From this "perpetual dusk" he looks out over "well-built chimneys that were never used now standing dark and mournful" (p. 12). The two gas burners, "where he sometimes cooks his food" (p. 3), are complemented by a gas light in the hall which he must tend. So did the ancients conceive of Hephaestus' workplace where monsters like the Chimera breathed the fires of the ignited gases. Also like the Olympian blacksmith, Hedger is physically powerful: "Hedger was medium height, but he practised with weights and dumb-bells, and in the shoulders he was as strong as a gorilla" (p. 11). He ascends easily an iron ladder that leads to the roof, and he lifts an iron door at the top that is "too heavy for any but Hedger's strong arm to lift" (p. 11). Hedger has the same features as the God of the Forge with thick black eyebrows hanging over defiant eyes and a "lean, big-boned lower jaw" (p. 46). Even the shapeless felt hat he pulls down over his bushy hair is like the oval cap that Greek sculptors showed on the head of Hephaestus. Both are vigorous and virile men, Hephaestus wearing a full beard as the ancients' symbol of this trait and Hedger always showing a "bluish stubble" over his "muscular jaws" (p. 15).

His background, too, is similar to Hephaestus'. Hephaestus, according to Hesiod,[7] was flung out of Olympus by his mother Hera, who was offended by the ugliness of her offspring. The infant fell into the sea and was rescued by the Nereid Thetis and Oceanid Eurynome, who raised him for nine years in a cave beneath the ocean. Upon his return to Olympus, Hephaestus learned the skills of an artisan, although he remained hostile to Hera. Only after becoming a master craftsman and building his own imperishable palace was he reconciled to his mother. The myth is much like the story of Hedger's life. Hedger was a foundling child, raised in a school for homeless boys, and the reader is reminded that his interest in marine life is strong. At sixteen, a Catholic priest took Hedger as a houseboy and introduced him to the world of art. Since that time Hedger has been a solitary person. His dog Caesar provides the same mute companionship that Hephaestus' robots, who worked

---

[7]   Hugh G. Evelyn-White, trans., "Homeric Hymn III: To Pythian Apollo" in *Hesiod: The Homeric Hymns and Homerica*, by Hesiod, ed. T. E. Page and others (Cambridge: Harvard Univ. Press, 1936), p. 347.

the bellows, must have provided him. Like Hephaestus, Hedger had no quarrel with women: "Not having had a mother to begin with, his relations with them, whether amorous or friendly, had been casual" (p. 21).

Most significant, though, is the parallel between Hephaestus' relationship with Aphrodite and Hedger's relationship with Eden. Paul Friedrich in *The Meaning of Aphrodite* analyzes the love goddess' marriage in this way:

> The marriage of Aphrodite and Hephaestus is itself an inversion of the usual union between a sky god and an earth goddess. Here a god who has been cast down from above and who works in the gloom with a forge is wed to a goddess who emerges from below and lives above in the sunlight, in the company of high-flying birds.... Moreover, it is Aphrodite who is dominant.[8]

Eden likewise dominates Hedger. He would prefer to see her as a white-skirted virgin and has not the least curiosity about "her everyday personality": "He wished that the girl who wore shirt-waists and got letters from Chicago would keep out of his way, that she did not exist" (p. 22). But, Eden's sensuousness forces Hedger to think of her as a sexual being and not as an undefiled goddess. Hedger had always prided himself on his strength of will, but after that first glance through the knothole, he is dominated by the sheer sensuality of woman:

> More than once he went out and tried to stay away for the whole afternoon, but at about five o'clock he was sure to find himself among his old shoes in the dark. The pull of that aperture was stronger than his will....(p. 20)

That "fatal aperture" (p. 23), as Cather calls it, clearly refers to female genitalia, the public exposure of which posed no trauma for Aphrodite, just as Eden is neither shy nor retreating in her nakedness. One would conclude that Eden would act no differently if she knew she were being observed. Her "consciousness of power" (p. 31) is great both on the streets and in the privacy of her apartment. The power of her sex is so strong that Hedger reacts to it with "a heathenish feeling; without friendliness, almost without tenderness"

---

8.   Paul Friedrich, *The Meaning of Aphrodite* (Chicago: The Univ. of Chicago Press, 1978), p. 65.

(p. 21). As he sits on the other side of the bolted doors, Hedger wonders "why a woman could do this to him" (p. 31), and, like Hephaestus, will soon be dominated by Aphrodite Charidotes, the Giver of Joy:

> He, too, was sure of his future, and knew that he was a chosen man. He could not know, of course, that he was merely the first to fall under a fascination which was to be disastrous to a few men and pleasantly stimulating to many thousands. (p. 31)

When, however, in her balloon descent, Eden publicly exposes her immortal beauty to the eyes of common mortals, Hedger becomes angry. In his mind, her purity has been violated but by her own choice. Hedger reacts much as did Hephaestus when he learned of his wife's unfaithfulness. The brutal story of the Aztec rain goddess, which Hedger coldly relates, serves the same purpose as the invisible net beneath which the Greek God of Fire trapped Aphrodite and her lover Ares in the throes of their ecstasy. Hedger wants to frighten Eden and to humiliate her into submission. The Rain Princess' death by fire, with which the story ends, is Hedger's message to Eden of his suppressed feelings, his anger, and his desire to punish her. Although Cather heard the tale from the young Mexican Julio on her trip to the Southwest in 1912, she was likely acquainted with similar fertility legends in the Mediterranean world. The earth goddesses of ancient Greece required the services of men at their temples where, especially in the case of Aphrodite, sacral prostitution was not only accepted but encouraged as assurance for fertility of the land and the people. Cather was also knowledgeable of Old Testament literature in which the practice of housing holy, professional prostitutes in temples served by castrated priests is recorded in stories like that of Jezebel (II Kin. 9:30-33). Taken from this perspective, the story within "Coming, Aphrodite!" seems less intrusive.

The Rain Princess legend, then, expounds upon those characteristics of Eden Bower (and Aphrodite) which exert such a strong control over Hedger and mortal men. Marilyn Arnold concludes, "The Rain Princess of the legend, like Eden, is both goddess and mortal, gifted with unworldly powers but cursed with worldly desires—desires for power, love, and, in Eden's case, success."[9]

---

9.   Arnold, pp. 115-116.

178

Against these desires Hedger must defend himself and his art. His love affair with Eden begins with cruelty, both in the story he tells and in the attack of his dog, but he only briefly holds sway over Eden. Their relationship begins on the roof where they stand like two figures from Hedger's paintings, "one white and one dark, and nothing whatever distinguishable about them but that they were male and female" (p. 49). But the primordial force of woman soon subdues Hedger. Like Hephaestus he cannot hope to be the sole possessor of the delights Eden offers. He casts aside his carefully formulated codes of life and art to accept, even if temporarily, the pleasures of love. He, like Samson, is cowed before a stronger force: "The woman was pulling the long black hair of this mightiest of men, who bowed his head and permitted it" (p. 51). Only after Eden leaves for Europe and is no longer a part of Hedger's life does he begin to recover from her Circe-like enchantment.

In the final section of "Coming, Aphrodite!" Cather thus returns to the issue of art and the bright Medusa. Frustrated by his failure to maintain a loving relationship with Eden, Hedger turns to his art. The immediate sensual gratification which governs Eden Bower's life had completely absorbed Hedger during their summer of passion, making art subordinate to life. Eden's presence is that of the devouring monster Medusa, eating up Hedger's creativity in erotic impulse. She yearns for success and fame and attempts to draw Hedger into the commercial enterprise of art. Hedger, however, battles this "bright Medusa" and relinquishes his love of Eden for his love of art:

> He had never in his life been so deeply wounded; he did not know he could be so hurt. He had told this girl all his secrets...all his misty ideas about an unborn art the world was waiting for; [he] had been able to explain them better than he had ever done to himself. And she had looked away to the chattles of [Ives'] uptown studio and coveted them for him! (pp. 53-54)

Like Perseus, Don Hedger triumphs over the Gorgon, returning to the ideals of art he had first associated with Eden Bower. Yet, Hedger does not escape unscathed. In his dignified defense of art he sacrifices a part of himself–his sexuality:

> He was hard hit. Tonight he had to bear the loneliness of a whole lifetime. Knowing himself so well, he could hardly believe that such a thing had ever happened to him, that such a woman had lain happy and contented in his arms. And now it was over. (p. 59)

Hedger's ultimate success as "one of the first men" among the modern school of painters (p. 62) offers some consolation for his loss, and, like the mythic hero Perseus, he "is able to escape from the perverse pursuit of his imagination, and to put himself–not only in intention but in fact, beyond the reach of exaltation of his bodily desires."[10]

For Hedger, Medusa is vanquished; she is not dead but merely driven from him. He triumphs in sublimating life to art. Perhaps Cather believed such a confrontation was necessary for every artist. She had long recognized that a writer could not serve two gods, and she, too, had traded human relationships in the bargain. Hazel Barnes reads, then, a larger truth into Hedger's battle with Medusa:

> Yet because Medusa stands for some kind of suprahuman abstract truth, The Poet must encounter her, though indirectly, by looking at her image in Athena's shield. When he has thus glimpsed the forbidden image without allowing himself to be captivated by it, Pegasus–the poem or the work of art–is born.[11]

Beauty from the death of ugliness–this is the theme which underscores the ancient myth and Cather's collection of stories. Cather was astute enough to realize, however, that resurrection of beauty in the modern world was becoming increasingly more difficult, and, in each victory over Medusa, the challenger must give up a little more humanness.

---

10.   Paul Diel, *Symbolism in Greek Mythology: Human Desire and Its Transformations*, trans. Vincent Stuart, Micheline Stuart, and Rebecca Folkman (1966; rpt. Boulder, CO: Sambhala Publications, 1980), p. 78.

11.   Barnes, p. 39.

A similar price is exacted of Eden Bower. The Medusa of success destroys not her sexuality but her "easy freedom of obscurity" and "sense of life over strong" (pp. 31, 47). Having given her life over to Aphrodisian impulses rather than to Artemisian ideals, Eden falls victim to the bright Medusa. Upon her return to New York, soft moonlight no longer envelops her; the street lamps flash ugly orange light upon her and neon lights glare her name. Her features are "hard and settled, like a plaster cast" (p. 63). Her humanness, too, has petrified.

In the magazine version "Coming, Eden Bower!" Cather ended her story with the theater marquee blazing forth Eden's next role, that of Clytemnestra. Cather changed this detail to "the golden face of Aphrodite" in her final version for *Youth and the Bright Medusa*. Although Bernice Slote suggests that Cather made the change to reflect a "more likely operatic role" for a performer in 1920,[12] Cather's use of the Aphrodite image is simply more consistent with both the theme of the story and with Eden's personality. Eden is nowhere the merciless and despicable Clytemnestra. The judgment is too hard, as Cather must have realized. What was coming, encroaching on the time-honored values of the matriarchy, was not the treachery and characteristically masculine violence with which Clytemnestra had tried to reorder her world. Cather had observed first-hand that civilization would survive such violence, though at great loss. What civilization might not survive was the dominance of Aphrodite whose Medusan lures of beauty become the ugliness of unrestrained or misdirected passion. This, Eden Bower represents. By expressing in mythic terms the love relationship between Eden Bower and Don Hedger, Cather manages to instill in her story a meaning beyond the immediacy of her characters' lives. *Youth and the Bright Medusa*, with "Coming, Aphrodite!" as its principal focus, signals a shift in both attitude and theme for Willa Cather. These short stories become the signposts for the novels of Cather's middle period, in which modern values would be tested against the standards of the past.

---

12. Slote, Introd., *Uncle Valentine and Other Stories*, p. xxi.

The harsh reality of World War I intruded upon Willa Cather in a variety of ways. Not only had her cousin died in the conflict, but former students who had enlisted in the cause visited frequently at her Bank Street apartment and brought friends with them. What most interested Cather about these soldiers was not the accounts of camp experiences and battles, although she did use some of these details in her next novel. Her keenest interest was in the changes which the war had effected in the personalities of these young men who, having come from widely diverse backgrounds, found a commonality of purpose in the war effort. Stimulated by these contacts, Cather spent four years in writing her "war" novel *One of Ours*, the story of a sensitive Nebraskan boy who confronts a world averse to his ideals. Cather's closeness to her character Claude Wheeler was so great that, even after the novel had come under severe attack by some critics, she still professed that she liked it best of all her books. So personally did she relate to the experiences of the central figure of *One of Ours* that she believed the title should have been "Claude."

Cather admitted that writing *One of Ours* drained her energy, although other events in her life between 1919 and 1922 also explain the strain she felt. Her relationship with Elizabeth Sergeant, for instance, had deteriorated. In 1914, Sergeant had left for Paris as a correspondent for *The New Republic*, and, while visiting a battlefield shortly before the Armistice, she had been wounded by the explosion of a supposedly dead grenade. Sergeant believed Cather's interest in the war was purely literary and found herself at odds with her friend on political issues as well. Fortunately, as this friendship weakened, Cather rediscovered a once deep friendship with Dorothy Canfield Fisher. The distance that had developed between the two friends since Dorothy Canfield's marriage and later success as a writer was dispelled by Dorothy's unsolicited and admiring review of *Youth and the Bright Medusa*. Also, during the four years spent composing *One of Ours*, Cather endured several illnesses, including a severe attack of influenza in the epidemic of 1918, and, in 1922, a recurrence of mastoiditis, resulting in a tonsillectomy, the complications of which placed her in a sanatorium in Pennsylvania. Cather had not been home to Red Cloud for two years and her mother's illness, too, preyed upon her mind. All in all, these years were not proving productive for Willa Cather, and even a retreat of several months to the Hambourg home in Toronto did little to ease the personal and professional burdens she felt.

It is surprising that the harsh criticism of *One of Ours*, which appeared upon its publication in the fall of 1922, did not have a more serious effect on Cather. Even some of her staunchest supporters, like H. L. Mencken, concurred with Elizabeth Sergeant that this novel romanticized the war, while reviews by Zoe Akins and Dorothy Canfield Fisher were, as might be expected, very defensive of the novel. Cather undoubtedly recognized the weaknesses in her novel but must have been truly dismayed that reviewers continued to consider *One of Ours* a war novel instead of the story of youthful idealism as she intended it to be. Occasionally a critical eye did not focus on the battle scenes which Hemingway sarcastically attributed to *Birth of a Nation*. When L. M. Field wrote in the *Literary Digest's International Book Review* that *One of Ours* was a tragedy, not a romance, Cather was surely pleased. Field saw in Claude the tragedy of an entire generation: "...in this world there is no place for the idealist, that just because Claude was fine and sensitive, clean-souled and aspiring, the best that can be wished for him was death."[13] Here was the problem about which Cather had written in *One of Ours*. Just as in her stories of *Youth and the Bright Medusa*, she was dealing with the clash of classical values in a modern world. The growing pessimism in her work of the early 1920's reflected her realization that the ideals which had sustained the pioneer culture of her youth no longer existed. Not by chance did T. S. Eliot's *The Waste Land* and Sinclair Lewis' *Babbitt* appear in the same year as *One of Ours*, for the modern wasteland was a harsh reality.

In depicting her concern for vanishing ideals, Cather again incorporates literary and mythic allusions in her novel. In *The Voyage Perilous*, Susan Rosowski analyzes the novel as "an American version of Arthurian legend that sets a would-be knight in search of a hero he could

---

13. L. M. Field, rev. of *One of Ours*, by Willa Cather, *International Book Review*, Jan. 1923, p. 58.

admire, an order he could join, and a chivalric ideal he could follow."[14] Such an interpretation seems in keeping with both the events of the novel and the sources with which Cather was well acquainted and to which she had previously made references in her works. Rosowski points to the many parallels with Tennyson's *Idylls of the King*, especially as the long poem provided prototypes for Enid and Claude, and argues that, in his almost quixotic quest for meaning in the apparently disordered modern world, Claude is a Parsifal figure.

Yet, the problem the novel explores is far older than the twentieth century or even the era of the legendary Arthur. The war alone, as a threat to youth and idealism, must have recalled to Cather the misspent heroism of young men like Protesilaus, Glaucus, Polites, and countless others in Homer's *Iliad*, a work which in itself serves as a condemnation of war. Moreover, her classical background provided the story of another youth whose purity and quest for truth set him apart. Hippolytus lived just such a life, and echoes of the Hippolytus myth do underscore *One of Ours*.

Although Cather's allusions to this myth are subtle and never intrude upon her narrative, Claude is very much like his ancient counterpart. At twenty-two Claude suffers greatly from his belief that there should be "something splendid about life, if he could but find it!"[15] Like Hippolytus, he turns away from the crudities of life, which he associates with men like his father and brother Bayliss, and he seeks a purer relationship with individuals whose spirits he believes seek the same ideals. Claude is repelled by the

---

14.   Susan J. Rosowski, *The Voyage Perilous: Willa Cather's Romanticism* (Lincoln: Univ. of Nebraska Press, 1986), p. 97. Rosowski further argues that Cather was well acquainted with Wagner's opera *Parsifal*, an "opera of salvation through compassion, renunciation, and suffering..." (p.106). In the role of Percivale, Claude finds his Gallahad in David Gerhardt, but unlike in Tennyson's "The Holy Grail" section of *Idylls of the King*, Cather's Percivale dies rather than returning to Arthur. James Woodress, in his most recent biographical study of Cather, agrees that the Parsifal motif is at work in the novel [*Willa Cather: A Literary Life* (Lincoln: Univ. of Nebraska Press, 1987), p. 329.]

15.   Willa Cather, *One of Ours* (New York: Alfred A. Knopf, 1922), p. 103. All further references to this novel will be cited in the text by page number.

184

brutal and vulgar ways of his father, much as Hippolytus resented the reputed licentiousness of his father Theseus, whose heroic adventures frequently included the violent subjugation of women like Hippolytus' own mother, Hippolyta.

Admittedly, Cather rarely followed myth exactly or purposely created a one-to-one correlation between her characters and their classical predecessors, but Nat Wheeler's portrait invites comparison to Theseus. Nat Wheeler has a heroic stature. He is "a very large man, taller and broader than any of his neighbours" (p. 3); he is "certainly the handsomest and most intelligent, man in the community" (p. 26). Yet, his selfishness and hardness lead him to chop down a cherry tree as a kind of practical joke on his wife and to insist that Claude haul smelly hides to town on the very day his son wishes to dress well and meet friends for an outing. Nat Wheeler is the monarch of his country, owning large tracts of land but doing little of the work himself. Like Theseus, he is often absent from his realm, traveling to conventions with Bayliss or to his Colorado ranch. Mr. Wheeler also hectors Claude because of the sense of pride which he detects in the boy:

> Mr. Wheeler had observed this trait in him when he was a little chap, called it false pride, and often purposely outraged his feelings to harden him, as he had hardened Claude's mother, who was afraid of everything but schoolbooks and prayer-meetings when he first married her. (pp. 26-27)

Mrs. Wheeler, too, is victimized by the authoritarian ways of her husband. Having come to Nebraska from the older new England culture, Evangeline Wheeler possesses a sense of beauty and an interest in intellectual pursuits which she passes down to Claude. Although Nat Wheeler did not abduct her as Theseus did the Amazon queen, Mrs. Wheeler also bears a son so different from his father that Claude understandably feels as did Hippolytus when he cried, "I would not wish on any of my friends a bastard's birth."[16] Mrs Wheeler is also a displaced person, like the Evangeline in Longfellow's poem, but she maintains a "personal life so far removed from the scene of

16.   David Grene, trans., "Hippolytus," by Euripides, in *Euripides I*, ed. David Grene and Richmond Lattimore (New York: Washington Square Press, 1967), p. 216.

her daily activities that rash and violent men could not break in upon it" (p. 69).

In his identification with his mother and her cultural sensitivity, Claude most assumes an Hippolytean role. Claude is deeply devoted to the ideals which Artemis would admire – purity of thought and abstinence from sensual indulgence. Even as a boy, "he imposed physical tests and penances upon himself" (p. 29), hardening himself against the elements so that he might more successfully confront forces hostile to his ideals. He prefers a life of almost monastic cleanliness, whether it be in wearing a linen coat rather than a colored shirt or in driving a washed car rather than a mud-spattered one. One might suspect Claude's motive for such behavior to be that of Hippolytus – to create by contrast a judgment against his father.

Claude's choice of companions is also reminiscent of the brotherhood which Hippolytus shared with his attendants, "such men/ as do no sin, nor offer wicked service,/ nor will consent to sin to serve a friend as a return for kindness."[17] The objectivity of Ernest Havel, the openness of the Erlich boys, and the cultural finesse of David Gerhardt attract Claude and bond his spirit to theirs. Yet, even Havel recognizes in Claude's blind devotion to his ideals a certain vanity characteristic of martyrs. Claude's tempestuous nature and defensive air make him a prime target for ridicule, and, as his mother realizes, he consequently suffers much more "over little things" (p. 68).

Like a worshiper of the Maiden Goddess, Claude withdraws from physical relationships with women. He resents the attentions of Anabelle Chapin, "a gushing, silly girl" (p. 32), and, after a brief interest in Peachy Millmore, avoids her whenever possible. Claude's awkwardness with women arises from their failure to meet his expectations, their failure to be both beautiful and chaste. His "sharp disgust for sensuality" (p. 56) is, in part, a reaction against the talk of hired hands which he has heard since childhood. Revolted by such coarseness, Claude searches for individuals to admire for their purity. He early develops a keen interest in Joan of Arc, and her ethereal beauty haunts him even when he is bringing in the cobs or pumping

---

17.   Grene, trans., p. 213.

water. Claude is, indeed, chaste and, as Cather writes, possesses "an almost Hippolytean pride in candour" (p. 56). This pose he retains even after marriage and throughout his war-time experiences. Unlike other soldiers, Claude apparently has no sexual encounters; his only close relationship is with David Gerhardt. Perhaps Cather intended to portray in this same-sex relationship a satisfaction unattainable in a heterosexual union. Cather herself had always shown a preference for homosexual friendships, and Claude, too, finds his selfhood less threatened by them.

Yet, in his perception of heterosexual love, Claude repeatedly hopes for a mother-son relationship. When the aviator Victor Morse displays a photograph of his mistress, Claude "would have preferred to believe that his relations with this lady were wholly of a filial nature" (p. 307). Claude had always found in his own mother a person of similar sympathies, and Cather makes clear this maternal identification in memorable scenes like Claude listening to his mother read aloud from the classics or pouring over a map of Europe with her as the war escalates. Both Claude and his mother are aware of a uniqueness that sets them apart from the scrambling materialism of their contemporaries and bonds them together.

A Freudian interpretation of this relationship might focus on the unnaturally strong son-mother bond and the fact that Claude's name means "lame." The Oedipal implications are strong, but one must remember that Cather almost universally rejected Freudian analysis.[18] But, Cather did not need to draw on Freud to develop a character who was crippled by his very nature. She writes, "Claude knew, and everyone else knew, seemingly, that there was something wrong with him" (p. 103).

Cather may have utilized the myth of Oedipus in naming Claude, but the Hippolytus story offered the same mythic element without the modern implications of Freudian analysis. Like Oedipus, Hippolytus identified with his mother rather than his father. Even his name was a matronym, the

---

[18] Phyllis C. Robinson, *Willa: The Life of Willa Cather* (New York: Holt, Rinehart and Winston, 1983), p. 221; E. K. Brown, *Willa Cather: A Critical Biography* (1953; rpt. New York: Discus-Avon Books, 1980),p. 173; Edith Lewis, *Willa Cather: A Memoir* (New York: J. B. Lippincott Co., 1953), p. 203.

masculine form of Hippolyta. Claude also identifies more fully with his mother than with his father, but Cather is certainly not consciously trying to rewrite the ancient legend. Rather, she explores a son-mother relationship which accounts for Claude's idealistic conception of what love should be. Evangeline Wheeler is not, after all, an Amazon queen waging war against a masculine, Greek world. In his mother, Claude finds the model for the ideal partner, since her wonderful human love is given without thought of personal gain (p. 196).

On his wedding night when he is rejected by Enid, Claude aches to return to his mother. The myth of Hippolytus, with its hints at possible incest between the devotee of Artemis and his young stepmother, may have been in Cather's mind as she described the close alliance between Claude and Evangeline Wheeler. When Mr. Wheeler and Ralph move to the Colorado ranch in the fall, Mrs. Wheeler enjoys herself, making new dresses from material Claude chooses and resting as she chooses. She remarks, "It's almost like being a bride, keeping house for just you, Claude" (p. 78). In other instances when they are alone, they show an unusual intimacy. At his final farewell, Mrs. Wheeler catches Claude in her arms, "smiling her little, curious intimate smile, with half-closed eyes" (p. 263). They share a secret understanding and physical closeness foreign to both their marriages:

> She passed her hands over his shoulders, down his strong back and the close-fitting sides of his coat, as if she were taking the mould and measure of his mortal frame.... Claude stood looking down at her without speaking a word. Suddenly his arms tightened and he almost crushed her. (p. 263)

In his unwavering love and loyalty to his mother, Claude reenacts a pledge like that of Hippolytus to Artemis, his mother-ideal and model of purity in a world corrupted by the powerful lusts characteristic of Aphrodite.

Claude continues to search for an unspoiled mother figure even when at college. He finds in Mrs. Erlich a woman upon whom he can attach his affection without a threat to his sexual abstinence. Augusta Erlich, whose name recalls both the cultural height of Imperial Rome and an epithet of highest respect and honor, seems, in Claude's opinion, "very young to be the head of such a family" (p. 40). He remarks on the beauty of her skin and his attentions are kindly and protective, as a dutiful son's should be. Mrs. Erlich, in turn, delights in the appealing figure he makes in evening clothes, and her friend Madame Schroeder-Schatz suggests that Claude might serve as more than a young escort: "...[I]f you were but a few years younger, it might not yet be too late. Oh, don't be a fool, Augusta! Such things have happened, and will happen again" (p. 60). What Claude searches for is a woman who embodies the chastity and nurture of an Artemisian figure, a power which can insulate him from the rapid changes in the world and can preserve for him the ideals of a primeval matriarchy. Such a desire causes Claude to turn toward Enid Royce, who is, in many ways, like his mother.

Although Claude maintains a disdainful guise that separates him from the coarse masculinity of the hired hands and men like his father, he is torn between his commitment to an asexual devotion to a mother goddess and the real physical needs of a twenty-two year old. Claude, like Cather's other heroes of the post-war generation, is victimized by both Artemis and Aphrodite. Deferring to his mother's wishes, Claude attends a strict religious college, where worldliness is discouraged; but, even in these surroundings, he wrestles with his natural impulses: "If an attractive woman got into the street car when he was on his way to or from Temple Place, he was distracted between the desire to look at her and the wish to seem indifferent" (p. 34). Such tension grows more acute as Claude recovers from erysipelas: "Waves of youth swept over him and left him exhausted. When Enid was with him these feelings were never so strong; her actual presence restored his equilibrium – almost" (pp. 144-145). His thoughts of Enid start up "like a sweet, burning pain...sensations he could neither prevent nor control." Yet, Claude is sure that he can master these urges and can be "infinitely patient, infinitely tender," never letting Enid know "how much he longed for her" (p. 145). His dilemma is Hippolytus', for even that ancient hero acknowledged the power of Aphrodite but worshiped her "from a long way off," as Euripides writes.[19] Later versions of the Hippolytus legend – Racine's *Phaedra*, for instance – introduce a love interest for the young prince as if in recognition of his humanness. One is reminded that Cather had read Racine in her French

---

19.   Grene, trans. p. 176.

classes while at the University of Nebraska, and she may have borrowed from such sources in introducing Enid. Enid, like Aricia in Racine's play, is an intelligent and chaste woman who arouses passion because of her purity.

Enid, whose name means "pure," projects an image of "'virtuous and comely Christian womanhood'" (p. 144), reminding the reader and Claude of the saintliness of Jeanne d'Arc. Claude is attracted to her smooth skin, graceful movements, and dignified expression. He remembers her as the one chosen for Sunday School tableaux vivants to play "the role of Nydia, the blind girl of Pompeii" or "the martyr in 'Christ or Diana'" (p. 123). Claude, who himself assumes a martyr role, believes that Enid must have found that something outside herself that makes life splendid, the very thing for which he searches. She comes to Claude's sick room like a goddess, letting in sunshine, scattering the fragrance of flowers, and enveloping him in her tranquil presence. Claude feels "unclean and abject" in comparison to her and, when he looks at her with longing, feels guilty "as if he must beg for forgiveness for something" (p. 145).

Although Claude is humbled before Enid's apparent goddess-like perfection, he is, as Stanley Cooperman has pointed out, aroused only by Enid's passivity.[20] What Cooperman fails to note, however, is that Cather draws her image from the myth of Pygmalion to explain the paradoxical nature of Claude's desires. Pygmalion, who had spurned women, fell in love with the perfect woman whom he had sculpted. In loving her, Pygmalion stroked the marble which softened to flesh under his touch, and he worshiped the woman he had awakened. So does Claude dream of loving Enid: "Even in his dreams he never wakened her, but loved her while she was still and unconscious like a statue. He would shed love upon her until she warmed and changed without knowing why" (p. 145). Claude believes that through Enid he can reconcile those opposing forces of desire and restraint, for she is, at once, the mother-ideal he worships, a chaste goddess, and a woman.

---

20. Stanley Cooperman, *World War I and the American Novel* (Baltimore: The Johns Hopkins Press, 1967), p. 132.

But, Claude is sorely disappointed. The traits which attract Claude prevent him from finding happiness in his marriage. In her initial rejection of Claude's proposal, Enid insisted that marriage was not for all girls, but Claude, like Jim Burden before him, continues to cling to his belief "in the transforming power of marriage" which "reduced all women to a common denominator; changed a cool, self-satisfied girl into a loving and generous one" (pp. 176-177). For Claude, marriage to such a paragon of virtue would be a natural and almost devotional act. Enid would "restore his soul" (p. 146), much as Tennyson's Enid did for Geraint. Claude, however, does not find his soul eased from the Aphrodisian desires which made him, prior to his wedding, guiltily keep one of Enid's lace corset covers which had blown away as she worked on them. Claude at first thinks he does not blame Enid for her dislike of the sweaty earthiness of men who had just finished their work, but her rejection of male sexuality is that of an Artemis who admits no man, including Claude, to her holy chamber. Although the novel does not specify when or if Claude's and Enid's marriage is consummated, Enid continues to appear as a virgin goddess. She wears white dresses, shoes, and stockings as she goes about her work and is unusually meticulous in the care of her linen. Although she is proud of Claude, she continues to find everything about a man's embrace distasteful (p. 210).

As much as these descriptions might lead the reader to expect mythic allusions to Enid as a virgin goddess, a Parthenos, that is hardly the portrait Cather offers. Just as Antonia and Lena do not live out the myth Jim Burden creates for them, Enid does not fulfill the role Claude envisions. She is not an inexperienced girl, waiting to be sexually awakened; rather, she responds to Claude's advances on their wedding night with almost frigid rejection and remains physically aloof, though not unkind, throughout their marriage. Cather again does the unexpected, not bringing her myth to its preset conclusion but introducing an ironic, and often satiric, thrust to the romance of myth by concluding with a harsh reality. In his devotion to the purity which Enid represents, Claude finds only death of spirit, not fulfillment. Enid never relinquishes her femininity nor will she submit to masculine approach. She is like Artemis, whose power lies "in her inviolability, which often makes her seem cold and cruel, disdainful of those who are more susceptible."[21] And, Claude is susceptible. Attracted to Enid's chaste appearance, he becomes like the bird trapped in the unfinished rooms of his new house. He can only "[flutter] wildly about among the partitions" (p. 177), seeking a way out of the blind corridor of misdirected passion.

Claude becomes, then, the classic, disappointed idealist. He had been "a well-behaved boy because he was an idealist," and he had "looked forward to being wonderfully happy in love and to deserving his happiness" (p. 210). But, like Hippolytus, he instead could shout, "Women! This coin which men find counterfeit!"[22] He chides the older generation for misleading him, for teaching him "to idealize in women the very qualities which can make him utterly unhappy..." (p. 251). Yet, Cather is not content to let Enid bear the entire burden for Claude's unhappiness. Claude remains a Hippolytean figure, an "unhappy neurotic," as Hazel Barnes writes, a man "so preoccupied with his own maladjustments that he is utterly incapable of forming normal human relationships."[23]

One such relationship could have been with Gladys Farmer. Claude silently censures her for what seems to be her interest in his brother Bayliss, but what he really censures is her apparent capitulation to sensuality and materialism. Claude had always thought of Gladys as a kindred spirit, as one who shared his fine feelings (p. 113). Gladys, whose name is the feminine form of "Claude," shared an implicit understanding "that all things which might make the world beautiful – love and kindness, leisure and art – were shut up in prison, and that successful men like Bayliss Wheeler held the keys" (p. 155). Claude, quite understandably, feels betrayed when Gladys begins to accept Bayliss' attentions. Only after he is assured that she has no intention

21. Christine Downing, *The Goddess: Mythological Images of the Feminine* (New York: Crossroad Publishing Co., 1984), p. 176.

22. Grene, trans., p. 197.

23. Hazel E. Barnes, "The Hippolytus of Drama and Myth," in *Hippolytus in Drama and Myth* (Lincoln: Univ. of Nebraska Press, 1960), p. 95.

of marrying his brother and only after he finds disillusionment in his own marriage does Claude forgive Gladys and accept her again as his companion in spirit. He recalls from the depth of his mind an old conception of Gladys that had "remained persistently unchanged" (p. 113). She, too, is a child of Artemis, a worshiper of the ideal. When the moon rises over the wheat fields, Claude's thoughts turn to Gladys. Along with his mother and Mahailey, he considers Gladys one of the "children of the moon, with their unappeased longings and futile dreams...a finer race than the children of the sun" (pp. 207-208).

Gladys also embodies those virtues of a simpler time; she is by name "a farmer," a woman associated with the earth. She has "strong feelings about places" (p. 151) and affinities with the land which place her in the company of other Catheran heroes. Trumpet vines cover the entryway of Gladys' low house, vases of flowers stand about on the tables of the parlor, and a garden of hollyhocks, catalpa, and mint spreads across the yard. Even the "long, uneven parlour" in which she meets Claude is a dusky room that "look[s] like a cavern with a fire at one end of it" (p. 258). An aura of sanctity exists in the room; it appears as a temple where an altar blazes to a benevolent and nurturing goddess. Gladys' presence fills the room with a "strange kind of calmness" (p. 258), and like the Demeter of Cnidus, she has a "settled composure" and the "air of one whose position is assured" (pp. 107-108). Claude is drawn to Gladys not only because she is an "exceptional person" but also because she projects the maternal protectiveness he seeks as a refuge from the life that seems to him so mysteriously hard (p. 154). But Gladys also exhibits a melancholy like that of Demeter, for she is fully cognizant of the passing of the old ways, of a falling away from traditional values. She admits that "Even her little life was squeezed into an unnatural shape by the dominance of people like Bayliss" (p. 155).

On her final visit to Claude's yet unfinished bridal home, Gladys senses "that she, too, had come to the place where she must turn out of the old path" (p. 181). Cather draws upon the myth of the Cretan Labyrinth to describe Gladys' feeling of entrapment:

> Claude descended in front of her to keep her from slipping. She hung back while he led her through confusing doorways and helped her over the piles of laths that littered the floors. At the edge of the gaping cellar entrance she stopped and leaned wearily on his arm for a moment. She did not speak, but he understood that his new house made her sad....(p. 181)

To Gladys, the new house also symbolizes a trap for Claude's spirit. The cellar entrance is like the entrance to Tartarus, and she shudders before it. Gladys thinks that in marrying Enid, Claude is doomed to become "one of those dead people that moved about the streets of Frankfort; everything that was Claude would perish, and the shell of him would come and go and eat and sleep for fifty years" (pp. 154-155). The prospect frightens her, and Claude feels her melancholy. In a reversal of the Theseus and Ariadne myth, he is reluctant to leave this maze and "would willingly have prolonged their passage, – through many rooms and corridors" (p. 182). Claude cannot rely on Ariadne's thread to free him. Rather, he must lead Gladys into the real world where he, too, will abandon her. Security exists for both of them only as long as they hide from the world. The devouring Minotaur lurks not in the labyrinth Claude has built but in the chilly world outside. Gladys and Claude have been drawn into a spiritual maze, into the world of Nat and Bayliss Wheelers.

In the last two books of *One of Ours*, however, Cather shifts her mythic emphasis. She turns to the idea of an epic adventure in which a young man like Claude may find some sense of purpose. Although Claude shows little of the adventuresome spirit of a classical epic hero, he does possess many of the physical traits. In the opening section of the novel, Claude appears as a young Odysseus, the red-haired, angry one, possessed of a "violent temper and physical restlessness" (p. 28). In spite of "a sharp physical fear of death," he sometimes feels that he will escape its clutches, that "he would actually invent some clever shift to save himself from dissolution." He would be "crafty and secret" (p. 50), the terms used by Homer to describe Odysseus. Claude also has the "catapult shoulders" of a hero, a phrase Cather seemed particularly fond of and had used in her portrait of Bartley Alexander. After the exhausting work in harvest season, Claude sinks onto his bed and sleeps "like the heroes of old" (p. 158) who knew their work had been accomplished. The reader is thus prepared for the transition from the Hippolytus myth to Claude's role in an epic journey. When coming home from his training camp in Omaha, Claude finds he must identify himself to others on the train as if he has come from foreign shores: "Like the hero of the Odyssey upon his homeward journey, Claude had often to tell what his country was and who were the parents that begot him" (p. 244). It is appropriate that Cather selects Odysseus as the hero to whom Claude is compared since his journey is more a struggle against gods and monsters than a conflict between humans, as in *The Iliad*. The tone of the Homeric epic is ever-present, and Claude's journey across the Atlantic is more like a homecoming than a departure.

Cather, however, had no reservations about combining Homeric and Vergilian details in her "epic." Her most evident borrowing from *The Aeneid* comes in the title of Book Four – "The Voyage of the Anchises." Claude boards this troopship in New York, and, on an epic scale, two thousand doughboys aboard the Anchises shout and wave as they pass from the harbor. They are "all young, all bronzed and grinning..." and are filled with "indomitable resolution" (pp. 273-274). So did Aeneas' sailors hang garlands in the sterns of their ships in the happy celebration of their departure from the African coast. The Anchises even sails before the image of its sanctioning deity, the Goddess of Liberty. Like a modern Calchas, an old clergyman imparts his blessing as the ship glides down to the sea. The epic overtones are clear, yet so is Cather's bitterness as she closes the chapter:

> That howling swarm of brown arms and hats and faces looked like nothing but a crowd of American boys going to a football game somewhere. But the scene was ageless; youths were sailing away to die for an idea, a sentiment, for the mere sound of a phrase...and on their departure, they were making vows to a bronze image in the sea. (Cather's ellipses, p. 274)

Cather evidently regrets and resents the wasting of young lives in the re-enactment of a ritual as old as human history.

Her choice of Anchises as the name for the troopship may reflect such feelings. Some critics have considered the name appropriate because it "recalls another epic journey in which youth came to the rescue of old age" or because in using the name "Cather hints at the fates that await Claude and his companions."[24] Although both suggestions offer some sound reflection on Cather's use of the Vergilian epic, neither is fully satisfying, for each

---

24.   David Stouck, *Willa Cather's Imagination* (Lincoln: Univ. of Nebraska Press, 1975), p. 92; Mildred R. Bennett, "How Willa Cather Chose Her Names," *Names*, 10 (1962), 33.

overlooks an important aspect of both the myth and Cather's novel. Anchises' name serves two thematic purposes here. First, Anchises was the victim of Zeus' wrath, having been lamed (or blinded, according to some accounts) for boasting of his love affair with Aphrodite. His pride in this sexual escapade was an offense even to the promiscuous Zeus. Second, Anchises was the one person fleeing from Troy to whom was entrusted the holy relics and the country's gods (*Aeneid*. II.717). These he brought safely to the new Troy where they were enshrined for later generations to worship.

Cather surely had these events in mind when she titled her chapter. The young Americans, too, are psychically lame, or blinded, like Anchises. If they are not emotionally crippled like Claude, they are, like Victor Morse, morally blind. In their cultural naivete, they venerate the gods of pleasure and gain, believing they can truly make the world safe for democracy while remaking the Old World into their new Troy. They carry into France a carelessness with money, which in its plentifulness is of little importance to them. They have only a shallow appreciation of the beautiful things which war destroys and have the vague idea that they must explore every cathedral and church they find. The Anchises bears to Europe representatives of an impaired culture whose love of Aphrodite (materialism) has made the worship of Artemis (aesthetic beauty) extinct. Only in a few rare men like David Gerhardt and Claude Wheeler does a genuine appreciation of the old ways exist. The French see in the Americans only "fictitious values," a "legend of waste and prodigality," and a threat to "everybody's integrity" (pp. 326-327).

Cather extends her reference to the ancient epics by including a modern adaptation of the Greeks' arrival on the island of Polyphemus. Just as Odysseus' troops, ravenous for fresh food, made landfall and glutted themselves on the Cyclops' cheeses, so do the young Americans trudge about town looking for cheese and, like wolves, fall upon the stock they find. The proprietress of the cheese shop is certainly not a Polyphemus, but the entire scene does encourage the reader to think about the "unwashed, half-naked" and "half-witted brother of the Chief Steward" aboard the Anchises who never spoke and "had only one eye and an inflamed socket" (pp. 317-318). Cather even describes the Steward's hand as soft and "cheesy" looking.

196

Cather's cyclopean figure is quite believable as a messenger for the crooked
Steward, and even if Cather is having a little fun in suggesting epic
associations with characters and incidents in her novel, she is quite serious in
their ties to her thematic concerns.

In keeping with the spirit of ancient epics, Claude's journey awakens
in him a sense of destiny: "The feeling of purpose, of fateful purpose, was
strong in his breast" (p. 312). He feels released from the meaningless routine
of his former life. While on the Anchises and surrounded by death, Claude
gives up his childhood and finds "a chance to correct one's ideas about life
and to plan the future" (p. 259). His survival of the raging epidemic is similar
to the epic hero's descent into the Underworld from which he arises renewed
and eager to fulfill the prophecy of his future. He finds a renewed
appreciation for the beauty of nature and the niceties of civilization, such as
the Jouberts maintain in the midst of chaos. Claude rededicates himself to
the idealism that marriage and life among selfish men has drained from him.
He believes that his new understanding is more realistic: "Ruin and new
birth; the shudder of ugly things in the past, the trembling image of beautiful
ones on the horizon; finding and losing; that was life, he saw" (p. 391). No
longer does he wear the guise of Hippolytean aloofness and haughtiness.
Claude develops an interest in the role passion plays in human life. He wants
to believe that the powers of Aphrodite and Artemis need not always be at
odds with each other. Hazel Barnes, in discussing the myth of Hippolytus,
explains the traditional dichotomy of these powers:

> Another way of putting it would be to say that Aphrodite
> represents that impulse in man which causes him to find self-
> fulfillment in emotional and physical contact with others,
> Artemis the yearning for self-sufficiency, the desire to keep
> one's inward being isolate from an encroachment by others
> which is felt to be a violation.[25]

In France, then, Claude seeks the union (alliance) of his divided self.

Male companionship in the army offers Claude his first chance for a
sustained and guilt-free human relationship, and in David Gerhardt he finds

---

25.   Barnes, "The Hippolytus of Drama and Myth," pp. 78-79.

a spiritual mentor. Although Gerhardt is cynical about the war fulfilling any promise of return to order and traditional values, he, at the same time, exhibits an artistic sensibility and suppressed idealism that appeal to Claude. With Gerhardt, Claude shares the natural beauty of the French landscape and the perfection of classical music. Gerhardt, who claims that he has become a fatalist, admits that the war has smashed "so many old things" (p. 409). Yet, he continues to believe that something unforeseen and unexpected must come out of such destruction:

> "You remember in the old mythology tales how, when the sons of the gods were born, the mothers always died in agony. Maybe it's only Semele I'm thinking of. At any rate, I've sometimes wondered whether the young men of our time had to die to bring a new idea into the world...something Olympian." (Cather's ellipses, p. 409)

Prior to the outbreak of the war and his acquaintance with Gerhardt, Claude had always viewed the world "like a business proposition" (p. 419). Gerhardt's musings, though, inflame Claude's imagination and his desire to contribute to a cause greater than himself.

Like an Aeneas, Claude wants to help to found a new age in which patriarchal values are harmoniously wedded to those of the matriarchy. During his company's weekend billet at the village of Beaufort, Claude observes what he believes is this new order. The American soldiers "came to life as if they were new men, just created in a new world" (p. 433). The town is inhabited almost entirely by women, and "The Americans found themselves in the position of Adam in the garden" (p. 436). The women are eager to feed, clothe, and house the soldiers whom Mlle. de Courcy had called "men of destiny" (p. 390). As commanding officer Claude makes no effort to interfere in the pleasure-making of his troops; he finds a certain innocence in their delight in living. The masculinity and gallantry of the soldiers harmonize with the femininity and sympathy of the village women.

Claude believes that worship of Aphrodite and Artemis can coexist, and the story of the Curé's niece confirms this for him. Cather retells the Pyramus and Thisbe myth in the relationship of this young French girl and her German lover, Lieutenant Muller. Claude is particularly drawn to the grave of Marie Louise, for she had killed herself for an ideal – purity of love. The wall that had joined the Curé's garden to the German cemetery – a convenient borrowing from the ancient myth – now divides the lovers' graves, and Claude, for the first time, contemplates a new "kind of misery" that stands out "in a world of suffering" (p. 439). The story recalls another scene Claude had watched on his first night in France. He had, without realizing it, followed two young lovers to the moonlit doorway of a church where "they clung together in an embrace so long and still that it was like death." Claude is no voyeur, but keeps watch over this tryst "like a sentinel, ready to take their part if any alarm should startle them" (p. 334). Perhaps he saw in the maimed soldier his own crippled self and in the wide blue, innocent-looking eyes of this country girl a purity which he thought was lost to the world. The scene is sanctified by the blessing of a sculptured bishop on the portal, and Cather describes the two as spiritual mother and son, a living Pietà:

> The girl sat down on the stone bench beside the door. The soldier threw himself upon the pavement at her feet, and rested his head on her lap.... The girl bent over her soldier, stroking his head so softly that she might have been putting him to sleep; took his one hand and held it against her bosom as if to stop the pain there. (p. 334)

Here was an idea Claude would willingly die for – virginal and motherly love, coupled with human passion, and given freely to the lamed victim of the world's lusts and greed.

As Claude develops a conviction that ideals are not "archaic things, beautiful and impotent," he is drawn toward "the bright face of danger" (p. 420). The mere presence of death on the battlefield dispels his feelings of inadequacy for confronting a world made by men like his father, a world opposed to his ideals. He, like Oedipus, is deceived into imagining himself a hero. In describing Oedipus' meeting with Sphinx, Paul Diel could be describing the new Claude: "...he is convinced that he is destined for the highest degree of spiritual achievement: he believes he has been called upon to free the country, symbol of the world."[26] In those final moments before his

---

26. Diel, p. 128.

death, Claude's blood is quickened by an excitement for what he is doing. He
no longer feels any weakness but is stimulated by a passion for those
"wonderful men" under his command, men with whom "he could do anything"
(pp. 452-453). Claude chooses death, believing that men are mortal but
unconquerable. Claude believes he has reconciled the warring factions of his
own nature. In his willingness to die for an ideal, he satisfies both the
Aphrodisian urges that make him human and the Artemisian loyalties that
are "the real sources of power among men" (p. 420).

Cather realized, as did Mrs. Wheeler, that men like Claude, "who in
order to do what they did had to hope extravagantly, and to believe
passionately" (p. 459), are doomed to disillusionment. Therefore, she protects
Claude from disillusionment by letting him die, adding a twist to epic
convention. Claude dies "believing his own country better than it is, and
France better than any country can ever be" (p. 458). Cather does not laugh
at Claude's innocence, but she knows that he is deceived. In the satiric thrust
of her title for the final book in *One of Ours*, Cather reflects the pessimism
which would become even more evident in her next novels. No epic
adventure awaits young Americans like Claude; the eagles of the West
cannot fly onward. A new force was emerging in western culture, and its
patron deity was not Artemis, but Aphrodite.

By the time Willa Cather learned that she had been awarded the
Pulitzer Prize for *One of Ours*, she had already completed her next novel, *A
Lost Lady*. Ironically, *A Lost Lady* had none of the weaknesses of her award-
winning work and was Cather's masterpiece of the novel démeublé, a concise
and powerful piece whose apparent effortless perfection belies the labor
required to produce it. Cather wrote part of *A Lost Lady* on Grand Manan
Island in the summer of 1923, and this remote island would, in the following
years, afford her a refuge, like the McClung's attic room, where she could
concentrate on her writing. The inspiration for *A Lost Lady* came during
Cather's stay with the Hambourgs in Toronto, at which time she learned of
the death of Lyra Anderson, once the wife of Governor Garber who had
made his home in Red Cloud. This name alone conjured up powerful
memories for Willa Cather. James Woodress notes that Cather once said "to
work well she needed to be carefree as if she were thirteen and going for a

picnic in Garber's Grove."[27] In the death of Mrs. Garber, Cather saw a loss of elegance and sophistication which were her personal memories of the Garber home. A tone of despair surfaces in the novel, a tone which naturally follows the bitter irony of Claude's death in *One of Ours*. In *A Lost Lady*, Cather returns to the narrative voice of a young man who, instead of finding fulfillment in memories of a glorious past as did Jim Burden, experiences the disillusionment of that glory gone awry. Niel Herbert, like his creator, confronts a civilization whose values are changing and learns that the Arcadian world of the pioneer west cannot be regained, its beauty lost to time.

Marian Forrester is both the symbol of that beauty and, for Niel, the symbol of the pioneer values betrayed. In creating a believable portrait of such a woman, Cather drew heavily upon classical myth, for in a blending of Artemis and Aphrodite she found the dichotomy of values which characterized American culture. Niel Herbert finds himself in a situation very similar to Claude Wheeler, for in worship of aesthetic ideals he discovers his own sexuality and an attraction to the image which would undermine those ideals. Cather continues to use the myth of Hippolytus to describe this dilemma.[28] Like Hippolytus, Niel is motherless, estranged from his father, and lives "with monastic cleanliness and severity," having "resolved to remain a bachelor."[29] He exhibits a reserve "which did not come from

---

27. James Woodress, *Willa Cather: Her Life and Art* (1970; rpt. Lincoln: Univ. of Nebraska Press, 1982), p. 199.

28. John J. Murphy, in his article "Euripides' *Hippolytus* and Cather's *A Lost Lady*," concurs with this conclusion and points out a number of details in the novel which lead Niel to resemble Hippolytus in both "temperament and outlook" [*American Literature*, 53 (March 1981) 72-73]. Beyond the more obvious plot details, Murphy even suggests that, as he grows older, Niel finds his greatest enjoyment in the company of men like Captain Forrester and Judge Pommeroy, who becomes his intellectual guide much as King Pittheus counseled Hippolytus.

29. Willa Cather, *A Lost Lady*, First Centennial Edition (1923; rpt. New York: Alfred A. Knopf, 1973), p. 29. All subsequent references to this novel will be cited parenthetically in the text by page number.

embarrassment or vanity, but from a critical habit of mind..." (p. 30). As a boy, Niel establishes a camaraderie with some of the local youths, and their outings become a simple relishing of the natural world where they behave like wild creatures. Yet, as he grows older, Niel turns to his uncle's Bohn library to satiate his curiosity not "about what men had thought" but "about what they had felt and lived..." (p. 78). Foremost among his choices is Ovid's *Heroides*, love stories that make him reevaluate his perspective of life and determine precisely what he wished his own relation with other people to be. As Niel comes of age, his interest in Marian Forrester changes, although he continues to delude himself into believing that "it was as Captain Forrester's wife that she most interested [him]..." (p. 74). As the favorite "son" of this aged railroad magnate, Niel shows an unusual interest in the Captain's wife, an interest that hints at the incestuous nature of the Hippolytus-Phaedra relationship.

Until directly confronted with Marian Forrester's adultery, Niel worships her as an undefiled, virgin goddess. His boyhood memories are of a beautiful woman who maintains an elegant home where the favored and rich bow down in adoration. Like Claude Wheeler's attraction to Enid, Niel is drawn to the apparently inviolable whiteness of Mrs. Forrester. Niel remembers her bestowing favor upon him and his companions as they asked permission to fish in the marsh, and the image of her white figure "coming rapidly down through the grove, under the flickering leaf shadows" (p. 13) remains with Niel into adulthood. Like Artemis in the forest, she appears bareheaded and admits to the picnicking boys that she often goes barefooted, picking up her skirts to go wading. (Among the ancients, only Artemis was depicted wearing a tunic-length garment.) Mrs. Forrester's name, too, calls forth the image of a nature goddess. Like Artemis, she is associated with groves and streams and offers a sanctuary to wild creatures, granting only to her followers permission to hunt or fish.[30]

---

[30]   John J. Murphy extends the comparison by suggesting that Mrs. Forrester's dislike of the snake-like Ivy Peters, and her concern that the boys should kill the "whopper" water snake they have found reflect Artemis' abhorrence of the Python which pursued her mother Leto ["Euripides' *Hippolytus* and Cather's *A Lost Lady*," pp. 78-79].

But, the primary parallel to Artemis exists in the unstained whiteness which surrounds Mrs. Forrester. After his accident, Niel awakes in her "white bed" in a room that is "cool and dusky and quiet" (p. 23). The sickroom, like Gladys Farmer's parlor, takes on the aspect of a temple where the attendant goddess soothes the pain of her devotee. Like Artemis, Marian Forrester applies the healing arts, touching Niel with soft fingers and bathing his forehead with cologne. In holy adoration, Niel notices "her white throat rising and falling so quickly" (pp. 23-24). Her choice of pearl earrings in the shape of fleur-de-lys reflects the purity of the moon goddess, and the moon is the one object of nature with which Niel most frequently associates her. After dining with the Forresters, Niel pauses at the end of the lane, remembering the first time he saw Mrs. Forrester. Above him hangs the "hollow, silver winter moon" (p. 38). Niel feels closest to Mrs. Forrester in the moonlight, even after he discovers she is not the goddess he wishes her to be. Upon returning to Sweet Water from college, Niel is haunted by his image of Marian Forrester and in "a night of glorious moonlight" wanders aimlessly until seeing her "white figure, standing on the bridge over the second creek, motionless in the clear moonlight" (pp. 120-121). In the Artemisian role which Niel assigns her, Marian Forrester characterizes the heroic age of first generation pioneers, who had made American civilization worthy of emulation in Cather's estimation.

Niel's discovery that Marian Forrester is not a chaste and divine being comes in the early summer after he has spent the winter eagerly reading the *Heroides*. Cather writes that Niel, through Ovid's elegiac poems, "had been living a double life, with all its guilty enjoyments" as he discovered "the great world that plunged and glittered and sumptuously sinned long before little Western towns were dreamed of" (pp. 78-79). Niel, awakening to his own sexual identity, places Marian Forrester among the heroines of these myths, making her, ironically enough, not more real but a woman of legend. Her failure to live up to his image is, therefore, devastating to his Hippolytean sensibility. Cather subtly prepares the reader for Niel's disturbing revelation. The first time Niel saw Marian Forrester she was alone, dressed in "a black silk dress all puffs and ruffles, and a black hat, carrying a parasol with a carved ivory handle." She alighted from her carriage in "a swirl of foamy white petticoats" out of which she "thrust a black, shiny slipper." From that moment Niel had recognized her "as belonging to a different world from any he had ever known" (p. 38). Marian Forrester is indeed from a different world, but her appearance is self-contradictory. She enters a church like a chaste worshiper but wears the black silks which stand in stark contrast to supposed purity.

Her pose of chastity throughout Part I of the novel is coupled with hints of sensuality. For example, from childhood Niel associates Marian with roses. On the day of his accident, she greets him with a pink rose in her hand and the wild roses in the fields are wide open. The fragile beauty of the rose is all the boy Niel associates with Marian Forrester, but some seven years later after reading "the most glowing love stories ever told" (p. 78), Ovid's *Heroides*, Niel offers up roses in tribute to his goddess, only to discover their Aphrodisian associations. Rising early in the morning to make his offering to Mrs. Forrester, Niel is unusually excited:

> There was an almost religious purity about the fresh morning air, the tender sky, the grass and flowers with the sheen of early dew upon them.... Out of the saffron east a thin, yellow, wine-like sunshine began to gild the fragrant meadows and the glistening tops of the grove. Niel wondered why he did not often come over like this, to see the day before men and their activities had spoiled it, while the morning was still unsullied, like a gift handed down from heroic ages. (p. 82)

Niel basks in the illusion of eoan purity in which earth deities like Artemis and Aurora preserve an "unstained atmosphere" (p. 82). The roses he places on the window-sill altar of Mrs. Forrester are "only half-awake, in the defencelessness of utter beauty" (pp. 82-83).

Kathleen Nichols proposes that these roses suggest the true source of sexuality encroaching on Niel's view of Marian Forrester. They serve as an emblem of Niel's own sexual jealousy, a greater threat to his untarnished vision of Marian than is Frank Ellinger's presence.[31] But, such a contention

---

31. Kathleen L. Nichols, "The Celibate Male in *A Lost Lady*: The Unreliable Center of Consciousness," in *Critical Essays on Willa Cather*, ed. John J. Murphy (Boston: G. K. Hall and Co., 1984), pp. 192-193.

only in part accounts for Niel's tirade against womanhood when he discovers that Frank Ellinger is sharing Mrs. Forrester's bedroom. Of equal significance is the affront he feels to his Hippolytean idealism. In a single moment he loses "one of the most beautiful things in his life" (p. 83). Marian Forrester is no longer "Maidy," as her husband calls her; she is no longer the partner of a marriage which Niel has assumed to be sexless. In his disillusionment, Niel condemns all women: "Beautiful women, whose beauty meant more than it says...was their brilliancy always fed by something coarse and concealed? Was that their secret?" (Cather's ellipses, p. 84). In similarly fierce terms Hippolytus reacted to the discovery of his stepmother's passion for him: "... the cursed creature/ rejoices and enriches [man's] heart's jewel/ with dear adornment, beauty heaped on vileness."[32] Although Niel goes on to declare, "It was not a moral scruple she had outraged, but an aesthetic ideal" (p. 84), Marian Forrester becomes more than a sullied Artemis. While continuing to profess disgust with Marian's unfaithfulness to her husband, Niel is more and more drawn to her, fascinated by her "magic of contradictions" (p. 75). Just as Claude Wheeler envisions marriage to Enid as the ideal union of body and soul, Niel ignores the doubt in the back of his mind and worships Mrs. Forrester as the incarnation of two quite different goddesses. Like the ancients, Niel worships at the shrine of both Artemis and Aphrodite, sacrificing to one out of respect and to the other out of fear.

Throughout Part I of *A Lost Lady*, Cather hints at the dual nature of Marian Forrester; only Niel's perception equates her with elegance, beauty, *and* purity. Niel's fear of his own latent sexuality blinds him to Mrs. Forrester's Cyprian role. He continues to associate her with the idyllic hours spent in her "inviolate Meadow" as Euripides calls it, and, like Hippolytus, believes he shares with no other man the privilege of worshiping her.[33] Yet, the traits of Marian Forrester clearly point to her role as the sensual and golden Aphrodite. Her "soft, musical laugh" reverberates throughout the

---

32.   Grene, trans., p. 198.

33.   Grene, trans., p. 174.

novel, whether she is teasing an awkward Swedish farmer or enthralling her dinner guests. Niel admits, "Compared with her, other women were heavy and dull; even the pretty ones seemed lifeless – they had not that something in their glance that made one's blood tingle" (pp. 37-38). Hers is the side-long glance of Aphrodite which years later Niel remembers as promising "a wild delight that he had not found in life" (p. 174). With Aphrodisian jealousy and vanity, Mrs. Forrester resents bright, animated eyes in other women. She reserves only for herself "the flashing eyes" of Homer's goddess of love. Her passionate nature is evident in the color of her jewels – garnets – and in the crimson scarf she wears on her sealskin coat. Her hands are adorned with glittering rings, which she claims she never leaves off except when working in the kitchen (p. 36). Niel feels a special closeness to Mrs. Forrester when she removes her rings to care for his broken arm, and he equates this action with a singular commitment to him. When, however, she meets Frank Ellinger before the fireplace, Mrs. Forrester has again taken off her rings. The symbols of her constancy are gone, but Niel is not there to see this.

Like Aphrodite, Marian Forrester is defined by male admiration and by her identification with flowers. Captain Forrester admits that she was never more captivating than on the day the new bull chased her through the meadow where she had gone to gather wild flowers. He is like Zeus attracted to Europa, and Marian Forrester's undeniable desirability flashes before the reader like the red parasol she carries. Her screams soon dissolve into laughter, however, and the scene then recalls the myth of Pasiphae's passion for the Cretan bull. Had Niel seen in this incident evidence of a perverse passion like Phaedra's rather than a threat to the safety of a virgin, he would not have reacted with such rancor upon discovering Marian Forrester's infidelity.

Similarly, Niel fails to see the two-fold meaning of the roses with which Marian is so often associated. Niel remembers the "old-fashioned blush roses" (p. 9) which decorated the Forrester parlor when he was a boy and the pink wild roses surrounding the house. Neither color suggests the full-blown sensuality of Aphrodite's red rose, but each offers the merest suggestion of a yet undeveloped passion and a source of embarrassment for the young man. Yet, when he is nineteen and makes a votive offering of roses to Mrs. Forrester, Niel selects roses whose petals are "stained with that burning rose-colour which is always gone by noon, – a dye made of sunlight and morning and moisture, so intense that it cannot possibly last...must fade, like ecstasy" (Cather's ellipses, p. 82). As the color of the rose deepens toward red in the novel so does Marian's role as Goddess of Love intensify, and Niel's crushing disappointment in finding his ideal ruined becomes imminent.

On his first visit to the Forrester home after his discovery of Mrs. Forrester's affair, Niel notes "the perfume of the mock-orange and of June roses" which blows in the open windows (p. 85). Roses and orange blossoms should call forth images of weddings and virginal sweetness, but these blooms now mock Niel and his worship of a chaste divinity. The flowers which Captain Forrester cultivates he prizes as belonging to Mrs. Forrester, and, in fact, they well suit the self-love of an Aphrodite. Throughout the winter months, the Forrester house was "full of the narcissus and Roman hyacinths, and their heavy, spring-like odour made a part of the enticing comfort of the fireside there" (p. 66). In Greek myth, the narcissus is the flower of self-love and the hyacinth of jealous love. Marian Forrester, therefore, assumes the role of Aphrodite Antheia, Aphrodite of the Flowers, around whose temple, altar, and statue were not the traditional paving stones but a luscious garden.[34]

Marian Forrester also revels in the attentions of men, particularly men of wealth and distinction like Cyrus Dalzell, President of the Colorado and Utah Railroad, or young men whose manners need polishing but whose eagerness to please is strong. Her seductiveness becomes her most powerful trait, and with coquettish ways she exacts worship from men of all ages – boys like Niel's companions, mature men like Frank Ellinger, and even those like her husband who surpass her in age by twenty-five years. Her relationship to Daniel Forrester is much like Aphrodite's to her husband Hephaestus. Captain Forrester is lamed by his stroke and, like the Olympian blacksmith, is quite content to sit next to his parlor fire. Mrs. Forrester expresses

---

[34]   Geoffrey Grigson, *The Goddess of Love: The birth, triumph, death and return of Aphrodite* (London: Constable and Co., 1976), pp. 95 and 143.

attentive concern for her husband's basic needs – warmth, food, and a pleasant home – but finds such existence bleak. She grievously misses the whirlwind of activities that wintering in Colorado Springs had offered.

Like Aphrodite, Marian Forrester finds satisfaction in an ongoing love affair. She is attracted by Frank Ellinger's physical appearance, much as the Goddess of Love was drawn to the impressive physique of Ares, God of War. Cather uses animal imagery to emphasize Frank's powerful physicality:

> Frank Ellinger was a bachelor of forty, six feet two, with long straight legs, fine shoulders, and a figure that still permitted his white waistcoat to button without a wrinkle.... His whole figure seemed very much alive under his clothes, with a restless, muscular energy that had something of the cruelty of wild animals in it. (p. 42)

When he and Marian Forrester go driving on the pretense of gathering cedar boughs, Frank tears off his glove with his teeth, devours his lover with his wolfish eyes, and crushes her hand in his grasp. The "something evil" (p. 42) that Niel senses in Frank is highlighted by his coarse black hair, black overcoat, and the black ponies he so skillfully manages. Mrs. Forrester's Arean-like lover has "the look of a man who could bite an iron rod in two with the snap of his jaws" (p. 42). What puzzles Niel is, "What did she do with all her exquisiteness when she was with a man like [that]?" (p. 97). Captain Forrester, though, is fully aware of his wife's extra-marital affair and, like Hephaestus, simply learns to live with her unfaithfulness without resenting it. When the Captain asks Niel to mail one of Mrs. Forrester's letters to Frank Ellinger, Niel is greatly embarrassed and tries to hide the envelope. Captain Forrester, however, examines it at arm's length, comments on his wife's fine handwriting, and reminds Niel that Mrs. Forrester, like her penmanship is "very exceptional" (p. 116).

Niel, even after two years' absence from Sweet Water, retains an image of the exceptional Marian Forrester as both chaste goddess and love object. He still envisions her as the white goddess of his youth. She is the last of the great and beautiful women of the heroic age and is married to one of the last great pioneers. Early in the novel, however, Cather describes a gruesome scene that prefigures the demise of pioneer ideals at the hands of the next generation. The scene also prefigures Marian Forrester's personal decline.

Ivy Peters, whose name suggests the invasion of life-choking vines into the idyllic forest along the Sweet Water, interrupts the innocent play of Niel Herbert and his friends who are fishing in the Forresters' marsh. Ivy sadistically fires a sling-shot at the female woodpecker and, after capturing it, slits its eyes. Upon its release, the bird whirls into the air in a corkscrew motion, blindly and desperately seeking safety. Niel's attempt to rescue the woodpecker and to put it out of its misery is unsuccessful and results only in his own injury. Much has been said of this scene, for the great detail which Cather uses indicates that the incident is intended to do more than shed light on the cruel and grasping ways of Ivy Peters. Most commentaries focus on the sexual implications of Ivy's sadistic act or on the symbolic blindness of Marian herself.[35]

Such suggestions are worthy of close attention, but Cather had at least twice before used the woodpecker in her novels. In each instance, the bird is associated with the awakening of intense physical longings. When Thea Kronborg learns that Fred Ottenburg will soon arrive at the ranch, she is filled with a bright sensation of aliveness and admits that she had always liked Fred better than other men. She feels that "A persistent affirmation – or denial – was going on in her, like the tapping of the woodpecker in one tall pine across the chasm." Similarly, Fred languidly listens to the persistent tapping of "the old woodpecker" until he spies Thea bathed in morning light on a cliff far above him. He sees her as one of those primitive women who, "dressed in their hair and a piece of skin," used to be caught in nets by

---

35.   Patricia Yongue, in "Marian Forrester and Moll Flanders: Fortunes and Misfortunes," suggests that the blinding indicates Ivy's attitudes toward all women and "images the fundamental predicament of a woman who has been mutilated to the point of blindness as to her own real needs and goals" [*Women and Western American Literature*, ed. Helen Winter Stauffer and Susan J. Rosowski (Troy, NY: The Whitson Publishing Co., 1982), pp. 204-205]. David Stouck finds the scene filled with sexual innuendos and foreshadowings of dangers for Marian Forrester [*Willa Cather's Imagination*, p. 61], while Beth Burch parallels the blinded bird's situation with the entrapment and restricted vision of the heroine ["Willa Cather's *A Lost Lady*: The Woodpecker and Marian Forrester," *Notes on Contemporary Literature*, 11, No.4 (Sept. 1981), 7-10].

invading soldiers (*The Song of the Lark*, pp. 307, 319-320). Cather refers to the bird again in *My Antonia* when Jim Burden is reluctant to leave the peaceful bower where a woodpecker hammers away in an old elm tree. The hired girls have just stopped to admire his gleaming body as he emerged from the water, and Jim is filled with a new appreciation of self and manhood (*My Antonia*, p. 234).

The woodpecker in *A Lost Lady*, however, is not tapping out a message of physical delight in being. This time it reels blindly about, striking trees, and searching desperately for its own hole. Cather has here returned to classical mythology to portray her concern with misdirected passion. What Niel, the Blum boys, and their friends observe is the failure of love in a world dominated by men like Ivy Peters. In Greek myth, the woodpecker was a prophetic bird which, like its cousin the wryneck, was also used to excite love. Pindar, whom Cather read in her study of Greek lyric poetry, calls the wryneck "the bird accurst,"[36] brought down from Olympus by Aphrodite as a gift to mankind. The bird generally was caught, fastened by its spread wings and feet to a small, four-spoked wheel, and revolved while incantations to Aphrodite were recited. The sole function of the twirling wryneck was to unite lovers. Supposedly the love of the desired person was irresistibly aroused when his or her image was tossed into the flames below the wryneck-spinner.

In her description of the bird's mutilation, Cather may be drawing upon these myths of Aphrodite's prophetic bird. Ivy Peters enters the sanctuary of Niel's "Artemis," violates one of the creatures she protects, and then mocks the goddess of love. Even as a child, Niel understands that Ivy puts no trust in the sanctioning power of the gods; he is one of the "new men" who makes his own destiny, taking whatever he wants, ignoring the standards of the past. In his crippling of the bird, Ivy enacts the crippling of all human passion that was once sacred and pure. Niel's attempts to rescue the bird are futile, for he can save neither the object of his youthful infatuation – Marian

36.   C. J. Billson, trans., "The Quest of the Golden Fleece" (Pythian IV), in *The Oxford Book of Greek Verse in Translation*, ed. T. F. Higham and C. M. Bowra (Oxford: The Clarendon Press, 1938), p. 310.

Forrester – nor the world of older, matriarchal values in which lovers' unions were blessed by the gods. Modern society was destined to fall into the hands of men like Ivy Peters. Niel would surely agree with Claude Wheeler's belief that "No battlefield or shattered country he had seen was as ugly as this world would be if men like his brother Bayliss controlled it altogether" (*One of Ours*, p. 419). And, Ivy Peters is a Bayliss Wheeler, though more blatantly cruel and grasping.

Cather extends her bird imagery to Niel's attempt to preserve his world against the onslaught of modernization. Upon his return from college, Niel first finds Mrs. Forrester in white and lying quietly in a hammock between two cottonwoods. Niel virtually ensnares her "like a bird caught in a net," acting out the first step of his fantasy to carry her off – "off the earth of sad, inevitable periods, away from age, weariness, adverse fortune!" (p. 109). She still enjoys her goddess-like pose, delightedly laughing at Niel's boyish eagerness and displaying the artifice of the alluring love goddess. Later in the summer Niel again observes Mrs. Forrester in the moonlight and resents the casual familiarity with which Ivy Peters addresses her. Niel is still offended by anything which might alter his perception of Mrs. Forrester. Even when Marian Forrester's perfection is besmirched by excessive drinking and a degrading phone call to Frank Ellinger, Niel refuses to accept her as less than goddess. Niel undresses her and puts her in his own bed, never entertaining the thought of violating a beauty so beyond the world in which it is trapped. He dutifully returns to the side of the invalid Captain, having betrayed neither his ideals nor Mrs. Forrester. Not even the farcical dinner party for the rough men of Sweet Water shatters Niel's commitment to his goddess. He still believes he can save her, as he wanted to save the woodpecker.

Only after he observes Ivy Peters in the kitchen with Mrs. Forrester does Niel give up his worship of an aesthetic ideal. Ivy's draining the marsh to raise wheat was an affront to natural beauty, but his "unconcernedly [putting] both arms around her, his hands meeting over her breast" was a violation of sanctity (p. 173). In Mrs. Forrester's failure to strike out against such an offense, Niel accepts what he had long tried to avoid. For the disillusioned Niel, purity of womanhood is a myth, and only Aphrodite reigns, both over women like Mrs. Forrester, who need love and adoration to survive, and over men like Ivy Peters, who see all of life as a commercial enterprise. Niel could and did believe in Mrs. Forrester as Aphrodite attended by the Graces, a goddess promising the niceties and felicities of civilization. Now from his point of view, she assumes another role – Aphrodite the Whore. Niel's abrupt departure from Sweet Water coincides with his Hippolytean resentment and judgment of Marian Forrester, with his scorning all lilies that fester. Niel is not yet able to accept Marian Forrester with compassion or understanding of her human weakness. Although he has longed for Mrs. Forrester as a sensual woman and worshiped her as the feminine ideal, he refuses to allow to her the very dichotomy of nature which he expects.

Cather, however, is not content to let Marian Forrester or women in general bear all blame for cultural decay. If "the world broke in two in 1922 or thereabouts," men were at least equally responsible. Men like Ivy Peters and the bright, young directors of Captain Forrester's failed bank exhibit none of the humanistic values which had civilized the frontier. They are as Gauls invading Rome, an image Cather used in her 1923 edition of *April Twilights*. Ivy Peters' brashness and unscrupulousness bring him material success, but he had "never dared anything, never risked anything" (p. 104) as had the great men who settled the plains. Men of his ilk are despoilers of classical beauty, as well:

> The space, the colour, the princely carelessness of the pioneer they would destroy and cut up into profitable bits, as the match factory splinters the primeval forest. All the way from the Missouri to the mountains this generation of shrewd young men, trained to petty economics by hard times, would do exactly what Ivy Peters had done when he drained the Forrester marsh. (pp. 104-105)

Cather's bitterness is strong, for in the draining of the marsh she undoubtedly saw a deeper meaning. This is a man's plan and an emblem of his dominance over the mother deities long associated with water, the life-giving source. Evelyn Helmick argues that "the swamp stage of civilization...represents the early matriarchate, [and] its drying up is a symbol not only of the human dominance of nature but also the male drive for knowledge that succeeds the

212

female acquiesence to nature."[37] The resultant male dominance parallels the triumph of the Olympian patriarchy, a situation which Artemis long resisted and which Aphrodite used to her own advantage. Marian Forrester is caught up in this transference of power. The usefulness of the feminine arts has declined; woman's identity is now shaped by male fantasies or expectations. She is, first, the Captain's objet d'art to be displayed before admiring guests. She is to Niel perfect woman and goddess, to Frank Ellinger a brief but delightful diversion, and to Ivy Peters a blinded bird dependent upon him for survival.

Understandably, then, the view Niel initially offers of the "lost lady" is a biased one, originating in his youthful romanticism and emergent sexuality. But, Niel's view is too limiting. Marian Forrester is neither virgin nor scarlet woman. Cather again utilizes classical myth in order to offer a more sympathetic portrait of Mrs. Forrester than that seen through Niel's eyes. Drawing upon the story of Jason and Medea, Cather portrays the plight of woman victimized by her own passion and by the boundaries men set for her. The blinding of the woodpecker becomes even more significant when one recognizes Marian Forrester's similarity to Medea, for as Pindar wrote, Aphrodite first presented the wryneck-spinner to Jason and "'Twas she taught Jason with what magic charm/ To draw Medea from her filial ways...."[38] Marian Forrester also possesses the enchanting beauty of Medea with "her long black hair rippling over her shoulders" (p. 7) and dark eyes whose beauty a veil cannot hide. While sitting in his uncle's law office one winter afternoon, Niel observes the spell her beauty casts:

> The frosty air had brought no colour to her cheeks, – her skin had always the fragrant, crystalline whiteness of white lilacs. Mrs. Forrester looked at one, and one knew that she was bewitching. It was instantaneous, and it pierced the thickest hide. (p. 31)

---

[37]. Evelyn Thomas Helmick, "The Broken World: Medievalism in *A Lost Lady*," *Renascence*, 28 (Autumn 1975), 45.

[38]. Billson, trans., p. 310.

Like Medea, Marian Forrester is a "foreigner," out of place in the highly opinionated and judgmental town of Sweet Water. Her background is shrouded in mystery, and even her marriage to the Captain does not dispel the gossip that she is a refugee, escaping from California with the taint of dishonor from her part in a love triangle. The women of Sweet Water are jealously curious about Marian Forrester and the regal appearance she maintains. So did Medea, rightfully a princess of Colchis, find herself an object of curiosity, rumor, and distrust when living in Corinth. Also like the mythic enchantress, Marian Forrester is a clever woman, a role which Euripides claims brings no profit to women but will make them "objects of envy and ill-will."[39] The townswomen, like Harpies, descend upon their "clever" woman's household after the Captain suffers a second stroke. They rummage among Mrs. Forrester's closets, boldly comment on her distracted behavior, and laugh at her weakness for alcohol. They soon discover that "they had been fooled all these years" and that there was "nothing remarkable about the place at all!" (p. 138). Marian Forrester proves to be like Euripides' Medea, merely a woman who both experiences joy and suffers pain.

It is this humanness that arouses both Cather's and Euripides' compassion for their heroines. Medea argues that "We women are the most unfortunate creatures,"[40] and, indeed, Marian Forrester feels the same way when deserted by her Jason. Frank Ellinger well fills the role of this Greek

---

39.   Rex Warner, trans., "The Medea," by Euripides, in *Euripides I*, p. 73. Cather could have drawn from a variety of ancient writers for her account of the Jason and Medea myth, and from her interest in and borrowings from Ovid's works, one might expect *The Heroides* or *The Metamorphoses* as her primary source. A close examination of Medea's letter to Jason in *The Heroides*, however, shows her pleading with Jason to remember how he had taken advantage of her as a naive young girl. Neither this suppliant nature nor guise of out-raged innocence appears in Marian Forrester. Moreover, Ovid stresses the cruelty and sorcery of a murderess in *The Metamorphoses* account, and these traits Cather virtually ignores. More probably, then, Cather returns to the older source of the myth, Euripides' play, in which Medea's desperate acts are more sympathetically portrayed. Cather knew Euripides' works well, having even performed as Electra, another of his suffering heroines.

40.   Warner, trans., p. 71.

hero. He has a heroic frame, a vigorous manner, and a "highly-coloured, well-visored countenance" which shines with "a good opinion of himself and of the world" (p. 57). His dark hair accents a strong-featured face whose "beaked nose" is "like the prow of a ship, with long nostrils" (p. 42). Ellinger's reputation precedes him, as did Jason's, and even in describing his attitude toward life, Cather uses imagery of a seafarer: "In Denver, Frank was known as a prince of good fellows; tactful, generous, resourceful, though apt to trim his sails to the wind; a man who good humouredly bowed to the inevitable or to the almost-inevitable" (p. 45). So must the Argonauts have perceived of their leader upon whom the gods seemed to smile. Women, like Constance Ogden, are attracted to Ellinger's good looks and manly behavior. His magnetism lures Marian Forrester to be unfaithful to her husband, a man who is more a father figure than lover, just as Jason enticed Medea to betray her own father and her country.

The closest parallels to ancient myth appear, however, in the powerful scene when Mrs. Forrester learns of Ellinger's marriage to Constance Ogden. Her resentment of Frank's desertion is coupled with humiliation. Like Medea, her strength comes from the singularity of purpose – to return hurt for hurt. Cather writes that Mrs. Forrester's "blue lips, the black shadows under her eyes, made her look as if some poison were at work in her body" (p. 131). Mrs. Forrester's appearance deteriorates as she becomes more confined to her home and turns to alcohol for solace. Like Medea, who in the opening scene of the ancient drama is wasting away in tears, Marian Forrester suffers intensely in her isolation and withers from her lover's betrayal. The poison in her soul reminds one of the magical arts of Medea, Circe's niece and worshiper of Hecate, whose potions could cure or destroy.

When she reads in a Denver paper that Frank is married, Mrs. Forrester takes extreme measures, even exposing herself to death by crossing a swollen creek on a partially washed-out bridge. She is a desperate woman but considers Constance Ogden a defeatable rival, just as Medea considered Jason's new wife Glauce a less than formidable enemy. After trying to maintain her composure and to allow reason to control her passion, Mrs. Forrester finally shrieks at her traitorous lover, "You know, Frank, the truth is that you're a coward; a great, hulking coward. Do you hear me? I want you to hear!" (p. 134). Medea had reviled her unfaithful husband with the same charge: "O coward in every way— that is what I call you,/ with bitterest reproach for your lack of manliness....."[41] Jason's only defense for his actions is that he married the princess Glauce so that Medea and his sons might live well and in comfort. Marian Forrester suspects Frank Ellinger of similar economic motives: "You've got a safe thing at last, I should think, safe and pasty! How much stock did you get with it? A big block, I hope!" (p. 134). In the final estimate, Frank is hardly better than Ivy Peters. He uses Marian Forrester for pleasure until it is in his best interests to ally himself with a younger and wealthier woman.

Cather surely concurred with the plea of the Chorus of *The Medea* when they sang of the inversion of roles in which women had traditionally been considered faithless:

> Flow backward to your sources, sacred rivers,
> And let the world's great order be reversed.
> It is the thoughts of *men* that are deceitful,
> *Their* pledges that are loose.
> Story shall now turn my condition to a fair one,
> Women are paid their due.
> No more shall evil-sounding fame be theirs.[42]

Marian Forrester falls victim to man's faithlessness as a new order evolves on the plains, displacing the golden age of matriarchy. New standards exist in her broken world and, like Medea, who was exiled by the "good" Creon, Marian Forrester must submit or escape. Cather clearly recognized, as did the ancient Greek playwright, that the primary forces disrupting the world's order were no more than blind passions. Of these passions, though, love like Marian Forrester's could offer little defense against the greed, ambition, and dominance of men like Frank Ellinger and Ivy Peters.

Niel is also caught up in patriarchal values of this new society and finds it easy to condemn woman for her fall from grace. He exerts a kind of

---

41.   Warner, trans., p. 79.

42.   Warner, trans., p. 78.

guardianship over Mrs. Forrester, cutting the phone cord before she muddies her reputation. He "chucks" school for a year to stay at the Forresters and to help them to regain their equilibrium. But, disguised by such protective measures lies an aggressive paternalism. When Marian Forrester fails to conform to his expectations out of gratitude for his manly "sacrifices," Niel, too, becomes a Jason, condemning her for not being willing "to immolate herself, like the widow of all these great men, and die with the pioneer period to which she belonged..." (p. 172). He resents that Marian will not accept the "end of an era," whose "glory was nearly spent" (p. 171). But, true to her Medean role, Marian Forrester goes on, preferring "life on any terms" (p.172). Her terms are a blending of the refined graciousness of Artemis, the fearful sorcery of Hecate, and the passionate vitality of Aphrodite. Just as Medea leaves behind the scene of her humiliation and betrayal, Marian Forrester disappears, supposedly going back to California. Only years later does anyone learn of her subsequent marriage to a wealthy Englishman who lives in Buenos Aires and who, like Medea's second husband, King Aegeus of Athens, has been married twice before. Such an end for Marian Forrester is quite apropos and is in keeping with the classical myth which underscores the novel. Moreover, the final scene allows Niel Herbert the opportunity to show his understanding of the changes taking place in his world.

One must consider as genuine Niel's remark that he is glad Marian Forrester "was well cared for, to the very end..." (p. 178). For, in spite of Niel's pose as a part of the ascendant patriarchy, he is one of the few who recognizes that in male dominance lies the death of a natural order of things. In his early worship of Mrs. Forrester as Artemis, a mother goddess, Niel associated her with inviolable beauty, chastity, and the wild things of nature. The bleakness of commercial success in a masculine world could offer him no such values. Time after time, Niel turns to his memories of Mrs. Forrester when he is "dull and tired of everything" (p. 67). She remains "a bright, impersonal memory" and a presence with "the power of suggesting things much lovelier than herself..." (pp. 174-175). The last glimpse both Niel and the reader has of Marian Forrester shows her, like a huntress-goddess, swathed in furs and wearing over her head a scarf, undoubtedly crimson in color. Her rich laugh is unchanged and her power to entrance, undiminished.

She is not Hippolytus' ideal, for she has been forced to compromise to Aphrodite in order to survive in a new age. What she evokes for Niel are beautiful memories and a sense of guilt. Unlike many of his male contemporaries, Niel realizes that Marian has lived only as men's expectations and her own misdirected passion have allowed her to. Caught between conflicting ideals in the post-pioneer era, Marian Forrester can only survive as a Medea, as beauty coupled with corruption. Cather's tone of despair is evident in this most perfectly wrought of her novels, and it foreshadows the pessimism of her next two novels, *The Professor's House* and *My Mortal Enemy*.

CHAPTER VIII
UNRECOVERABLE ORIGINS: THE MYTHIC QUESTS OF GODFREY ST. PETER AND MYRA HENSHAWE

Affected by a growing sense of alienation and pessimism in the early 1920's, Willa Cather searched for an unshakable support for the ideals and traditions which she believed essential to both her own well being and society's. Her decision in 1922 to join the newly established Episcopal Church of Red Cloud is an indication of her efforts to come to grips with the doubts, disillusionment, and general malaise which she was then experiencing. These feelings surface in *The Professor's House*, a novel which Cather began writing in 1923. Like her principal character, Godfrey St. Peter, Cather was soon to be fifty-two years old and found herself in a world which no longer advocated the values of pioneer ancestors, but preferred the ease and glittering comforts of modernity. St. Peter confronts the same situation, and his story becomes what James Woodress calls "a kind of spiritual autobiography"[1] for Willa Cather. The sense of retreat and the physical withdrawal displayed by Prof. St. Peter parallel Cather's own increasingly private style of living, a style which assured her a means of self-preservation as an artist. Grand Manan Island and her Bank Street apartment became havens like the Professor's attic room where one could look out on the world,

---

1.   James Woodress, *Willa Cather: Her Life and Art* (1970; rpt. Lincoln: Univ. of Nebraska Press, 1982), p. 207.

as if through the open window in a Dutch painting, without being an active participant in that world.

Criticism of *The Professor's House* has largely concentrated on these biographical parallels or on thematic studies. Susan Rosowski in *The Voyage Perilous* accords the novel a central position in her discussion of the romantic imagination as the means of directing salvation, while Merrill M. Skaggs argues for the novel as initiating a "four novel span of works" which explores the relationship between art and religion in an increasingly materialistic society.[2] Other critics have focused on source studies, ranging from movements in art (see Particia Yongue on Dutch genre painting and Jean Schwind on nineteenth-century precedents) and musical parallels (see Richard Giannone). While these analyses provide some illuminating insights, they prove inadequate for understanding the concomitant imagery which characterizes *The Professor's House* and makes it a key transitional work in the Cather canon.

The Professor's House begins more explicitly to develop Cather's dialectic between the imagery from classical myth and allusions to Christian myth. In Book I of the novel, "The Family," Cather draws upon the pattern of imagery through which she had expressed her bitterness at the loss of Artemisian and pioneer ideals in *A Lost Lady*. Professor St. Peter's world, like Niel Herbert's, is distorted by the Aphrodisian drive for immediate gratification, an impulse which results in materialism, greed, and envy. Even the Professor's life has been affected by money. The Professor's recently awarded Oxford prize for history brings him five thousand pounds and an international reputation. He is intolerant of "depressing and unnecessary ugliness,"[3] such as he finds at Prof. Crane's house, and recognizes the selfish pleasure his friend takes in "doing without many so-called necessities" so as to have a few personal luxuries (pp. 26-27). Lillian St. Peter is even more affected by such materialism and delights in the lavish wealth of her son-in-law Louie Marsellus. Rosamond engages in spending sprees in Chicago, and

2.   Merrill Maquire Skaggs, "A Glance Into *The Professor's House*: Inward and Outward Bound," *Renascence*, 39, No. 3 (Spring 1987), 422.

3.   Willa Cather, *The Professor's House* (New York: Alfred A. Knopf, 1925), p. 142. All further references to this novel will be cited parenthetically in the text by page number.

Louie enthusiastically applauds the tasteless montage of styles which will "grace" their country retreat. This undeveloped aesthetic sense, which Cather believed characterized the post-war generation, is a far remove from the Artemisian values of a Claude Wheeler, Thea Kronborg, or Alexandra Bergson. *Ars gratia artis* (art for the sake of art) has given way to *ars gratia ostentationis* (art for the sake of show).

Like Edith Wharton, Cather portrays in *The Professor's House* the turmoil of the world within the microcosm of the family, as familial love decays before the love of gold. Kitty and Scott McGregor feel only envy for the Marselluses' wealth, which they consider an affront to their honest, but insubstantial income. Money initiates a jealous vengeance, and Kitty feels hate coming toward her when Rosamond approaches. Jealousy and spite also cause her to ridicule Louie for being a Jew, and Scott's monetary grievance leads him to bar Louie from the Arts and Letters Club. John Gleason, in "The 'Case' of Willa Cather," proposes that the dichotomy between the two verbs "to love" and "to buy," both of which Cather singles out in the novel (pp. 264 and 154), becomes the focus of *The Professor's House*, for in their juxtaposition, Cather defines "the polarities of the old American and the new."[4]

But, Cather may not have emphasized these words to indicate their opposition. The infinitives "to love" and "to buy" both define Aphrodisian impulses, and the former is not necessarily the pure and unselfish love which Gleason supposes Cather intends. St. Peter confesses to having conjugated "to love" in his youth, a comment which implies the elementary stages of learning Latin when *amo* is the principal verb studied. Cather was enough of a Latinist to know that *amo* (interestingly phonetically similar to *emo*, "buy") connotes pleasure and passion, as opposed to *diligo*, connoting esteem and high regard. Prof. St. Peter has been victimized by both the forces of passion and acquisitiveness; he is as much a "new" American in this sense as is Louie. His compulsion "to love," he remarks, "reached its maturity" when he met Lillian and "From that time...existence had been a catching at

---

4.   John B. Gleason, "The 'Case' of Willa Cather," *Western American Literature*, 20 (Winter 1986), 293.

handholds...had been shaped by all the penalties and responsibilities of being and having been a lover" (pp. 264-65). Rather than juxtaposing these verbs, then, as a means of identifying St. Peter with the "old American" (solely the aesthetic lover) and Louie Marsellus with the "new" (the profligate buyer), Cather reinforces her mythic imagery with these selected verbs and shows Aphrodite as the dominant power affecting both St. Peter and her other characters (the deceased Tom Outland excepted).

The theme was not new for Cather. In *A Lost Lady*, she had depicted Marian Forrester as a devotee to the pleasures of life offered by Aphrodite, and only through cooperation with the grasping Ivy Peters could she survive in the manner she desired. What Godfrey St. Peter discovers, however, is that he is not suited to such a world and, as Niel Herbert says of Marian Forrester, should have died with the period to which he belonged. His career was meaningful when he struggled, unrecognized, to create a book worthy of praise. But prosperity undermines the nobility of the struggle and, like the American society itself, his life is cheapened accordingly. The physical fatigue which descends upon St. Peter is an acknowledgment of his "falling out of all domestic and social relations, out of his place in the human family..."(p. 275).

In Book I, then, St. Peter embodies the concerns and regrets of Willa Cather as she grieved over the loss of pioneer values. In her first novels, Cather had heralded the mythic matriarchy whose values were tied to the land. This Golden Age she had seen decline before a patriarchal system which worshiped Aphrodite, instant gratification, and crass materialism. *The Professor's House* becomes her vehicle for a search for origins, for the recovery of a world untainted by materialism and dedicated to the struggle to create something lasting.

This is a mythic quest, and in Book II Cather chooses a world of mythic dimensions as her landscape for the search. In "Tom Outland's Story," a tension develops between classical and Christian mythic allusions, a tension which foreshadows the religious dimensions of the later novels, *Death Comes for the Archbishop*, *Shadows on the Rock*, and *Sapphira and the Slave Girl*. The account of Tom Outland's adventures, though, reflects Cather's continuing concern with the demise of the matriarchy, a loss of a Golden

Age, while introducing a search for a patriarchy which could serve as a suitable substitute for undergirding society. In this search, the Blue Mesa and its archaeological remains become the novel's focal point for understanding the tension which obtains between Cather's imagery from classical and Christian myth.

The Blue Mesa, like the lost civilization of ancient Crete, stands as an ageless symbol of the greater human family and of cultural sophistication, an idea which Father Duchene first notes:

> "The shapes and decorations of the water jars and food bowls is better than in any of the existing pueblos I know....I have seen a collection of early pottery from the island of Crete. Many of the geometrical decorations on these jars are not only similar, but, if my memory is trustworthy, identical." (pp. 219-220)

As in the early Cretan culture, these vanished Indians celebrated the arts of peace, raising no fortifications but finding delight in cultivating crops, crafting objects of art, and observing religious ceremonies. These were the values of a matriarchal system, an origin-culture like Crete, presided over by a fertility goddess to whom both the serpent and cow were sacred. The Cretans, too, had a "genuine taste for intimacy and a peaceful domestic life ....[They] excelled in the so-called minor arts: painted pottery, jewellery and finely carved precious stones."[5] On her first visit to Mesa Verde in 1915, Cather had been immediately aware of the tranquillity of ancient life on the Mesa and of the Cliff Dwellers' "successful evasion of ugliness." Her article, published on January 31, 1916, in *The Denver Times*, goes on to praise their "tempered, settled, ritualistic life, where generations went on gravely and reverently repeating the past, rather than battling for anything new."[6] The Cliff Dwellers' pottery, so similar to that which she undoubtedly recognized from her classical studies, was merely an emblem of such satisfied living.

Cather carefully weaves together images of the Cretan world and the Blue Mesa, making the remnants of this southwestern culture the reminder of "some extinct civilization" (p. 202), of a lost Golden Age. The cliff villages hang like beehives on the canyon walls, and one is reminded that the bee

5. Henri-Paul Eydoux, *In Search of Lost Worlds*, trans. Lorna Andrade (New York: Hamlyn, 1972), p. 176.

6. Willa Sibert Cather, "Mesa Verde Wonderland Is Easy to Reach," 31 Jan. 1916, *The Denver Times*, rpt. in Susan J. Rosowski and Bernice Slote, "Willa Cather's 1916 Mesa Verde Essay: The Genesis of *The Professor's House*," *Prairie Schooner*, 58 (Winter 1984), 84-85.

224

was, for the ancients, both the symbol of order and of the Earth Mother. These dwellings form a jumble of houses, "nestling close to one another, perched on top of each other, with flat roofs, narrow windows, straight walls..." (p. 201). Cather's description could as easily apply to the labyrinthine palace of Minos at Knossos where an entire cultural family lived together in harmonious proximity. Such a parallel to Crete may have arisen, in part, from Cather's acquaintance with Gustaf Nordenskjold's 1893 work *The Cliff Dwellers of the Mesa Verde*. Besides his detailed analysis of the artistic and agricultural achievements of this people, Nordenskjold frequently alludes to the readily apparent labyrinthine aspects of the cañons and dwellings.[7] Moreover, just as Crete was a thalassocracy, an empire isolated and protected by the seas around it, the Blue Mesa is surrounded by "an ocean of clear air" (p. 213) and is encircled by a deep, fast-flowing river.

In describing Tom Outland's first journey to the Mesa, Cather relies heavily upon the account of Richard Wetherill's discovery, a story she heard from Wetherill's brother, but she adds a new dimension to that account by suggesting classical comparisons. Nordenskjold's early work describes Richard Wetherill and Charley Mason's accidental discovery of the Cliff Palace "as they were riding together through the piñon wood on the mesa, in search of a stray herd":

> They had penetrated through the dense scrub to the edge of a deep cañon. In the opposite cliff, sheltered by a huge, massive vault of rock, there lay before their astonished eyes a whole town with towers and walls, rising out of a heap of ruins.[8]

Such understated phrases as "astonished eyes" and the objective recounting do credit to Nordenskjold as a scientist but hardly accord with the feeling of suspense Cather recorded in her 1916 essay:

> [Richard Wetherill] rode off with one of his cow men and they entered the mesa by a deep cañon from the Mancos river, which flows at its base. They followed the cañon toward the heart of the mesa until they could go no farther with horses....After a long stretch of hard climbing young Wetherill happened to glance up at the great cliffs above him, and there thru a veil of lightly falling snow, he saw...the cliff palace....[9]

---

7.   D. Lloyd Morgan, trans., *The Cliff Dwellers of the Mesa Verde, Southwestern Colorado, Their Pottery and Implements*, by G. Nordenskiold (Chicago: P. A. Norstedt and Soner, 1893; rpt. New York: AMS Press, 1973), pp. 12 and 60.

8.   Morgan, trans., p. 12.

9.   Cather, qtd. in Rosowski and Slote, pp. 83-84.

Some nine years later, the story reemerged in *The Professor's House* and was then charged with religious awe. The Mesa "loom[s] up above the dark river like a blazing volcanic mountain" and the lightning plays around it (pp. 192-193). Tom Outland, like a Moses before the Mountain of God, is both bothered and tempted by the rock's presence. His climbing to the "sacred mountain" expands into several pages, with each step of the discovery taking on greater import, like the exploits of some mythic hero.

Tom overcomes his first obstacle by swimming the cold river in a kind of baptism of the spirit. As he crosses the valley beneath the Mesa, Tom thinks that nothing "tasted so pure as the air in that valley," and it produces "a kind of exultation" in him (p. 200). (While the crossing offers comparison to Christian baptism, it likewise suggests crossing Lethe into the Elysian Fields, a classical image which surely did not escape Cather.) Abandoning his horse, Tom scrambles among the rocks in his ascent, successfully evading "a slip of the foot [that] might cripple one" (p. 210). His heroic endeavor is rewarded with the first glimpse of the cliff city:

> I wish I could tell you what I saw there, just *as* I saw it, on that first morning, through a veil of lightly falling snow. Far up above me, a thousand feet or so, set in a great cavern in the face of the cliff, I saw a little city of stone, asleep. It was as still as sculpture – and something like that.... Such silence and stillness and repose – immortal repose. That village sat looking down into the canyon with the calmness of eternity. (p. 201)

His wonderment is that of the singular man suddenly confronted by the immense and the eternal. Cather imbues her scene with the same sense of awe as did Keats in "On First Looking Into Chapman's Homer." Like "stout Cortez," Tom stares in wonder, "Silent, upon a peak in Darien." The historical record of the Mesa's discovery assumes a larger meaning, "a reality that goes deeper than the bustling business of the world," as Cather wrote.[10]

Cather extends the sense of romance even further by allowing Tom's experience to echo that of another classically heroic figure – Theseus – who, perhaps inadvertently, led to the despoiling of a culture. In his pursuit of the cattle which have wandered into Cow Canyon, Tom is much like the ancient

---

10.   Cather, qtd. in Rosowski and Slote, p. 86.

hero recapturing the herds carried off by Pirithous. Tom Outland, too, crosses the water to enter a Minoan-like world where the cow-goddess was worshiped and where the horns of the wild goat made "something noble about him ... like a priest" (p. 214). A religious solemnity engulfs the Mesa, and Father Duchene verbalizes Tom's own feelings:

> "Like you, I feel a reverence for this place. Wherever humanity has made the hardest of all starts and lifted itself out of mere brutality, is a sacred spot. Your people were cut off here without the influence of example or emulation, with no incentive but some natural yearning for order and security. They built themselves into this mesa and humanized it." (p. 221)

Father Duchene further suggests that perhaps Cliff Dwellers were "too far advanced for their time and environment" (p. 221) and fell victim to invaders who felt no reverence for this culture, situated in "pure and uncontaminated" air (p. 200). The Mycenean invasion of Crete offers a parallel. The patriarchal and war-like forces of the Greek mainland must have little appreciated the civilization they subdued. Like the Cliff Dwellers, after this invasion all that remained of the Minoan Golden Age was "the calmness of eternity" (p. 201). What Tom Outland and Prof. St. Peter find in the great mesa, then, is what Cather saw in looking back to a noble past – the dignity of human striving and its harmonious resolution. Here begins Cather's and her characters' search for a replacement, but not a return to, lost roots, a search for a mythic golden age.

Tom Outland's search for roots becomes the prototype for St. Peter's search and explains to a great degree St. Peter's dissatisfaction with life. While the novel's insert narrative, "Tom Outland's Story," may be "a technical mistake that has damned the book," as Alfred Kazin claims,[11] it is no thematic mistake in light of the novel's substructure of mythic quest. Outland's story is the quest of the male, epic hero who, cast out from his homeland, strives to find a *patria* which preserves his own heritage. Unlike the epic hero of classical literature, and Vergil's Aeneas specifically, Outland (as well as St. Peter) is displaced in time rather than by geography. As an

---

11.   Alfred Kazin, "Elegy: Willa Cather," in *Modern Critical Views: Willa Cather*, ed. Harold Bloom (New York: Chelsea House Publishers, 1985), p. 22.

orphan, Tom searches for paternal origins; he moves about in a world of men accompanied by his own "faithful Achates," Roddy Blake. Cather stresses that while studying the cliff-dwelling culture Tom turns again and again to Vergil's *Aeneid*, an ancient record of the fall of civilization before barbaric forces. Undoubtedly Cather saw in post-World War I society the same demise of values, religion, and the arts which Vergil pictured in the Greek conquest of Troy. Upon his return from Washington, Tom, who is sensitive to this loss, approaches the Mesa with Vergilian filial piety:

> The excitement of my first discovery was a very pale feeling compared to this one. For me the mesa was no longer an adventure, but a religious emotion. I had read of filial piety in the Latin poets, and I knew that was what I felt from this place. I had formerly been mixed up with other motives but now that they were gone, I had my happiness unalloyed. (p. 251)

Tom's respect for this lost civilization quells his youthful adventuresome spirit, much as Aeneas is committed to fulfilling his destiny after descending to Hades and hearing his father's prophecy. For the fatherless Tom, the Mesa offers a restorative and nurturing relationship with paternal origins. He has wandered without direction much like the outcasts about whom he reads – Gulliver, Robinson Crusoe, and Aeneas. The round tower in the middle of the "pale little houses" draws Tom's attention and is the symbol of the paternity for which he searches:

> It was beautifully proportioned, that tower, swelling out to a larger girth a little above the base, then growing slender again. There was something symmetrical and powerful about the swell of the masonry. The tower was the fine thing that held all the jumble of houses together and made them mean something. (p. 201)

Father Duchene later suggests that the tower is not a watch tower for war but for astronomical observation, the ancients' means of determining the future and individual destinies. Tom turns to paternal order, to an Olympian hierarchy, as a means of ordering his universe. He draws upon "solar energy in some direct way" (p. 251), finding a new source of strength in what seems the natural order of things. The sun is a mythic, masculine power, displacing the goddesses of earth as did Apollo in subduing the Python.

228

But, Tom's epic quest is not a consoling one, for the myth upon which it is based is one of loss as well as triumph. He commits to memory long passages of Book II of Vergil's epic, and this book begins with foreboding:

> Infandum, regina, iubes renovare dolorem,
> Troianas ut opes et lamentabile regnum
> eruerint Danai, quaeque ipse miserrima vidi
> et quorum pars magna fui. (II. 3-6)

> "Beyond all words, O queen, is the grief thou
> bidst me revive, how the Greeks overthrew Troy's
> wealth and woeful realm – the sights most piteous
> that I myself saw and whereof I was no small part."[12]

Tom is deceived in his devotion to a patriarchal order as a means of redeeming his culture. Tom's "fidus Achates" proves unfaithful to his dream and innocently sells the Indian artifacts to the highest bidder. Tom cannot preserve his new-found utopia, nor can he find a patriarchal system supportive of beauty and peace. What Tom Outland fails to realize is that filial piety, Vergilian *pietas*, constitutes love of *mother*, as well as love of God and country.[13]

And, inherent in Tom's search for paternity is a rejection of traditional matriarchy. Cather describes this search in terms of Christian rather than classical myth, and Christian myth, while celebratory of the Virgin, simultaneously points to woman as the cause of a lost utopia. In his desire to recover the peace and orderliness of Eden before the Fall, Tom must reject Eve and, in so doing, violates *pietas* as well. (One is reminded that Aeneas' demonstrated *pietas* involves devotion to his mother Venus, a figure often associated with Eve and the passions that corrupted a male-dominated system.) No Eve exists in Tom's Eden; only he, Henry Atkins, and Roddy Blake disturb the quiet of the mesa. Eden, at first, seems recoverable since neither a tempter nor temptress is present.

---

12. H. Rushton Fairclough, trans., *The Aeneid*, by Vergil, in *Virgil: Eclogues, Georgics, Aeneid I-VI*, ed. T. E. Page, E. Capps, and W. H. D. Rouse (New York: G. P. Putnam's Sons, 1929), p. 295.

13. I am indebted to my colleague John Shields, whose on-going work on *The American Aeneas: Classicism and Early American Culture*, inspired the following reading of Tom Outland's story in light of the Roman ideal of *pietas*.

The great adobe tower rises undisturbed and triumphant from the cedar-fringed grotto, a female symbol. Yet, in his paternal tower Tom finds betrayal. The governmental agents in Washington, D.C., representatives of the country's fatherhood, reject Tom's appeal to preserve the Cliff City. Like the great god who drives his finest creation from the garden, Washington rejects its children, both Tom Outland and the Cliff Dwellers. The serpent in this Eden is materialism, and Cather does not omit the symbol in her story. Henry Atkins dies from rattlesnake bite.

The most evident Edenic association occurs in Tom's naming the preserved Indian corpse "Mother Eve." From her acquaintance with Nordenskjold's work and from her own visit to the Mesa, Cather gleaned the archaeological details about such mummies and recorded faithfully the details of burial. Yet, she departs markedly from the historical text by having Tom observe "Mother Eve" to have died "as if she were screaming" (p. 214) and with a gaping wound still evident in her side. No speculation about such agonizing death was recorded by Nordenskjold, and, in most cases, he did not even attempt to determine the sex of mummified remains. Cather, however, uses such details to highlight the personal quest of Tom Outland and to underscore Tom's failed sense of *pietas*. While Tom claims to revere Mother Eve as the most precious of all his finds, he apparently accepts Father Duchene's explanation that the woman's violent death was the result of her infidelity:

> "I seem to smell," he said slyly, "a personal tragedy.... Perhaps her husband thought it worth while to return unannounced from the farms some night, and found her in improper company. The young man may have escaped. In primitive society the husband is allowed to punish an unfaithful wife with death." (p. 223)

Mother Eve becomes just another woman as betrayer, the Helen of an Indian Troy and the spoiler of a masculine paradise.

Tom, perhaps unconsciously, reveals his preference for a patriarchal system where men do escape the natural corruption of womanhood. Tom wants to establish identity with mankind and to recover Eden; he would prefer to blame womankind if that recovery proves impossible. In *The Professor's House* this expulsion from Eden, whether described as the extinction of Minoan Crete or of the Cliff Dwellers, ends in death. The paternal protection Tom seeks fails to save him. Tom Outland's death in World War I – the action of a male-dominated society – ensures that he will not face the disillusionment of the failed patriarchy. Tom never becomes, then, fully the classical epic hero, for he fulfills only a part of the demands of *pietas* and rejects "love of mother." Instead, his failed search and unconscious bias toward patriarchy characterize the tension between pre-Olympian and Christian values which Cather illustrates throughout *The Professor's House*. For Cather, too, the matriarchy is gone and the masculine world of the twentieth century offers no redemption for paradise lost.

Godfrey St. Peter's situation is Tom Outland's; he, too, searches for a lost self, which in his case lies behind the "secondary social man" (p. 265). St. Peter has found little consolation for his predicament as a castaway in time, and he rejects the modern representatives of womanhood whom he considers the source of distorted values. In his search for a lost self, for the freedom and simplicity of a child on the prairie, St. Peter resents the interference of women. He takes on the appearance of an ancient warrior waging a silent battle against the established matriarchy. His southern European look is heightened by silky black hair and by a deep tan in summer – the color of terra-cotta. His son-in-law notes that the Professor's head in its swimming visor "looked sheathed and small and intensely alive, like the heads of the warriors on the Parthenon frieze in the tight, archaic helmets" (p. 71). Furthermore, St. Peter finds his greatest freedom in male companionship, when in his garden or at the beach, two places unfrequented by the women of his household. He relishes the long summers when his wife and daughters vacation in Colorado, leaving him to be "a bachelor again" (p. 15) and letting him work in his garden under the trees. This carefully planned French garden has all the orderliness of Tom's catalogued shelves of Indian relics, and here St. Peter and Tom sat and talked throughout summer nights. It is an Edenic garden, rampant with blooming flowers and glistening shrubs set against a white wall. Similarly, the beach front St. Peter owns is a haven for only himself, his sons-in-law, and a few male acquaintances. The blue of Lake Michigan awakens his memories of the Mediterranean, where fifteen years earlier he was inspired to write his history of the Spanish adventurers. No women played a role in his creative inspiration; no women are present in his retreats to spoil his dreams.

This is not to say that Prof. St. Peter feels no affection for his wife and daughters, but for him, women interfere with creativity. Such an opinion stands in direct contrast to the role Cather believed women had held in earlier years. As pioneer mother, woman had stimulated growth and encouraged creativity, but as Cather shows in *A Lost Lady*, the world had changed. Aphrodite ruled and whetted the appetites of men for both possessions and power but left women to make their ways by wiles and deceit. The Professor is not unaware of this change and does exhibit genuine regret for both his personal and society's collective loss. While at the opera, St. Peter is touched by the youthful gentleness that returns to Lillian St. Peter's countenance, and he remarks, "We should have been picturesquely shipwrecked together when we were young" (p. 94). Significantly, though, when that night he envisions such a shipwreck, "his wife was not in it":

> Indeed, nobody was in it but himself, and a weather-dried little sea captain from the Hautes-Pyrenees, half a dozen spry seamen, and a line of gleaming snow peaks, agonizingly high and sharp, along the southern coast of Spain. (p. 95)

St. Peter returns to the scene of his moment of greatest creativity, and, as in Tom's discovery of Cliff City, women are conspicuously absent.

The Professor is likewise disappointed in his two daughters. Rosamond parades her wealth, most of which she has acquired through exploitation of Tom Outland's engine design, and only grudgingly shares it with others. St. Peter attributes such lack of generosity not just to Rosamond but to all women. The Professor is, however, very defensive of his own paternal role. Upon returning from a shopping trip with Rosie to Chicago, he remarks, "I am quite ready to permit myself a little extravagance to be of service to the women of my family. Any other arrangement is humiliating" (p. 155). St. Peter will not admit an inferior position, not even a financial one, to any woman; he must not succumb to the power of what be believes to be a corrupted matriarchy. He rather shallowly concludes that he is much like Euripides who fled to a cave to live out his years, and St. Peter wonders "whether it was because he had observed women so closely all his life" (p. 156).

The pettiness of his younger daughter Kitty makes St. Peter even more wary of womanhood. His "special kind of affection" (p. 88) for Kitty is dampened when she actually becomes green with envy for her sister's good fortune. From their father's view, Rosie has indeed grown thorns and Kitty's claws are bared. The petty vindictiveness, which St. Peter observes in his own family, he projects onto an entire sex, and he then muses with an almost misogynistic cruelty that perhaps Euripides had offered a solution: "When a man had lovely children in his house, fragrant and happy, full of pretty fancies and generous impulses, why couldn't he keep them? Was there no way but Medea's, he wondered?" (p. 126). The situation of the ancient drama is, of course, reversed in Cather's novel, for here the father, not the mother, contemplates destroying not sons, but daughters. St. Peter certainly does not consider seriously this course of action, but the female powers which once initiated growth and encouraged creativity had changed. Was there no way to regain that better time?

Cather offers perhaps the most obvious exploration of this theme in her description of St. Peter's attic room and its sewing mannequins. St. Peter is particularly attached to these mock images of women which he shares with Augusta but refuses to relinquish to her. The forms are, at once, both attractive and repulsive, drawing him to them as representatives of an unspoiled, primeval matriarchy and driving him from them as symbols of forces undermining the patriarchal utopia he longs for. The matronly "bust" appears soft, but when touched, the form is lumpy and hard, "the most unsympathetic surface imaginable" (p. 18). The "full-length female figure in a smart wire skirt with a trim metal waist line" (p. 18) is woman as erotic creature, an alluring Aphrodite, appealing in physical beauty but hollow inside. As St. Peter rather smugly comments, "He had his blind spots, but he had never been taken in by one of her kind!" (p. 19). Godfrey St. Peter's refusal to give up the forms is both an assertion of masculine domination and an admission of masculine needs. They recall to him "certain disappointments" and "cruel biological necessities" (p. 21). His study room is not Tom Outland's open spaces of the Mesa where the male symbol (the tower) stands triumphant over female symbols (the grotto). In the attic room, St. Peter is, instead, haunted by forms of what women seem to have become – cold Dianas or alluring Aphrodites. His only hope of survival is to possess these women, and to possess them exclusively, as Leon Edel argues.[14]

Since Prof. St. Peter thinks he is out of step with the new culture, which spends money so easily and craves amusement more than it appreciates beauty, he feels cast adrift even from his own family. St. Peter embarks upon the same search for paternal roots that Tom Outland followed. In many ways, St. Peter is also fatherless. He tells Augusta, "You'll never convert me back to the religion of my fathers now..." (p. 24), and he rejects the inherited family name "Napoleon." When Rosamond displays a cool and "faultless purchasing manner," St. Peter remarks that she is "like Napoleon looting the Italian palaces" (p. 154). In his refusal to be Napoleon, St. Peter breaks with a cultural heritage of grasping materialism and destruction of beautiful things. But, orphaned in a new age, St. Peter begins a mythic quest to recover a strong, paternal figure. Although be finds Louie Marsellus "magnanimous and magnificent" (p. 170), St. Peter cannot accept unequivocally the "new man" any more than he can accept the "new woman." Whereas Marsellus sees nothing sinister about the new order that he and others like him – engineers and financiers – are establishing, St. Peter turns back in pursuit of mythic origins, and particularly of a masculine world unaffected by "women's corruption."

St. Peter's attempted recovery of the patriarchy leads him not to age but to youth – to Tom Outland. Tom satisfies St. Peter's need for spiritual companionship,[15] and Tom becomes for St. Peter a mythic father. He brings St. Peter to a rebirth, a self-genesis through rediscovered filiation. On first

---

14. Leon Edel, "A Cave of One's Own," in *Critical Essays on Willa Cather*, ed. John J. Murphy (Boston: G. K. Hall and Co., 1984), p. 207.

15. Bernice Slote, in her Introduction to *Uncle Valentine and Other Stories: Willa Cather's Uncollected Short Fiction 1915-1929*, supports this view, describing the relationship between St. Peter and Tom as "emotional harmony." Slote points out that in several of Cather's works – *Alexander's Bridge*, "Her Boss," and *My Antonia* – a mature man, divided from the wife he loves but does not fully understand, finds companionship in a young person and that this communion assumes as archetypal significance (p. xiv).

meeting Tom Outland, St. Peter noted those fine lineaments and inherent strength of pioneer fathers:

> The first thing the Professor noticed about the visitor was his manly, mature voice – low, calm, experienced....The next thing he observed was the strong line of contrast below the young man's sandy hair – the very fair forehead which had been protected by his hat, and the reddish brown of his face, which had evidently been exposed to a stronger sun than the spring sun of Hamilton. The boy was fine-looking, he saw – tall and presumably well built.... (p. 112)

Tom exudes an elemental strength of association with the earth but couples this with an unusual aesthetic appreciation. St. Peter admires the delicacy with which Outland handles the ancient Indian water jars and later comments that Tom's hand "never handled things that were not the symbols of ideas" (p. 260). In such a man St. Peter easily finds a spiritual ally. When the Professor admits Tom to his inner sanctum, the attic room, Lillian St. Peter becomes cold toward the young man with whom she had previously found no fault. This alliance between the two men prevents the women of the St. Peter household from exerting power over the direction of their thought.

Within this same sex friendship that inspired creativity, roles are also inverted. St. Peter's relationship with Tom recalls the Professor to the role of sonship rather than fatherhood. The Professor virtually courts the boy in the summer months when the women of his family are absent, as if trying to win again a place in the primitive patriarchy which Tom represents to him. St. Peter prepares exquisite dinners for Tom, laying before him food fit for the gods:

> When he cooked a fine leg of lamb, saignant, well rubbed with garlic before it went into the pan, then he asked Outland to dinner. Over a dish of steaming asparagus, swathed in a napkin to keep it hot, and a bottle of sparkling Asti, they talked and watched night fall in the garden. (p. 176)

This is man's Eden, untainted by the female presence. Here St. Peter shares with Tom the philosophy of Lucretius, whose sentiments are much like the Professor's. Lucretius begins his *De Rerum Natura* by acknowledging the power of Venus (Aphrodite), without whose procreative urge the world would not move onward. Yet, Lucretius, like St. Peter, dismisses any deific powers at work in daily life, condemns luxury, and celebrates the simple life and beauty of nature. Lucretius applauds a time when under kingship – the earliest patriarchies – men were justly allotted wealth and success:

> They made division of the herds and lands
> According to men's qualities, their strength,
> Their wit, their beauty – virtues highly prized
> In those old days....

Such values, however, disappeared in Lucretius' world as they had in St. Peter's, primarily due to greed and vanity, the results of Aphrodite's influence:

> ...but later on, with wealth
> And the discovery of gold, the strong,
> The beautiful, all too easily forsook
> The path of honor ... [and] craved
> Power and fame, that their fortunes might stand
> On firm foundations, so they might enjoy
> The rich man's blessed life. What vanity![16]

Similar sentiments echo throughout Tom Outland's diary and cause St. Peter to remember a simpler time, namely his own youth. In his search for paternal roots, St. Peter strives to find again the "primitive" he was, the "original, unmodified Godfrey St. Peter" who communed with the natural world (pp. 263-265):

> He was not nearly so cultivated as Tom's old cliff-dwellers must have been – and yet he was terribly wise.... He seemed to know among other things, that he was solitary and must always be so; he had never married, never been a father. He was earth, and would return to earth. (p. 265)

The primal self for which he searches is not defined by gender and exists outside the limits imposed by gender.

Even the opera St. Peter attends with his wife underscores his search for his elemental self, from which he has been cut off by time. *Mignon* presents a search for identity which is the inverse of St. Peter's. Mignon remembers nothing of her childhood and is unknowingly transported to the homeland where her illness and pain of a lover's rejection are soothed by the discovery of her own father. Whereas Mignon, as daughter, finds a father in her *le pays*, St. Peter, a disaffected son, cannot recover his birthright. His

---

16.   Rolfe Humphries, trans., *Lucretius: The Way Things Are,* by Lucretius (Bloomington: Indiana Univ. Press, 1968), p. 191.

236

quest for mythic parentage never reaches a satisfactory conclusion. All the things that had "nothing to do with the person he was in the beginning" (p. 264)–his career, wife, and family–interfere with his attempt to define his sonship. The only parental figure St. Peter recovers after Tom Outland's death is Louie Marsellus, whose racial origin, as John N. Swift notes, "evokes the ancient patriarchy of Judaism, and ultimately the first father of Eden." Swift goes on to argue that Louie's "archetypal fatherhood" becomes a reality at the end of the novel when he and Kitty are soon to become parents.[17] This announcement becomes, however, a precipitating cause for St. Peter's willing withdrawal from modern life, for in this new paternity is also inherent the death of the old system of pioneer values, a system of which St. Peter so desires to be part.

The Professor retreats to his attic room in his search for elemental truths, but he finds no nurturing mother there. The dress forms stand like empty vessels, offering no sustenance for growth. Nor is any paternal figure evident to guide St. Peter's psychological quest. He fails to attach himself to any ancient order of things: "Falling out, for him, seemed to mean falling out of all domestic and social relations, out of his place in the human family, indeed" (p. 275). Unable to ally himself with a mythic past, St. Peter finds the thought of "eternal solitude" no longer terrifying (pp. 272-274). In reveries about Tom Outland, the Professor briefly touches the elemental self which he had lost in his domestic and professional life. That self is recoverable only in the imagination, the repository of Truth, where gender distinctions are meaningless. In reawakening from his near-death state, St. Peter recognizes in Augusta the embodiment of this ideal: "St. Peter, with half-closed eyes, lay watching her–regarding in her humankind, as if after a definite absence from the world of men and women" (p. 279).

Cather does not allow a character, whose situation is so much like her own, to submit to "accidental extinction," as she calls it (p. 282). While writing the novel, Cather had passed through a period of personal crisis, but, as James Woodress notes, she "picked herself up" and began to get used to her

17.   John N. Swift, "Memory, Myth, and *The Professor's House*," *Western American Literature*, 20 (Winter 1986), 308.

growing fame, although she still required solitude for her writing.[18] So she considers it important that the Professor pick himself up or have someone do it for him. The timely arrival of Augusta, the St. Peter's seamstress, results in the Professor's revival, but Augusta is not a mother woman who comes to rescue an orphaned child. St. Peter does not relax his disdain for a dominant matriarchy and does not cling to the breast of a woman savior. She is neither female nor male to St. Peter but is only "solid earth...matter-of-factness and hard-handedness, kind and loyal" (p. 281). The primary trait she embodies is pioneer-like endurance of a petty life.

In accepting Augusta as one of the many in the world "with whom one was outward bound" (p. 281), Prof. St. Peter reflects that part of Willa Cather which Edith Lewis claimed was buried beneath the "legend of [her] inaccessibility and love of seclusion...." Lewis writes that Cather was always interested in people, perhaps because of "her instant recognition of their common humanity, of the fact that their claim on life was equal to her own."[19] St. Peter becomes part of the human family, having lost his driving passion to recover prehistorical patriarchy. The traditional values in which he believes will continue to be threatened by greed and materialism, but he can endure now, even if apathetically: "Theoretically he knew that life is possible, may be even pleasant, without joy, without passionate griefs. But it had never occurred to him that he might have to live like that" (p. 282). His lesson "on the nature of things" was long coming. St. Peter had conveniently overlooked this same message in his reading of Lucretius:

> Whereas, if man would regulate his life
> With proper wisdom, he would know that wealth,
> The greatest wealth, is living modestly,
> Serene, content with little.[20]

The Epicurean poet defined pleasure as the calm which proceeds from absence of pain and desire in one's life. In dying for an ideal that he still believed existed, Tom Outland had circumvented learning the lesson.

---

18. Woodress, p. 212.

19. Edith Lewis, *Willa Cather Living: A Personal Record* (New York: Alfred A. Knopf, 1953), p. 135.

20. Humphries, trans., p. 191.

In his quest for mythic origins, then, Prof. St. Peter commits himself to a new ideal, to the marriage of art to religion. This religion is not, for St. Peter or Willa Cather, the worship of mythic deities who contend with one another in quarrels and struggles for power. Such a conclusion on Cather's part may account for the developing dialectic between classical and Christian myth in this novel. A conflict of ideals raging between Aphrodite and Artemis, the quest of the epic hero, and the struggle for Olympian supremacy over the earth-mothers work with (and not against) Christian myth. Cather turned toward the selflessness of Christianity, coupled with the discipline of art, as the only means of coping with a materialistic world. St. Peter reconciles himself to his world, not by abandoning the noble past, but by transcending it. His "out-of-body," near-death experience takes on all the implications of a religious awakening, not unlike Tom Outland's baptism of the spirit. He becomes, like his namesake, a rock, impervious to personal desire, unscathed by the mundane world, but immovable in his devotion to the ideals of art.

When *The Professor's House* was published in September of 1925, Cather had nearly completed her next and perhaps most problematic work, *My Mortal Enemy*. Both Edith Lewis and Elizabeth Sergeant are unusually silent in reference to this novella, which stands as Cather's finished example of the unfurnished novel. But, the biographers' reluctance to deal with the circumstances surrounding the writing of *My Mortal Enemy* does not indicate an inferior artistic achievement. Cather felt that the book was important enough to be bound as a separate volume in spite of its brevity. The decision was not altogether pleasing to the critics in 1926 and may, in part, account for some of the negative opinions hurled against the work even forty years later. An early reviewer commented on "a creative tautness that robs it of warmth," and one modern critic views it as nothing more than "a hymn of hate against the present, so violent that it is not too surprising that in subsequent works she turned entirely to the past."[21] Indeed, a reader might easily agree with James Woodress that *My Mortal Enemy* is "the bitterest piece of fiction

---

21.   Rev. of *My Mortal Enemy*, by Willa Cather, *Dial*, 27 Jan. 1926, p. 73; John H. Randall, III, *The Landscape and The Looking Glass* (Boston: Houghton Mifflin Co., 1960), p. 155.

[Cather] wrote" but that it retains the "nostalgic, elegiac tone" of her best fiction.[22] In this alone, *My Mortal Enemy* seems closely tied to the pervasive mood of *The Professor's House*. But its importance in the Cather canon and to a study of her allusive art is more evident if one considers the mythic images which underscore the novel.

In keeping with the pattern of images developed in *One of Ours* and *A Lost Lady*, Cather describes her heroine as Greek goddess, this time as a combination of Artemis, Aphrodite, and Hera. Unlike Enid Royce, who conveniently passes out of the reader's view, and unlike Marian Forrester, who is whisked away to a better life in a remote land, Myra Henshawe does not fade into the background. Nor is a bitter diatribe leveled against womanhood on her account as occurs in *The Professor's House*. Rather, Cather brings to a conclusion the struggle for the supremacy of values which she had long described in mythic terms. Myra Henshawe dies, and with her dies the mother-figure. The novella is, therefore, of central importance in understanding Cather's reconciliation with the passing of this matriarchy and with her own world.

The view which Cather offers of her principal character is filtered through the eyes of young Nellie Birdseye, whose name alone signals the limitations of her insight into Myra's personality. Nellie is quick to perceive but is only one-sided in her view. With adolescent romanticism, Nellie sees Myra as the heroine who has sacrificed family and fortune for love. As Myra comments, Nellie is "moon-struck"; the girl sees Myra's elopement as fairy-tale romance and believes Myra's life "as exciting and varied as [hers] was monotonous."[23] The portrait Nellie draws of Myra is of a regal beauty, charming and, at the same time, threatening with a sarcasm "so quick, so fine at the point – it was like being touched by a metal so cold that one doesn't know whether one is burned or chilled" (p. 7). Whether Nellie's discomfort stems from feeling like a belittled and victimized daughter or from her immediate and strong attraction to Oswald Henshawe, the sense of something fearful about Myra is real.

22.   Woodress, pp. 213-214.

23.   Willa Cather, *My Mortal Enemy* (1926; rpt. New York: Random House, n.d.) pp. 26, 4. All further references to this work will be cited parenthetically in the text.

240

Nor is this the first instance in Cather's works of a woman in whose nature lurks a malignant evil. In 1916 Cather had depicted in "The Bookkeeper's Wife," an exquisitely beautiful woman who was the star on which the hard-working and morally upright Percy Bixby fixed his affection. Stella Bixby proves to be a selfish and cold wife who considers "position and pleasure worth the sacrifice of any other life."[24] Stella, though, is not totally responsible for the unhappiness in her marriage. Like Bertha Gray of "The Willing Muse" (1907) and Virginia of "The Profile" (1907), Stella Bixby is the victim of masculine expectations, which circumstances prevent her from fulfilling. These women are, like Marian Forrester, lost ladies, seemingly insensitive and malicious but not devoid of affection. The struggles they face as women of a new century are echoed in Lillian St. Peter, who succeeds in adapting to a society founded on money primarily because she has money. Myra is, therefore, not a sudden departure from the portrait of woman as Cather had presented her in previous works. Instead, she is an extension of some earlier wifely figures whose callousness or viciousness stems directly from disappointed passion. Cather need not enumerate the changes Myra's personality undergoes from the time of her "moon-struck" youth to her middle age; the resentment and prejudices she shows are the natural consequences of a matriarchy gone awry, of old values crushed by the new.

As described in Part I of the novel, Myra embodies the traits of an aging goddess of love whose regal hauteur becomes more reminiscent of Hera than Aphrodite. Myra retains a "beautiful voice, bright and gay and carelessly kind..." and a "playful curiosity in her eyes" which make her the mistress of her salon and admired by all those around her (p. 6). She impulsively expresses affection, throwing her arm around Nellie when seeing that the young girl's sensibility has been hurt. Just such impulsiveness prevents Myra from becoming a strictly stylized figure, from mirroring detail for detail her mythic models. Cather allows to Myra a human dimension that denies the scenario written for her by the ancients and reinforced by those stereotypes which the western world had since imposed upon women. However, her playfulness is, like Aphrodite's, sometimes difficult to

---

24.   Slote, Introd., *Uncle Valentine and Other Stories*, p. xii.

interpret, as Nellie notes: "And I was never sure whether she was making fun of me or of the thing we were talking about" (p. 7). Although the effects of age are beginning to show on Myra – she is growing plump and double-chinned – she is still excited by "her" man, and "his presence gave her lively personal pleasure" (p. 8). With the teasing tone of the love goddess, Myra dismisses Oswald's objections to her having given his six new shirts to the janitor's son, and she emerges as laughter-loving Aphrodite with a mirth which has "a spark of zest and wild humour in it" (p. 10). Myra's keen wit had always been a point in her favor with her adoptive father and great-uncle John Driscoll, who admired its earthiness, "Native and racy, and none too squeamish" (p. 12).

Myra's origins are obscure. She was a parentless child, as was Aphrodite Urania when she stepped ashore on Cypris. And, like Aphrodite, Myra had once accepted the attentions of numerous courtiers while she secretly planned an escape with Oswald Henshawe. She traded everything for love on a winter night when she left the Driscoll house and "gave the dare to Fate" (p. 17). For the ancients, too, only Love could begin to challenge all-powerful Fate, and even the mightiest of gods – Zeus himself – cowered before both forces. Even Myra's life reflects the role of Aphrodite. She is "fond of helping young men along" in their love affairs (p. 29), reliving her dreams of passion long after her own marriage has proved less than satisfactory.

Whereas Aphrodite never grew weary of her own powers, though, Myra is disappointed in love and especially in its consequences. In this aspect, Cather deviates again from myth. However, in Part I of the novel, age, illness, and regret have not yet completely subdued Myra's fascination with romance. She vacillates between human disillusionment in and deific celebration of love. "Love itself draws on a woman nearly all the bad luck in the world...," she remarks to Ewan Gray (p. 28); but, with an eagerness which typifies Aphrodite, Myra delights in the jewels Ewan shows her and relishes in the fact that he wishes to share with her the verses he has written to his sweetheart. Yet, Myra is well aware of the pain as well as the pleasure that love can bring. She vows no longer to play with love, never to meddle again, because "very likely hell will come of it!" (p. 31). Only in quiet moments, untouched by the scrambling for wealth and power, does Myra assume her role as the goddess whose gifts could bring peace and unmitigated joy. "When she was peaceful, she was like a dove with its wings folded," Cather writes (p. 35).

Although she strives to keep up the appearance of Goddess Aphrodite, swathing herself in furs and jewels and a hat "with a single narrow garnet feather sticking out behind" (p. 20), Myra is, as John Murphy writes, clearly "a dispossessed goddess, larger than life, haughty, imperious, and extravagant...."[25] She decries the loss of her powers as love goddess and assumes instead the stance of Hera, disappointed in her marriage and offended by her husband's unfaithfulness. Cather prepares her readers for the conversion of love goddess into imperious queen of the gods by naming the town of Myra's origin "Parthia." Although Cather could have borrowed the name from any history text that discussed the ancient and war-like Parthians, she was equally as likely to have borrowed the name from the myth of Hera. A variety of ancient writers, all of whom Cather had studied, – Callimachus, Apollonius Rhodius, and even Varro – identify as the place of Hera's birth Parthenia (also known as Samos), the island of the virgin.[26] Here Hera was the undisputed ruler of a matriarchal domain until Zeus arrived, an intruder vying for her power. He wooed Hera as a cuckoo, the bird which lays eggs in other birds' nests. After first resisting his advances in spite of a strong attraction she felt for the young god, Hera eventually defied the matriarchal incest prohibition and married her brother. Myra, too, left Parthia as a virgin bride, spurred on by Aphrodite but defiant of a patriarchal ban on marriage. Her marriage, like Hera's, brought not an increase in power but a loss of authority. As Hera came to be the patron deity of wifehood and marriage, but not of love in marriage, so Myra Henshawe assumes a despotic power which masks the demise of the matriarchy.

---

25. John J. Murphy, "The Dantean Journey in Cather's *My Mortal Enemy*," *Willa Cather Pioneer Memorial Newsletter*, Special Literary Issue, 30 (Summer 1986), 11.

26. C. Kerenyi, *Zeus and Hera: Archetypal Image of Father, Husband, and Wife*, trans. Christopher Holme, Bollingen Series 65 (Princeton: Princeton Univ. Press, 1975), pp. 156, 165.

Myra desires power and control, the things she had given up in marrying Oswald. Oswald is no Zeus, but his supposed infidelity–a thing Cather neither confirms nor denies in the novel–provides the motivation behind Myra's struggle for dominance. She declares a willingness to perjure herself, not for a man but for pearls, symbols of chastity and purity. Myra's declaration is an ironic one, for in marrying Oswald she has perjured herself for a man, giving up both youth and chastity. Myra realizes that the passion of youth has faded and that, as a result, her marriage is less fulfilling for both herself and Oswald. As if admitting defeat, the long garnet feather of her hat then droops behind her (p. 54). Unlike Hera, Myra cannot turn to the magical charms of Aphrodite to regain the love of her husband (cf. *Iliad* Bk. XIV). Nor can she through parthenogenesis produce offspring for their childless union. She can only do as did Vergil's Juno when she found her power thwarted:

> Quod si mea numina non sunt
> magna satis, dubitem haud equidem implorare, quod
> usquam est;
> flectere si nequeo superos, Acheronta movebo.
> (*Aeneid.* VII. 310-313)

> Very well!
> Suppose the power of my godhead be too weak–
> I would not shrink from seeking aid elsewhere,
> Wherever I can find it–If I cannot
> Prevail on Heaven I shall let loose Hell![27]

Although the Latin passage conveys the ancients' concept of "powers above" (*superos*) and, through metonomy, the special powers beneath the earth which work harm (*Acheronta*), Cather most likely thought of Juno as calling forth the powers of Heaven and Hell, thus Christianizing the myth as had Dryden in his translation of the *Aeneid* with which Cather would have been best acquainted: "If *Jove* and Heav'n my just Desires deny,/ Hell shall the Pow'r of Heav'n and *Jove* supply." At this juncture in her writing, Cather, with greater frequency than in the earlier works, allows such a cross-over of myths

27.   Patric Dickinson, trans., *The Aeneid*, by Vergil (New York: The New American Library, 1961), p. 155.

from pagan to Christian, for that dialectic expresses the changes taking place in her own life and in her perception of the larger human problem.

Myra Henshawe thus becomes "saeva Juno," holding tyrannical sway over all those about her. She surrounds herself in cold, royal purple, wearing a necklace of carved amethysts, traditionally the gem of royalty and "reputed to be a cure for drunkenness including the drunken passion of those over-excited by love."[28] Her New York apartment is surrounded by "violet buildings, just a little denser in substance and colour than the violet sky" (p. 26). "Plum-coloured curtains" frame the front windows and her velvet chairs are "like ripe purple fruit" (p. 26). Even the air Myra sniffs as she holds her head high is a "purple air" (p. 41).

Myra's queen-like appearance is heightened by a mass of black hair "done high on her head, a la Pompadour" (p. 6). She stands like a primitive statue of Hera, goddess of fertility, who wears a crown of creeping vines and grasses woven into a high headdress.[29] Her haughtiness is often marked by a laugh very different from the lilting mirth of her youthful, Aphrodisian role. Sometimes she has "an angry laugh," which Nellie shivers to remember (p. 10), and "a curl about the corners of her mouth that was never there when she was with people whose personality charmed her" (p. 40). When she stoops to entertain Oswald's business friends, Myra exhibits the same lofty manner Hera would in accepting the humble offerings of her mortal worshipers:

> Among these people Mrs. Myra took on her loftiest and most challenging manner. I could see that some of the women were quite afraid of her. They were in great haste to rush refreshments to her, and looked troubled when she refused anything. (p. 39)

Yet, like the queen of Olympus, Myra can be generous at the most unforeseen times, paying a cab driver a much too large fee or sending an expensive holly tree as a gift to an old friend. But, with her enemies, Myra shows no mercy and is forever mindful of the wrong done to her. "I've never

---

28.   Kathryn T. Stofer, "Gems and Jewelry: Cather's Imagery in *My Mortal Enemy*," *Willa Cather Pioneer Memorial Newsletter*, Special Literary Issue, 30 (Summer 1986), 20.

29.   Joan O'Brien, "Who Was Hera Before Zeus Tamed Her?" Illinois Classical Conference, Urbana, IL, 12 Oct. 1985.

forgiven him," Myra says of a young author who had once failed to stand by her husband (p. 44). Although she suffers in her bitterness, Myra goes over and over such past offenses in her mind, repeatedly "arguing, accusing, denouncing" (p. 44). Myra, therefore, reflects the two-sided nature of Hera, a goddess who could shower kindness upon one hero (Jason) and direct the greatest enmity toward another (Aeneas or Heracles). Myra not only tries to direct her own destiny but, with a deific pose, attempts to control the destinies of others as well. She becomes the embodiment of Moira, the Greek personification of fate.[30]

Myra is not, however, just a dispossessed matriarch seeking to regain her authority. Her nature is more complex than that of the queen of the gods, who will continue to reign despite reversals in fortune. She is, after all, a woman, haunted by the memories of what might have been. Myra is much like Godfrey St. Peter in this respect, for she has been caught up in a world delighted by materialism but only occasionally made aware of what has been lost in the bargain. Myra Henshawe complains that "[I]t's very nasty, being poor!" but the conscious recognition of her real poverty comes in a memory from lost youth, in a glint of light from a statue, or in the seductive air from an old song. In each instance, Myra is haunted by images of Artemis, the sanctity of art, and the inviolability of time-honored values. Just as Cather uses references to the moon to show Nellie's innocent perception of the world, the pure moonlight of Artemis awakens a sense of guilt in Myra (p. 31). Even her home in Parthia has become a Roman Catholic convent, the symbol of celibacy and obedience. Here the Sisters of the Sacred Heart devote their lives to the worship of another virginal figure, Mary, whose name anagrammatized could be Myra. Mocked by her own name and taunted by regret, Myra cannot escape the power of the chaste goddess or her own sense of failure. In New York, Nellie twice is confronted by the flashing, golden image of St. Gaudens' Diana, a sculpture Myra Henshawe has told her about. The goddess seems to "[step] out freely and fearlessly into the grey air" (p. 25), and the reader is reminded that Cather had used the

---

30.   John J.Murphy in "The Dantean Journey in Cather's *My Mortal Enemy*" also hears echoes of the classical term in Myra's name (p. 11).

image before in "Coming, Aphrodite!" when Eden Bower chose the way of Aphrodite instead of her rival goddess. Nellie must learn to cast aside her dreams of romance, and Myra, as experienced woman and not aloof goddess, is best suited to teach the lesson.

The most evident reference to Myra's failure to remain committed to Artemisian ideals comes when Madam Modjeska sings the Casta Diva aria from Bellini's *Norma*. Like a hymner to Artemis, Madam Modjeska sits by the window "half draped in her cloak, the moonlight falling across her knees" (p. 47). Myra crouches low at her side like a suppliant before the altar of an offended deity. The opera's tale is one of bitter passion, and the aria begins "like the quivering of moonbeams on the water" (p. 47). As Richard Giannone points out in *Music in Willa Cather's Fiction*, Cather selected the ideal piece for her novel. Both the novel and the opera "treat a heroine's reconciliation of the opposing obligations of sacred and profane love."[31] Norma's decision to defy both her Druidical vows and her patriotic commitment for the love of an "enemy" parallels Myra's decision to leave Parthia with one who may become her "mortal enemy." When betrayed in love, as Myra believes she has been, Norma unleashes pitiless wrath against Pollione, the father of her two children. In her desire to make him as unhappy as she is, Norma considers the revenge of Medea – killing both her children and her husband. But, like Norma, she can do little but pray to the Casta Diva, the moon goddess, invoking aid in a silent avowal to return to her worship. Whereas Norma is reconciled in death to Pollione, Myra no longer shares any spiritual bond with Oswald and upon him she conveniently attaches the label of "mortal enemy."

In Part II of the novel, then, Cather works out Myra's atonement for her transgressions by employing the same combined allusive schemas as she had done in *The Professor's House*. Cather never abandons the classical, mythic pose for Myra but adds a Christian dimension to Myra's final days. Now poverty-stricken, fatally ill, and living in a seedy boarding house, Myra nevertheless retains what trappings of regalness she can afford. Her now faded plum-colored curtains hang at the window, and even the violet ink,

---

31.   Richard Giannone, *Music in Willa Cather's Fiction* (Lincoln: Univ. of Nebraska Press, 1968), p. 180.

with which Oswald had inscribed her book of Heine's poetry, is faint with age. The powerful and fearful aspects of her personality hold sway as she exacts vengeance on the one who she believes has diverted her from a path to happiness. Myra's appearance more than ever confirms her former remark that hers "was no head for a woman at all, but would have graced one of the wickedest of the Roman emperors" (p. 63). Her mouth still curls "like a little snake" when she is scornful (pp. 54, 89), and she contends that in age she has lost everything "even the power to love" (p. 89). What Myra knows, however, is that the ability to love is inextricably bound to the other side of Aphrodite's nature – the desire to possess. "I was always a grasping, worldly woman; I was never satisfied," Myra admits (p. 88), but such an admission in no way reduces her vengeance toward Oswald:

> "People can be lovers and enemies at the same time, you know. We were....A man and woman draw apart from that long embrace, and see what they have done to each other. Perhaps I can't forgive him for the harm I did him. Perhaps, that's it." (p. 88, Cather's ellipses)

Cather relegates to Myra an honesty, straight-forwardness, and admission of weakness that hardly are in keeping with the role of Hera, Aphrodite, or Artemis. In her sharing with Nellie what she has learned of life, including its bitterness and disappointment, Myra demonstrates a heroism uncharacteristic of her mythic antecedents. Myra was trapped by what she had long believed to be true about life and romance. One must applaud both her willingness to admit her wrong-sightedness and her human concern for those, like Nellie, who are bound to follow her.

Yet *My Mortal Enemy* is more than an indictment of the falsity of romance. It is also a harsh commentary on the acquisitive instinct, whether for power or money. Cather associates both forces with the mythic Aphrodite, and in this work Cather is finally ready to abandon the goddess to the world in which she has wreaked havoc. No longer will Cather, like Claude Wheeler, Niel Herbert, or Godfrey St. Peter, struggle to reconcile Aphrodisian forces to the pioneer and artistic values which she associated with the mythic Artemis. Myra's death is, as Elizabeth Sergeant describes it, a "heroic failure against odds."[32] Although, in her limited view, Nellie

---

32. Elizabeth Shepley Sergeant, *Willa Cather: A Memoir* (New York: J. B. Lippincott Co., 1953), p. 219.

248

Birdseye sees only Oswald's "indestructible constancy" (p. 103), she does come to understand the source of Myra's degeneration: "Violent natures like hers sometimes turn against themselves...against themselves and all their idolatries" (p. 96, Cather's ellipses).

Nellie's comment might refer as well to the unnamed malignancy which Cather had felt encroaching on her life and on all human affairs, a newly arisen mortal enemy. In the new century Cather had blamed ambition, cruelty, and desire for the decline of civilization. But Myra, not Oswald, embodies these traits. She, not just Oswald, is her own mortal enemy. The seeds for destruction of the matriarchy lay not only in the threatening patriarchic power of commercialism but also in those human relationships which the mother-goddesses sanctioned. When Myra chooses to die alone on a cliff overlooking the sea, she is not a totally despairing figure, however. She has reconciled herself to her own humanness and to a world hostile to her values. She lays to rest the bitter and imperious Hera in dying beneath the tree of the goddess' origin, the cedar.[33] Myra leaves unchanged the clause in her will which Oswald honors: "I shall scatter her ashes somewhere in those vast waters" (p. 103). Aphrodite, too, is put to rest, returning to the sea from which she had emerged. Myra's death comes at dawn, a time of new beginnings, and *My Mortal Enemy* signals a new beginning for Cather's fiction. In Cather's subsequent works, her characters would, to an even greater degree, move beyond the limiting roles prescribed by myth and perpetuated by society's acceptance of such roles. Instead, Cather would increasingly describe human struggles in religious terms, never abandoning the allusions from classical myth which were such an integral part of her thought, but subordinating those images to a larger dimension of Christian allegory.

---

[33] Joan O'Brien explains that recent archaeological discoveries at Samos substantiate literary evidence that Hera's birth was supposed to have occurred beneath a lygos tree and that worship of the juniper – one of many cedar trees – was also part of the goddess' cult. Cather was undoubtedly acquainted with the myth of Hera's origin and worship since Hellenistic historians and poets, as well as classical authors, refer to the myth. Since Cather prided herself on being an amateur naturalist, she probably knew the relation between the juniper and cedar.

Although *My Mortal Enemy* is far from a happy novel, it is, like *The Professor's House,* a basically religious work. The Christian reconciliation with which the book ends does reflect a new direction in Cather's work. Within the short space of *My Mortal Enemy,* Cather depicted an individual journey from secularism to religiosity. Bernice Slote has convincingly argued that Part I celebrates the pagan festivals of Artemis and a Druidic priestess. Part II, however, is dominated by the Easter season, and even the tree under which Myra dies takes on sacrificial significance. The novel as a whole, then, follows Myra from East to West (literally, from New York to California), from paganism to Christianity.[34] In leaving the "house of her father" in Parthia, Myra symbolically divorced herself from her past and found only suffering and loss of human affection. In religion she recovers what the saints of the early Church discovered, that "...in religion seeking is finding":

> She accented the word "seeking" very strongly, very deeply. She seemed to say that in other searchings it might be the object of the quest that brought satisfaction, or it might be something incidental that one got on the way; but in religion, desire was fulfillment, it was the seeking itself that rewarded. (p. 94)

Stephen L. Tanner, in his recent article "Seeking and Finding in Cather's *My Mortal Enemy,*" questions the sincerity of Myra's "conversion" and sees this change in her as "more a matter of aesthetic than of theology."[35] Indeed, Myra's conversion and well-planned death scene seem self-indulgent, romanticized, and hardly genuine. Yet, as Tanner concedes, the apparent irony of the conversion may lie in Myra's actions alone, not in authorial attitude. The problem of Myra's "conversion" is a primary reason for the paucity of commentary about this novel démeublé, and understandably so. But, as this study of Cather's imagery reveals, many of the critical problems associated with Myra's death can be unraveled by noting how she completes a mythical pattern and emerges as a dispossessed Hera, taunted by unrecoverable origins (Artemisian values), as was Godfrey St. Peter, and

---

34. Bernice Slote, "Willa Cather: The Secret Web," in *Five Essays on Willa Cather,* ed. John J. Murphy (North Andover, MA: Merrimack College, 1974), p. 19.

35. Stephen L. Tanner, "Seeking and Finding in Cather's *My Mortal Enemy,*" *Literature and Belief,* Willa Cather Issue, 8 (1988), 35.

250

betrayed by modern acquisitiveness (Aphrodisian impulses), as was Tom Outland. The wide-ranging interpretations of *My Mortal Enemy*, then, overlook a principal aspect of Cather's work which would, to some degree, clarify authorial intention. I would argue that Cather does not intend to show a wholly sanctified woman, "restored to grace, if not fully purged for her sins," as John J. Murphy contends; neither does she, through irony, intend to omit all "religious overtones," as John H. Randall, III, concludes.[36] Rather, Myra, the pagan "goddess," is no more and no less than fully human – willful, contradictory, and sometimes even unloving. She dies while still seeking the answers to life's apparent injustice, and religion offers her serenity, but not all the answers. That Myra finds no great enlightenment or redemption does not dismiss the inherent religiosity of the work or Cather's conviction that in religion lies a means of dealing with both personal and societal dilemmas.

In Myra's quest for a "new Parnassus" (p. 80), Cather finds what Bartley Alexander, Thea Kronborg, and Claude Wheeler had not. Religion offers what the marriage of memory and desire could not, what the mythic matriarchy could not, namely a bulwark against the decay of time. The tragedy of Myra Henshawe's life is that she learns this too late; she has already squandered her potential for greatness. But, Cather assures her readers that Myra "must have died peacefully and painlessly" (p. 101). The mythic images of *My Mortal Enemy* confirm that Cather had made a truce with the world in which she lived but to which she still did not belong. If the world broke in two for Willa Cather in 1922 or thereabouts, by 1925 she was gluing it back together. *My Mortal Enemy*, therefore, stands as a watershed between Cather's early work and the quite different works of her final period – *Death Comes for the Archbishop, Shadows on the Rock, Lucy Gayheart,* and *Sapphira and the Slave Girl.*

---

36.   Murphy, p. 13; John H. Randall, III, p. 237.

CHAPTER IX
TOWARD A CHRISTIAN MYTHOS: WILLA CATHER'S
LAST NOVELS AND STORIES

The Professor's House (1925) signaled a point of departure for Willa Cather as she moved away from classical myth as a primary pattern of imagery for structuring her works. Whereas the heroic myths had seemed appropriate for conveying the struggles of individuals like Bartley Alexander, Alexandra Bergson, or Antonia Shimerda as they confronted situations or environments hostile to their ambitions, the values in the myths seemed out of place to Cather in the fast-paced world of the Twenties. She expressed her growing weariness with life in the tumultuous quests of such characters as Claude Wheeler, Marian Forrester, and Myra Henshawe, whose search for values she depicted as a classic struggle between mythic powers. Then in her next two novels – *Death Comes for the Archbishop* and *Shadows on the Rock* – Cather's spirit seems to revive, finding new strength in the quietude and order of another mythos – Christianity. Her search for a New Parnassus now focused on the Rock of the New Testament rather than on the myths of Greek literature.

Death Comes for the Archbishop reflects an inner peace which settled upon Cather after joining the Episcopal Church in 1925 and visiting again the Southwest, the landscape of which offered her a model of the permanent and the enduring. While reading among obscure books which described Bishop Machebeuf's experiences in this region some three centuries earlier, Cather discovered in the Church's history ideals and greatness similar to those she found in heroic myth. She sets the Prologue to her novel in Rome, a city steeped in both classical and ecclesiastical heritage, but in a time (the mid-nineteenth century) when the Church leaders no longer "conveniently discuss[ed] contemporary matters in Latin."[1] They, like the gods of Olympus, gather at a sumptuous table. There old Father Ferrand, "an Odysseus of the Church" (p. 3), admits that the time of his wanderings has ceased and acknowledges the need for a new man to carry on the spread of civilization. Heroic challenges still exist in the New World, and missionary Ferrand describes such challenges in classic terms:

> "The old mission churches are in ruins. The few priests are without guidance or discipline. They are lax in religious observance, and some of them live in open concubinage. If this Augean stable is not cleansed...it will prejudice the interests of the Church in the whole of North America." (p. 5)

The scene is of great significance, for it reveals Cather's blending of religious and classical imagery in describing an aesthetic endeavor. The mission Father Latour undertakes is an aesthetic one – to bring order out of chaos; in religious terms, to redeem the lost; and, in classical terms, to effect a Roman peace.[2] In *Death Comes for the Archbishop*, Cather does not abandon the imagery of Graeco-Roman myth. She does, however, subordinate it to Christian myth, the strength of which supported her at that time.

The journey upon which Father Latour embarks has, then, overtones of both an epic quest and redemptive mission. His piety is that of an Aeneas, who unlike Achilles or Odysseus, was destined to found a new civilization. Like Aeneas, Latour is haunted by memories of his homeland (France), childhood, and the refinements of a highly developed culture. He is sustained by an unshakable faith in the protection and guidance of a deity who is personally involved with his fate. The echoes of Aeneas' adventure are clear. Latour, like the hero of the Roman epic, found himself shipwrecked on the

---

1.   Willa Cather, *Death Comes for the Archbishop* (New York: Alfred A. Knopf, 1926), p. 3. All further references to this novel will be cited parenthetically in the text by page number.

2.   John J. Murphy, "Willa Cather's Archbishop: A Western and Classical Perspective," *Western American Literature*, 13 (1978), 146.

coast "of a dark continent" (p. 18), wandering in a land which was much like the sea itself:

> Across the level, Father Latour could distinguish low brown shapes, like earthworks, lying at the base of wrinkled green mountains with bare tops, – wave-like mountains, resembling billows beaten up from a flat sea by a heavy gale.... (p. 19)

Also like the ancient hero, Father Latour is not alone in this unknown land but is accompanied by a faithful Achates, Father Joseph Vaillant, "his boyhood friend, who had made this long pilgrimage with him and shared his dangers" (p. 20). Vaillant stands in the same relationship to Latour as did "fortis Achates" to "pater Aeneas," the valiant joined to the tower of strength.

Additionally Latour finds supernatural guidance from a deific intermediary, not Venus, but the Holy Mother. When wandering about the New Mexican desert and hampered by thirst, Latour does not encounter a goddess whose rosy neck and ambrosial hair betray her, but he kneels in devotion before a cruciform juniper and is later discovered by a young girl who brings him to a lush settlement, Agua Secreta. Latour gazes down upon the Mexican village "in the midst of the wavy ocean of sand" (p. 21) much as Aeneas, led by his mother Venus to a hill overlooking Carthage, gazed in amazement upon the city which rose miraculously out of the sands of Libya. At Agua Secreta, Father Latour's memories of the Old World are revived when he recognizes this spot as "a refuge for humanity" that is "older than history, like those well-heads in his own country where the Roman settlers had set up the image of a river goddess, and later the Christian priests had planted a cross" (p. 30). Such a supplanting of one system of symbols by another was occurring in Cather's fiction, too, and with great artistic skill Cather makes the transition in *Death Comes for the Archbishop*.

Father Latour's heroic efforts are not unlike those of Cather's Nebraskan pioneers who struggled to live harmoniously with their environment. In exerting such efforts, Latour has none of the misgivings of Godfrey St. Peter nor is he confused about his purpose. He needs no prophetic utterings, as did Aeneas, to apprize him of his mission to reclaim a people for his God. Yet, like an epic hero, Latour makes a descent into the Underworld. Cather's debt to Dante as an intermediary source for Latour's

254

descent also should not go unacknowledged.[3] Like his predecessors in Medieval accounts, Latour encounters not the shades of great heroes and the ghost of his father, but the embodiment of the Christian deadly sins – the gluttony of Father Baltazar, the lust of Padre Martinez, and the greed of Old Marino Lucero. New Mexico is not an Edenic garden, and the evils which undermine classical ideals are present. Latour finds himself seeking refuge in a huge stone cavern where, according to Indian legend, children had been sacrificed to the great serpent god and where the terrifying power of "one of the oldest voices of the earth" resounds "under ribs of antediluvian rock" (p. 132). Latour realizes that he cannot hope to triumph by force over a world fragmented by superstition, evil, and ignorance:

> There was no way in which he could transfer his own memories of European civilization into the Indian mind, and he was quite willing to believe that behind Jacinto there was a long tradition, a story of experience, which no language could translate to him. (pp. 92-93)

Latour cannot, like the hero of a Roman epic, brandish a sword and subdue the primitive tribes of his world. Instead, his mission becomes a redemptive one, to bring into existence, by slow degrees, discipline and beauty and order.

In Father Latour's mission Cather must have found comfort and, perhaps, for this reason she considered *Death Comes for the Archbishop* her best book. Cather had found a rock to sustain her in a time of disillusionment and dispiritedness:

> The rock, when one came to think of it, was the utmost expression of human need; even mere feeling yearned for it; it was the highest comparison of loyalty in love and friendship. Christ himself had used that comparison for the disciple to whom He gave the keys of His Church. (p. 98)

Whereas Prof. St. Peter had never found the spiritual support which the great Blue Mesa could have provided, both Latour and Cather do. They share a sense of the past coupled with a clear perception of the present. Latour's role

---

3.   James Woodress, *Willa Cather: A Literary Life* (Lincoln: Univ. of Nebraska Press, 1987), p. 408. John J. Murphy has also examined extensively the influence of Dante in shaping what he calls Cather's "Catholic Trilogy" ["The Dantean Journey in Cather's 'Catholic Trilogy,'" The Third National Seminar – Willa Cather: The World and the Parish, Hastings, Nebraska, June 17, 1987].

in the novel is Cather's role as a novelist – to revitalize the human spirit and to redefine contemporary society's place in the larger scheme of human history. And behind each stands immovable and secure the Rock of belief, not just the Olympus of old but also the mountain of the Christian god.

In her discussion of Cather's heroic design, Patricia Youngue argues that this "Hero as Priest" is the necessary replacement for the "traditional frontier hero, represented by Latour's friend Kit Carson, [who] is defunct as a viable ordering force."[4] The age of frontier heroism has faded and, with it, many of Cather's mythic images. This is not to say that a figure like Latour has no ties to the tradition of classical civilization. Rather, he assimilates the past, Christian or pagan, and reorders a fragmented world. For Latour, a properly made onion soup is more than a delight to the palate; it is "a constantly refined tradition...[with] nearly a thousand years of history in [it]" (p. 38). The Mexicans' devotion to their little wooden icon of the Virgin is part of this long heritage. Draping her in homemade laces and silver chains, these simple people follow in the footsteps of pagan sculptors who "were always trying to achieve the image of a goddess who would yet be a woman" (p. 259). This was the goal pursued by painters like Raphael and Titian, great composers, and great architects. Father Latour even delights in the Moorish origin of his great bell, finding as the wellspring of its beauty the blending of religion with art, even the art of "infidels" (pp. 44-45).

In this "missionary" role for the artist, Cather found a restorative power for her own life. By 1927, Cather was beyond the crisis of her middle age, had experienced fame, and had earned a comfortable fortune. She was secure as an artist and, apparently with calm assurance, understood that Latour's purpose was an artistic one. Her personal struggles against the onrush of civilization seem to have lessened as had her struggle against the reshaping of her relationship with Isabelle McClung Hambourg. Cather had come to accept that Isabelle would live abroad and that their lives had, indeed, separated. Like her celibate hero, Cather seems to realize that "...this was a final break; that their lives would part here, and that they would never

---

4.   Patricia Lee Youngue, "Willa Cather on Heroes and Hero-Worship," *Neuphilologische Mitteilungen*, 79 (1977), 61.

work together again" (p. 253). Just as Latour's and Vaillant's separation is a "natural" one, the two friends were still "bound by early memories" (p. 254). A sense of personal loss does not weigh heavily on Latour, as it did on Godfrey St. Peter at the death of Tom Outland. Instead, "that feeling of personal loneliness was gone, and a sense of loss was replaced by a sense of restoration" (p. 257). So was the case with Cather herself, and this, in part, accounts for the prevailing mood of *Death Comes for the Archbishop*, a mood of contentment and achievement.

In seeing the New World in terms of the Old–Latour's purpose as David Stouck describes it[5]–the priest fulfills the pattern of both Cather's life and art. Although Cather never abandons her stance that material progress may not mean improvement of the human condition ["Men travel faster now, but I do not know if they go to better things." (p. 294)], she does, through religion, reconcile herself to the present. The land still provides a mythic revitalizing power by which Latour's sensual perceptions are awakened, as were Cather's in her return visits to the Southwest in 1925 and 1926:

> In New Mexico [Latour] always awoke a young man; not until he rose...did he realize that he was growing older. His first consciousness was a sense of the light dry wind blowing in through the windows...a wind that made one's body feel light and one's heart cry "To-day, to-day," like a child's. (p. 276)

What Latour finds in this unchanging landscape is a perpetual youth, an immutability that nourishes him and dissolves the tension between past and present. Even his out-of-body experiences, initiated by the ringing of the Angelus, change throughout the course of the novel. Whereas on first awakening to the bell Father Latour was "carried out of the body thus to a place far away" (p. 43), even to his childhood in the south of France, later the ringing of the church bell reminds him of the present, of his place in the scheme of things:

> As the darkness faded into the grey of a winter morning, he listened for the church bells,–and for another sound, that always amused him here; the whistle of a locomotive. Yes, he had come with the buffalo, and he had lived to see railway trains running into Santa Fe. He had accomplished an historic period. (p. 274)

5.   David Stouck, "Cather's *Archbishop* and Travel Writing," *Western American Literature*, 17 (May 1982), p. 12.

Latour fulfills his destiny as an Aeneas of the Church and discovers the satisfaction of being "dissolved into something complete and great" (*My Antonia*, p. 18).

The peace that Archbishop Latour finds when confronting death is not that of Myra Henshawe who, defeated and alienated from those around her, turned to religion and the past out of penance and long suffering. Rather, the Archbishop finds personal completion in religion. Just as the Archbishop in his old age chooses not to return to France, to the scenes of his youth and the foundation of his values, Cather chooses no longer to concentrate on a mythic past in attempting to define the spiritual dimensions of human life. Using Christian imagery, Cather makes the Archbishop's journey of the spirit her own: "...it was the Past he was leaving. The future would take care of itself" (p. 292). If the writing of *Death Comes for the Archbishop* was "the most unalloyed pleasure of her life,"[6] as Cather told Ida Tarbell, then surely this mood arose from Cather's coming to terms with her world, and, in a spiritual sense, from her coming home. Like her Bishop, Cather had found a revitalizing air that did not deny the past but redeemed it:

> He did not know just when [that air] had become so necessary to him, but he had come back to die in exile for the sake of it. Something soft and wild and free, something that whispered to the ear on the pillow, lightened the heart, softly, softly picked the lock, slid the bolts, and released the prisoned spirit of man into the wind, into the blue and gold, into the morning, into the morning! (p. 277)

The profound comfort which Cather found in religion became her mainstay throughout the four years following the publication of *Death Comes for the Archbishop*. Willa's father, Charles Cather, died in March of 1928, and in December of the same year her mother suffered a debilitating stoke. Not only was her familial home at Red Cloud now abandoned, but Cather also made regular and very tiring transcontinental trips to California to stay with her bed-ridden mother. Her personal grief was great, but the book that she had begun in the autumn of 1928 sustained her during this time. This work

---

6.   James Woodress, *Willa Cather: Her Life and Art* (1970; rpt. Lincoln: Univ. of Nebraska Press, 1982), p. 225.

was *Shadows on the Rock*, a novel inspired by Cather's three visits to Quebec between 1928 and 1930. The Catholic heritage of Quebec became her focus, and the novel developed along themes similar to *Death Comes for the Archbishop*. The pattern of images in the novel reflected again Cather's new-found means of describing the human experience. Classical echoes, particularly Vergilian ones, are undeniably present, but religious images dominate. Lionel Trilling argues that in religion Cather found a goal more satisfying for contending with life's dilemmas than was the pioneering struggle she had long admired[7] and had described in classical or mythic terms. What surfaces, then, in *Shadows on the Rock* is a serenity of spirit that Cather admitted made the reader like the book in spite of its lack of energy. As Euclide Auclair, one of the novel's principal characters, believes, "That was the important thing – tranquillity."[8]

Just as Cather had depicted religion as an aesthetic force which ordered life in Archbishop Latour's chaotic world, so does cultural heritage and faith order life in *Shadows on the Rock*. Madame Auclair had, shortly before her death, advised her daughter Cecile that "...your father's whole happiness depends on order and regularity, and you will come to feel a pride in it. Without order our lives would be disgusting, like those of poor savages" (p. 24). Such order Cather had believed to be a classical ideal, first describing it as one of the jealously guarded refinements of the Troll Garden and then as the emblem of an Olympian hierarchy. In Christianity Cather finds her final expression of an ordered universe, the basic element of which is the family unit, the very thing she had so recently seen disrupted by the death and illness of her parents. In the Auclair household Cather describes the sense of order and stability which had been, in part, the wellspring of her own art. Cather had long contended that "Art must spring out of the very stuff that life is made of,"[9] and life, for her, was the family, whether Antonia's "rich

---

7.   Lionel Trilling, "Willa Cather," in *Modern Critical Views: Willa Cather*, ed. Harold Bloom (New York: Chelsea House Publishers, 1985), p. 10.

8.   Willa Cather, *Shadows on the Rock* (1931; rpt. New York: Vintage Books, 1971), p. 157. All subsequent references to the novel will be cited in the text by page number.

9.   Willa Cather, qtd. in Mildred Bennett, *The World of Willa Cather*, rev. ed. (Lincoln: Univ. of Nebraska Press, 1961), p. 168.

mine of life" or Latour's Holy Family. Art brought together both the classical and religious ideals of order, but, as Cather noted, such art could be of the humblest kind:

> "The German housewife who sets before her family on Thanksgiving Day a perfectly roasted goose, is an artist. The farmer who goes out in the morning to harness his team, and then pauses to admire the sunrise – he is an artist."[10]

So are the heroic figures of both *Death Comes for the Archbishop* and *Shadows on the Rock* artists. To criticize either novel for its excessive attention to the trivial aspects of living, such as the tradition of French cookery, is to miss Cather's point. Domestic life itself was art and the foundation of civilization.

In addition, Cather turns to Christian imagery rather than to classical myth to describe the family as a household of faith, untainted by the wranglings and petty jealousies of Olympian deities. Just as the Ursuline Sisters maintain "their accustomed place in the world of the mind (which for each of us is the only world), and they had the same well-ordered universe about them..." (p. 97), so did the Auclair household maintain a cultural stability defined by religion. The Church offers to the motherless Cecile a security in its maternal figure, a figure for whom many of Cather's earlier characters had searched, whether in the guise of Demeter, Aphrodite, Hera, or Artemis. Not only does the Holy Mother now replace these protective deities, but she, like the Church on Cap Diamant, also represents order in a fast-changing world:

> Notre Dame de la Victoire was a plain, solid little church, built of very hard rough stone. It had already stood through one bombardment from the waterside, and was dear to the people for that reason. (p. 49)

Like the rock on which it sits, this church is the symbol of permanence, order, and immutability. In again using the Christian symbol of the rock, Cather creates a kind of stasis in the world she describes, where all life seems to rest in frozen harmony: "...the whole rock looked like one great white church, above the frozen river" (p. 136). Religion, with its matriarchal protector,

---

10.   Willa Cather, qtd. in Bennett, p. 168.

provides a stay against time. The Auclairs' life becomes Cather's fictive vivant tableau untouched by the "change [that] is not always progress..." (p. 119). These words, spoken by Euclide Auclair could easily have been those of the author herself.

Yet, Cather never totally abandons those mythic patterns which had been integral parts of her earlier works. The seasonal motif, which underscored works like *My Antonia* and *O Pioneers!*, appears again in *Shadows on the Rock*. Just as Marie wrestled with her love for Emil in the winter of his absence and just as Antonia faced her impending motherhood in winter, Cecile's exposure to harsh realities and threats to ordered existence come in the winter. She listens in rapt attention to Father Hector Saint-Cyr's stories of adventures in the dark forests beyond the rock of Quebec, where death awaits even the most pious. And, Cather describes this outside world in terms reminiscent of the classical Hades:

> ...the black pine forest came down to the water's edge; and on the west, behind the town, the forest stretched no living man knew how far. That was the dead, sealed world of the vegetable kingdom....The forest was suffocation, annihilation; there European man was quickly swallowed up in silence, distance, mould, black mud, and the stinging swarms of insect life that bred in it. The only avenue of escape was along the river. (pp. 6-7)

Along this river Pierre Charron travels, and although he hardly has the dark and mean aspect of the Greek boatman of Hades, his name and his shallop recall the role of the mythic ferryman. Charron also provides the means by which Cecile first journeys beyond her protected environment. Cecile, like an uninitiated Persephone, finds unbearable a life across the river at the Harnois home, and she mourns the loss of her mother's world:

> She began to cry quietly. She thought a great deal about her mother, too, that night; how her mother had always made everything at home beautiful, just as here everything about cooking, eating, sleeping, living, seemed repulsive. (p. 192)

Cather's sense of personal loss is strong here, for her mother's illness had made her acutely aware that for happiness "one had to have kind things about one, too..." (p. 197). *Shadows on the Rock* was published in the same month that Mary Virginia Cather died (August, 1931), and Cather's growing appreciation of her own position in the family unit was, undoubtedly, foremost in her mind. Like Cecile, she may have come to a clearer understanding of self at this time, an understanding that life was an art just as much as art made life:

> [Cecile] did not feel like a little girl, doing what she had been taught to do. She was accustomed to think that she did all these things so carefully to please her father, and to carry out her mother's wishes. Now she realized that she did them for herself, quite as much. (pp. 197-198)

Cecile's marriage to Pierre Charron is not unexpected in light of Cather's now strong conviction that the future would take care of itself. Cecile had journeyed into the Underworld, only to return more appreciative of cultural tradition. In response to her father's comment, "I do not wish to outlive my time," Cecile emphatically states, "I have got to live on into a new time..." (p. 261).

In that "new time," Cecile Auclair will become the Lavinia of her race, bearing strong sons to found a new civilization which will not abandon the faith of the old. As her father later says with pride, "She is bringing up four little boys, the Canadians of the future" (p. 278). The reader at once is reminded of Antonia, whose many children would be the Americans of the future, sharing with their mother a pride in the Old World heritage, from the very goods they eat to the Bohemian language in which they converse about the most private things. Yet, the strength Antonia passes on is one of earth, of a steady struggle against obstacles, a literal survivalism against the odds. Cecile fills a somewhat different role than that of biological mother of the race. She emerges as the spiritual mother of her race, a role which, as Susan Rosowski explains, is in keeping with Cecile's actions throughout the novel. As a child, she serves as gentle corrector and intercessor for Jacques Gaux, just as "the Virgin Mother is a mediator for all living...." In her selflessness, tenderness, and unfailing devotion to her father and her faith, Cecile, like Father Latour, lives a saint's life, and the novel, as Rosowski contends, portrays "the apotheosis of a French girl into a Canadian Holy Mother."[11]

---

11. Susan J. Rosowski, *The Voyage Perilous: Willa Cather's Romanticism* (Lincoln: Univ. of Nebraska Press, 1986), pp. 184-185.

Cecile's strength lies in a quietude of the soul, developed not in the aftermath of great struggles but in the presence of an enduring faith.

Epic parallels, much like those in *Death Comes for the Archbishop*, are subtly interwoven throughout this novel. The memories of a finely developed culture that Euclide Auclair carries with him into Quebec are like those Aeneas brings with him out of Troy. Like Vergil's epic hero, Auclair brings his household gods, traditions, and cultural refinements into a new world. Cather alludes to *The Aeneid* early in the novel and sets the stage for this implicit comparison of the classic text to her own:

> *Inferretque deos Latio.* When an adventurer carries his gods with him into a remote and savage country, the colony he founds will, from the beginning, have graces, traditions, riches of the mind and spirit. (p. 98)

Like Aeneas, Auclair is careful to preserve his heritage by teaching his child the language of his faith – Latin – and by instilling within her a loyalty to Count Frontenac, the figure-head of a finer and older way of life.

When the Count dies, Auclair recalls the poignant cry of Aeneas, who saw his faithful men drowned by Juno's wrath: "Not without reason, he told himself bitterly as he looked up at those stars, had the Latin poets insisted that thrice and four times blessed were those to whom it befell to die in the land of their fathers" (p. 263). Auclair's paraphrase is taken from Vergil's *Aeneid*, Book I: "O terque quarterque beati,/ quis ante ora patrum Troiae sub moenibus altis contigit oppetere" (ll.94-96). Yet, the circumstances surrounding this utterance are far different from Auclair's.

Euclide Auclair is not the target of superhuman powers, nor is the Count the victim of a god's wrath. Both men are, like Aeneas' crew, dispossessed of their native land, but the land they have left behind is hardly a devastated Troy. Again Cather does not hesitate to change the Roman myth, making the old Count a reflection of Aeneas' other face, the warrior-hero. The Count is not guided to Canada by gods' visitations and dreams; he had been sent to Canada by an unappreciative sovereign. Yet, in this strange, new land, he accomplishes his tasks: "He had chastized the Indians, restored peace and order, secured the safety of trade" (p. 238). The Count demonstrates the military might of the hero of the *Aeneid* who subdues

Turnus and establishes a peace with the Latins. Cather, however, does not force either Auclair or Count Frontenac into a role which exactly follows the ancient epic. Her "new world" epic does not celebrate a Rome founded "to impose upon the nations/ The code of peace; to be clement to the conquered,/ But utterly to crush the intransigent" (*Aeneid* VI.851-853).[12] Rather, as Auclair concludes in the closing lines of the novel, his fortune, along with his grandsons', lies in living in a country "where nothing changed...where the death of the King, the probable evils of a long regency, would never touch them" (p. 280). Cather's epic adventure will not end as did Vergil's. The Count is not whisked away by the gods in the midst of battle, leaving his power in the hands of a most capable son. He dies unreconciled to his king, feeling no "deep regret that his son had died in youth" (p. 247) but reconciled to "his new position in the world and what was now required of him" (p. 262).

In his admiration for the Count, Auclair becomes his hymner, the Vergil of Cather's prose-poem. Auclair lays before the reader those other traits of the old Count which made him heroic: "...he was always courteous and considerate. He belonged to the old order; he cherished those beneath him and rendered his duty to those above him, but flattered nobody, not the King himself" (p. 261). Like Auclair, Cather mourns the passing of such strength, but in Cecile, rather than a Iulus, her hope for the future resides. Cecile learns much of endurance from the Count and much of compassion from her father. In the marriage of the two qualities, Cather recognizes the importance of a heritage from two worlds – Graeco/Roman and Christian. Auclair even characterizes Blinker, the beggared wood carrier, in terms Aeneas once heard: "You remember, when Queen Dido offers Aeneas hospitality, she says: *Having known misery, I have learned to pity the miserable.* Our poor wood-carrier is like Queen Dido" (p. 163). The values Auclair upholds – sympathy, loyalty, and piety – are shared by both classical and Christian writers. As epic heroes, then, both Count Frontenac and Euclide Auclair are markedly different from their classical predecessors. They do not

---

12.   Patric Dickinson, trans., *The Aeneid*, by Vergil (New York: Mentor Book-The New American Library, 1961), p. 144.

exhibit the endless striving of the ancient adventurers but a quiet strength, like the rock of Quebec itself. For them, human values supersede god-like endeavor.

Likewise, even those who have consciously decided to live out their lives as Canadians embody the classical as well as Christian ideals. Father Hector, like his namesake, "has good breeding and fine presence"; he is "strong and fearless and handsome" (pp. 146-147). He is magnanimous and devout, displaying the spirit of an ancient hero, but is "peculiarly susceptible to the comforts of the fireside and to the charm of children" (p. 149). So it is that Homer describes Hector in Book VI of the *Iliad*. Priam's son reluctantly takes leave of his beloved family, reassuring Andromache of his safe return and playfully tossing Astyanax in the air after the child is frightened by the waving plume of his father's helmet (ll. 390-493).

In his vow never to return to France, Father Hector exhibits his ancient counterpart's loyalty to his nation, and in this Cecile finds much to admire. She shares his compulsion to make a place in the New World for the Old. Cecile dutifully learns of other great heroes from Plutarch's *Lives*, and she seeks a similar figure in her own time and place. She imagines that the recluse Jeanne Le Ber must be such a hero since she has chosen solitude and given herself to one thing "altogether and finally," as Father Hector would say (p. 149). Jeanne Le Ber serves, for a time, as Cecile's model for creating the beautiful and the lasting. From the recluse's spinning wheel comes "the beautiful altar-cloths which went out from her stone chamber to churches all over the province..." (pp. 134-135). As stories spread from fireside to fireside about the recluse, Jeanne Le Ber's faith and devotion assume saint-like proportions; her life becomes heroic and her art the evidence of a greater miracle – "the actual flowering of desire" (p. 137). For Cecile, Jeanne Le Ber's cell becomes, as Judith Fryer argues in *Felicitous Space*, "a place of vision and power," like the dwelling place of the Sibyl, "'the primordial prophetess who mythically conceived all women artists.'"[13] Once again, Cather creates an aesthetic image by synthesizing religious and classical ones.

---

13.   Judith Fryer, *Felicitous Space: The Imaginative Structures of Edith Wharton and Willa Cather* (Chapel Hill: The Univ. of North Carolina Press, 1986), p. 340.

But, Cecile is deceived by her beautiful image of the heroic Jeanne Le
Ber. Cecile is absent, having gone to bed, when Pierre Charron narrates his
account of watching the recluse at her prayers. In isolated commitment she
has sacrificed, along with the comforts of the world, an elemental humanness.
Her face is "like a stone face [that] had been through every sorrow" (p. 182).
It is Pierre who hears her groan and sob in resignation and despair. The
heroism of stories about the recluse is undermined by Pierre's recounting, yet
Cather allows Cecile to remain unaffected by harsh realities, to remain
entranced by the rapture of miracles. One can only speculate that Cather had
herself suffered the private griefs of one committed to art and separated by
that dedication from the human "family." *Shadows on the Rock* stands as
evidence of Cather's coming to terms with the death of her own mother and
of her reconciliation to the art that often separated her from her family.
Cecile Auclair would undoubtedly grow into a new understanding of heroic
commitment, never relinquishing her admiration for piety and self-sacrifice,
but adding to these the active heroism of a Father Hector or Pierre Charron.
Leaving behind the imaginings of youth, Cecile finds in Pierre the classic
heroism of her world: "But he had authority, and a power which came from
knowledge of the country and its people; from knowledge, and from a kind of
passion. His daring and pride seemed to her even more splendid than Count
Frontenac's" (p. 268).

Shadows on the Rock, therefore, grows out of Cather's commitment to
religious faith as a means of preserving those customs which define
civilization. The orderly and serene life that Auclair, like Latour, preserves in
the New World is Cather's safeguard against personal losses and against the
decay of twentieth-century society generally. Although Cather still lauded the
pioneering spirit of expansion and conquest, such epic, heroic values now
became secondary to a civilized domesticity and tranquillity. In many ways
the crystal bowl of glass fruits, which the Count wills to Cecile, is the emblem
of such a civilization. In its fragile beauty is an other-worldliness that makes
it, as Cecile remarks, "much lovelier than real fruit" (p. 60). That for which
Cather's characters had long searched – for a monument more lasting than
bronze – is not hammered out in the steel of Bartley Alexander's bridge nor
planted into the furrows on a Nebraskan tableland. Civilization, instead, lay

in that "which might have been a lost ecstasy," unless infused with a religious significance and "made an actual possession [which] can be bequeathed to another" (p. 137). Cather credits Christianity with much of the remarkable ability for civilization to endure and be passed on to subsequent generations. For Cather, the tradition of coupling labor and religion finds its place not in the founding of an empire, but in the most fundamental unit of civilization – home and family.

Memories of her own family haunted Cather as she sat at her mother's bedside, and here she began the three stories which would later comprise *Obscure Destinies* (1932). all three stories – "Neighbour Rosicky," "Old Mrs Harris," and "Two Friends" – are colored by a nostalgic longing for the irretrievable. In "Two Friends," Cather acknowledges this mood as "...the feeling of something broken that could so easily have been mended; of something delightful that was senselessly wasted, of a truth that was accidentally distorted – one of the truths we want to keep."[14] The somber mood of *Obscure Destinies* is, nevertheless, touched by the same religiosity that reached its peak in *Shadows on the Rock*. While none of the stories' principal characters are heroes in the traditional sense, all display a silent strength and a belief in old ways and values that lend support to the new generation.

In *Obscure Destinies* Cather exalts the individual by showing the conjunction of separate lives on an often obscured path of life. Just as the two friends Mr. Dillon and Mr. Trueman advise their young listener that she might never again see in a lifetime the occultation of Venus with the moon, so Cather shows the crossing of some human paths to be brief instances of Christian love. Cather had often shown the tragic consequences of the clash of those mythic powers symbolized by the planet Venus and the moon, but this same meeting in Cather's late works assumes Christian overtones. Instead of a violent clash of sensuality and sensibility, the two forces touch briefly before passing on.

---

14. Willa Cather, "Two Friends," in *Obscure Destinies* (1932; rpt. New York: Vintage Books, 1974), p. 230. References to this story and others in the volume – "Neighbour Rosicky" and "Old Mrs Harris" – will be cited parenthetically in the text by page number.

So is the case in "Neighbour Rosicky," the first of the stories in *Obscure Destinies*. Cather portrays the now aged characters of *My Antonia* in a new light, renaming Antonia as "Mary" and adding a religious aspect to the already mythic dimension of her tale. Rosicky accepts with saintly resignation his own impending death and sets out in his "quiet, unobtrusive" way (p. 66) to soothe the strain between Rudolph and his American wife Polly. Rosicky's "special gift for loving people [was] something that was like an ear for music or an eye for colour," Cather writes (p. 66). Again, Cather equates a religious ideal with aesthetic achievement. The moment of spiritual communion which Rosicky and Polly share becomes one of those chance and never-repeated junctures of two spirits. Rosicky's exceptional nature reaches out to "resurrect" Polly, with all his moral strength and understanding evident in "a warm brown human hand": "Polly remembered that hour long afterwards; it had been like an awakening to her. It seemed to her that she had never learned so much about life from anything as from old Rosicky's hand" (p. 67). In that human hand is incarnate a Christ-like spirituality, and a blessing is bestowed upon Polly. The story itself becomes a Christian parable, and Rosicky's death becomes expiatory, making his life "complete and beautiful" (p. 71), not through heroic or mythic exploit but through Christian transcendence.

Cather carries through the same theme in her next story, "Old Mrs. Harris." In depicting three generations of women in the Templeton household, Cather drew more directly upon her childhood experiences than she had in any other work. In "Old Mrs. Harris," Cather takes her last step in exploring the roles of women, and such a step is expected if one keeps in mind the shift in imagery that had occurred in her works since the earliest stories. As Susan Rosowski concludes in "Willa Cather's Women," Cather had moved "from women as mythic goddess and earth mother to the more specifically cultural myths of women as aesthetic ideal and romantic heroines and, finally, to women who live apparently ordinary lives...."[15] But, in spite of the restrictions of ordinary lives, women like Old Mrs. Harris (the fictional

15. Susan J. Rosowski, "Willa Cather's Women," *Studies in American Fiction*, 9 (Autumn 1981), 274.

268

equivalent of Willa's Grandmother Boak) assume heroic dimensions, sharing with the younger generations those "certain unalterable realities, somewhere at the bottom of things" ("Two Friends," p. 193). When the paths of Mrs. Rosen and Mrs. Harris cross, that instant of genuine affection shapes the destiny of Vickie Templeton. Oblivious to the personal sacrifices her grandmother has made to ask for financial assistance from Mrs. Rosen, Vickie, like the anxious, young Willa Cather, only wonders, "What were families for, anyway?" (p. 186). Eagerly pursuing her classical studies in the Rosens' library, Vickie is, as Ellen Moers explains, the "brightest and strongest" of the women in the household. Her mother Victoria is "the most beautiful, the most spoiled, the most helplessly adored." Like an Artemis and Aphrodite, they overlook their resident Athena, Grandma Harris, "the noblest and the wisest."[16] But, Old Mrs. Harris' triumph is hardly the victory of a Greek goddess. Her death, like Rosicky's, is sacrificial, having offered up to the new generations the universal values of the old. Cather, writing from the perspective of one growing old, is sure that Grandma Harris' influence will reach even beyond her death: "They will think a great deal about her, and remember things they never noticed; and their lot will be more or less like hers" (p. 190).

In her final selection, "Two Friends," Cather touches the same idea of "transference of experience" (p. 218), but, in this case, she shows by negation the importance of the Christian values of understanding, tolerance, and forgiveness. As a child, the narrator shared in life's possibilities by listening attentively to the evening conversations of two local businessmen who were good friends. When the two disagree on the subject of William Jennings Bryan and the Populist Party, the equilibrium of life disappears. The brief conjunction of two great natures ends only in "a real loss" to their young admirer, whose existence they had hardly noticed (p. 229). The tone of regret in "Two Friends" stands in contrast to that of "Neighbour Rosicky" and "Old Mrs. Harris," yet this tone, too, serves Cather's purpose. Mr. Dillon and Mr. Trueman are "merely pictures, vivid memories, which in some unaccountable

16.   Ellen Moers, *Literary Women* (Garden City, NY: Doubleday and Co., 1976), p. 242.

way give us courage" (p. 193). Memories became, at this point in Cather's career, the force which sustained her art and made life bearable.

With the writing of *Lucy Gayheart*, which she began in the spring of 1933, Willa Cather retreated even further into personal memory. Although Cather set the novel in a small prairie town, something she had not done since *A Lost Lady* (1923), she colored the approach to both setting and character with a sentimentality clearly influenced by changes in her own life. Willa Cather was now in declining health and plagued by a number of chronic ailments. She had again moved her residence in an effort to seek congenial surroundings, and her family home at Red Cloud, no longer serving as a stable center for her life, was sold. Willa Cather was, frankly, growing old, and *Lucy Gayheart* is in many ways an old woman's book. Its writing dragged along, and when the novel was nearly completed, Cather wrote to Zoe Akins that she had "lost patience with her silly young heroine."[17] Lucy's development never involves the reader, just as Lucy is not actively involved in her own growth. She is not a Thea Kronborg who struggles against conflicting desires to achieve greatness. She is, instead, a dreamer to whom things happen by chance. Her character is not her fate; only her humanness is. But, in this alone, lies Cather's growing interest in the Christian mythos. Like its immediate predecessors, *Lucy Gayheart* then is an essentially religious novel.

Cather begins her work by characterizing Lucy Gayheart as a "mercurial, vacillating person" whose unrestrained vitality makes life seem to lie "very near the surface in her."[18] She has a nymph-like beauty and litheness which make her other-worldly:

> When the old women at work in their gardens caught sight of her in the distance, a mere white figure under the flickering shade of the early summer trees, they always knew her by the way she moved....There was something in her nature that was like her movements, something direct and unhesitating and joyous, and in her golden-brown eyes. (p. 4)

She possessed the entrancing traits of a nymph with her rather dark skin, deep red lips and cheeks, and a "warm and impulsive" mouth (p. 5). Even her

<hr>

17. Woodress, *Willa Cather: Her Life and Art*, p. 251.

18. Willa Cather, *Lucy Gayheart* (New York: Alfred A. Knopf, 1935), pp. 18, 5. All other references to the novel will be cited in the text by page number.

eager response to the first fine music she has ever heard has pagan overtones. Clement Sebastian sings of a mariner, worshiping at the temple of Castor and Pollux and laying down his oar as a votive offering. Lucy is affected by "a kind of large enlightenment, like daybreak" (p. 30). As her name implies, Lucy is both a source of light and is enlightened by art. Cather again shows the merging of classical and religious imagery into an aesthetic image, as she had done in both *Death Comes for the Archbishop* and *Shadows on the Rock*:

> The song was sung as a religious observance in the classical spirit, a rite more than a prayer; a noble salutation to beings so exalted that in the mariner's invocation there was no humbleness and no entreaty. (p. 29)

In her rapture for art, Lucy shifts her devotion to the creator of such art, to Clement Sebastian, and he, in warm appreciation of her youthful vitality and innocence, expands Lucy's artistic sensibilities.

In describing the relationship between Lucy and Clement Sebastian, Cather inverts the expected seasonal cycle for the origin, blossoming, and death of love. Like the song that haunts Lucy, *Die Winterreise*, the novel is a winter's tale. Lucy's romance begins in winter, the lovers separate in summer, her beloved dies in autumn, and she, in winter. As Richard Giannone goes on to point out, though, the prevailing mood of the *Die Winterreise* "derives not from a falling out of human love but from a disaffection with all life."[19] After Sebastian's death, Lucy's similar "disaffection with all life" necessitates, from Cather's religious stance, a resurrection to a belief in living. Cather prepares her reader for this shift back to life by introducing Mendelssohn's *Elijah* as the first song for which Lucy accompanies Sebastian. Just as Elijah was the Biblical prophet who recalled the backsliding Israelites to the worship of their true god, so does the song foreshadow Lucy's return to her true god, not art but life itself.

The Elijah of Mendelssohn's oratorio is much like Clement Sebastian, who also fulfills a prophetic role in warning Lucy of life's pain and suffering, even while demonstrating compassion and understanding. Elijah in the

---

[19]   Richard Giannone, *Music in Willa Cather's Fiction* (Lincoln: Univ. of Nebraska Press, 1968), p. 216.

musical score is, only in part, the Biblical prophet who chastized the Israelites. For Lucy, at first, Sebastian fills the role of one who recalls her to the true art of music and introduces her to the garden of delights, which in Cather's early work was jealously guarded by the trolls. When Sebastian asks, "Have you ever heard the *Elijah* well given, Miss Gayheart?", Lucy admits that she has not, having been diverted by the music of "fashion." Sebastian's comment that "people are interested in music chiefly to have something to talk about at dinner parties" (p. 42) reveals his cynicism about art when laid before unappreciative forest children. But his interest in awakening the sympathetic conscience of Lucy to the beauty of fine music is genuine. The *Elijah*, perhaps better than any other musical opus, serves Cather's purpose here. Prince Albert wrote to Mendelssohn in 1847, after the second London performance of the work, addressing the composer as "the noble artist who, surrounded by the Baal-worship of false art, through genius and study has been able, like a second Elijah, to remain true to the service of true art...."[20] Sebastian is likewise Lucy's Elijah, directing her in the worship of their true "god."

Yet, the *Elijah* offers a second portrait of the prophet, as well, a portrait which varies from the historical, Old Testament image of a "powerful, unbending prophet." As Eric Werner explains in his definitive work on Mendelssohn, Elijah also emerges as the symbolic "forerunner of Jesus,"[21] whose sympathy, understanding, and forgiveness arise from a first-hand knowledge of pain and suffering. Such was the case for Clement Sebastian. In this capacity Sebastian fulfills his second role in influencing Lucy. As the Christian implication of his name indicates, he shows compassion for this young girl. His song recounts the despair not only of the prophet's life but also of his own. He sings the aria as one who has tasted of troubles and is ready to give up his life: "It is enough, O Lord, now take away my life, – I am not better than my fathers!" (*Elijah*, No. 26). Lucy responds emotionally to the pathos of his song, but never deigns to speak her feelings

---

20.   Eric Werner, *Mendelssohn: A New Image of the Composer and His Age* (London: The Free Press of Glencoe, 1963), p. 482.

21.   Werner, p. 461.

aloud. She senses his weariness with life, and yet the memory of the *Elijah* sustains and revitalizes her after Sebastian's death. The oratorio offers hope and direction to those who would see beyond the prophet's despondency in the wilderness. An angel awakens Elijah, slumbering under a juniper tree, and promises, "Shouldst thou, walking in grief, languish/ He will quicken thee, He will quicken thee" (*Elijah*, No. 28). Similarly, Lucy is "resurrected" to life in her orchard, remembering Sebastian's songs. Her belief in living is restored as she comes to understand that, as in the Oratorio, only the presence of God can rescue one from a weakened will to live: "O rest in the Lord, wait patiently for Him, and He shall give thee thy heart's desires..." (*Elijah*, No. 31). In choosing Mendelssohn's *Elijah* as the song which introduces Lucy to a new life in art, Cather also selected the song which, as a memory, would reintroduce Lucy to life itself with all its desires.

Upon returning to Haverford, Lucy also finds compassion in the person of Mrs. Ramsay, who in earlier novels Cather might have depicted as a kindly Greek Moira guiding Lucy's destiny. Such was the case in "The Joy of Nelly Deane" (1911), the prototype story for *Lucy Gayheart*, in which three kindly old women watched over and cared for Nelly's child. Mrs. Ramsay is not a mythic goddess but is "Divine compassion," whose interest in other people has taken on a "less personal, more ethereal" aspect than the "quick, passionate sympathy that used to be there for a sick child or a friend in trouble" (p. 147). It is she who assures Lucy, "Accomplishments are the ornaments of life, they come second. Sometimes people disappoint us, and sometimes we disappoint ourselves; but the thing is, to go right on living" (p. 165). When Lucy finally consents to attend a performance of *The Bohemian Girl*, she finds her spirit reborn. Cather does not describe Lucy's spiritual renewal as the reconciliation of Bacchic and Apollonian impulses. Rather, she uses the hushed scene of Christian prayer and adoration:

> What if—what if Life itself were the sweetheart? It was like a lover waiting for her....She opened the window softly and knelt down beside it to breathe the cold air. She felt the snowflakes melt in her hair, on her hot cheeks. Oh, now she knew! (p. 184)

The scene is one of religious ecstasy, and Lucy recalls the words from *Elijah*: "If with all your heart you truly seek Him, you shall surely find Him." These words take on a wider meaning than the mere longing for a lost lover.

In the final book of *Lucy Gayheart* Cather's religious focus is strongest. Lucy's accidental drowning, like the sacrificial death of an innocent, fundamentally alters the behavior of Harry Gordon whose callous rejection of Lucy's love marred her newly recovered enthusiasm for living. E. K. Brown observes that the same calmness and quietude that characterize *Death Comes for the Archbishop* and *Shadows on the Rock* envelops Book III of *Lucy Gayheart* and makes this section the "finest part" of the novel.[22] Even if one criticized Cather for mawkish sentimentality which leads Harry to buy the Gayheart home and to protect the sidewalk where Lucy's light footprints are preserved in the concrete, the sincerity of Harry's actions are beyond question. His deep concern for old Mr. Gayheart becomes "somewhat like an act of retribution" as "the sense of guilt he used to carry had gradually grown paler" (p. 222). Cather uses Christian images of penance and contrition to praise individual behavior and to applaud what Lucy Gayheart herself displayed – an intense interest in people and in life itself.

Cather's use of Christian imagery as a pattern for shaping her fiction culminates in her final novel, *Sapphira and the Slave Girl*. Although not overtly concerned with Catholic themes, this novel is deeply involved with religious concepts. Cather virtually ignores the possibility of presenting the novel's central conflict in mythic terms, even though an imperious mother-figure's actions against a slave whom she suspects of disloyalty offer numerous parallels to classical myth. Instead, Cather reaches farther into her own past, returning, for the first time in her longer fiction, to a Virginia setting. James Woodress suggests that writing the book "eased the hurt of bitter sorrow, because when the present was painful, it was a help to turn back to those early memories."[23] And, Cather's present was painful. She began the book in the fall of 1937, but within the next year, she suffered the

---

22. E. K. Brown, *Willa Cather: A Critical Biography* (1953; rpt. New York: Avon Books, 1980), p. 230.

23. Woodress, *Willa Cather: Her Life and Art*, p. 261.

loss of both her brother Douglass and Isabelle McClung. Douglass' death was quite unexpected, but Cather had spent much of 1935 with the ailing Isabelle who had returned to the States with her husband for a temporary stay. Cather was aware that death was close for Isabelle. Out of such personal griefs arose *Sapphira and the Slave Girl* (1940). But, the further decay of her "family" did more than reawaken her interest in the memories of childhood. It also led her to a reconciliation with life, and this Cather expressed in terms of Christian reconciliation.

Although L. V. Jacks asserts that "many aspects of this work recall the young African playwright [Terence]" and that the "conventional happy ending would have been dear to a Roman audience,"[24] the text itself offers little evidence leading one to suppose that Cather was purposefully imitating the Roman dramatist in either plot or theme. Moreover, although Susan Rosowski's close analysis does point to elements of the novel which lie within the Gothic tradition of dark romanticism,[25] Cather was not writing a Gothic novel. Her purpose lies within a Christian tradition of sin, repentance, and forgiveness. Even the characters' names are far different from those in her early works which recalled classical heroes and gods. Here the reader returns to the Old Testament world of Sapphira, Sampson, Sarah, Rachel, and Jezebel, whose names had both historical and mythic implications for Cather.

Indeed, Sapphira holds sway over her household like a powerful goddess, demanding and expecting devotion and loyalty. She is, however, much more like Myra Henshawe in Part II of *My Mortal Enemy* than like a deity secure in her position. Like Myra, she is an ailing woman, jealous, suspicious, and vindictive. Henry Colbert, too, is reminiscent of Oswald Henshawe. Neither is a particularly impressive man, and Henry's moral weakness stands in direct contrast to his wife's strength, even if her values are distorted by tradition, upbringing, and personal prejudice. Henry is a "good" man who searches through his Bible and *Pilgrim's Progress* in an effort to fathom human life:

---

24. L. V. Jacks, "The Classics and Willa Cather," *Prairie Schooner*, 35 (1961), 295.

25. Susan J. Rosowski, "Willa Cather's American Gothic: *Sapphira and the Slave Girl*," *Great Plains Quarterly*, 4 (Fall 1984), 220-230.

> We must rest, he told himself, on our confidence in His
> design. Design was clear enough in the stars, the seasons, in the
> woods and field. But in human affairs–? Perhaps our
> bewilderment came from a fault in our perceptions; we could
> never see what was behind the next turn of the road.[26]

Mr. Colbert's bewilderment could have been Willa Cather's as she saw the decline of values she held dear and as she grew more and more to believe herself really old. If one were to seek the enduring, where could one turn except to religion?

Cather may have recreated in Rachel Blake's situation the isolation from the family group that she had felt as the demands of her art kept her physically, and sometimes spiritually, from her parents' home. The relationship between Sapphira and her daughter Rachel may indicate Cather's own sense of now being closed out of the family unit. Nancy, the slave girl, is also thrust out of the family. Her youth and simplicity recall that of the mythic Kore, but to equate Nancy with a Persephone, abandoned by Ceres and shoved into the path of a would-be rapist and Plutonian figure, is to distort Cather's purpose.[27] Sapphira is certainly not an attentive earth goddess whose love and compassion nurture her world. Although she is capable of demonstrating genuine concern for individuals like Old Jezebel and Tansy Dave and although she spends long hours in her well-tended garden, Sapphira exhibits a cruelty and deceitfulness of which Demeter is hardly capable. Cather's portrait of Sapphira is not a mythic one. Sapphira suffers and is redeemed by Christian standards, not pagan.

In keeping with a pattern of Christian images, then, Betty becomes, like Lucy Gayheart, the innocent who is sacrificed to redeem the sinner. Only after the child's death by diptheria – not an uncommon event of the time, but still a convenient plot detail – does Sapphira relent and forgive her daughter for defying a mother's authority and helping Nancy to escape to freedom. Likewise Henry Colbert is reconciled to the wife he "had never

---

[26]   Willa Cather, *Sapphira and the Slave Girl* (New York: Alfred A. Knopf, 1940), p. 111. Subsequent references to this work will be cited in the text by page number.

[27]   Sharon O'Brien suggests just such a parallel in her article "Mothers, Daughters, and the 'Art Necessity': Willa Cather and the Creative Process," in *American Novelists Revisited: Essays in Feminist Criticism*, ed. Fritz Fleischmann (Boston: G. K. Hall, 1982), p. 294.

understood...very well" but of whom "he had always been proud" (pp. 267-268). In a blatantly confessional scene, Henry Colbert kneels before his wife's chair, buries his face in her hands, and reveals his deepest feelings. Sapphira also discloses her regrets for past behavior and wonders if perhaps "We would all do better if we had our lives to live over again" (p. 269). When Sapphira faces death, maintaining her courageous solitariness, she insists that four lighted candles be set on her tea-table so "that the candle-flames inside were repeated by flames out in the snow-covered lilac arbour" (p. 294). The image has connotations of Christian penitence and serves as Sapphira's statement to the outside world of the need for prayer to release her soul from torment.

The final book of *Sapphira and the Slave Girl* is, significantly, the only place in which Cather included herself as a part of her fiction. Recalling the scene of Till's reunion with her daughter Nancy some twenty-five years later, Cather narrates the incident from the view of a sick child – herself at age five. Although this narrative technique has been widely criticized as fatal to the artistic design of the novel, the intensely personal nature of the concluding book enhances Cather's thematic concern. Just as old Till has long since forgiven Sapphira for the injustice she perpetrated, the reader can believe that Cather has at last been reconciled to her world. John H. Randall, III, is justified in contending that the novel's ending undercuts its moral realism and that Cather's "later view of life definitely interfered with her handling of the novel..."[28] but a kind of personal triumph still surfaces in the conclusion, a triumph of Christian forgiveness.

A similar mood of forgiveness exists in Cather's last two finished stories, "The Best Years" and "Before Breakfast." Willa Cather's later years were far from "the best" physically, and she withdrew more and more into a quiet life to which only a few select friends like the Menuhin family were admitted. Yet, the bitterness against life, which characterized the aged sophisticate of "The Old Beauty" (1936), seems to be tempered by a conciliatory tone in these final stories. Although the young school teacher

---

28.   John H. Randall, III, "The Protestant Past: 'Sapphira and the Slave Girl,'" in *Modern Critical Views*, p. 68.

Lesley Ferguesson dies in "The Best Years," no profound and unalterable grief follows this loss of innocence. Lesley's death is only temporarily tragic. Cather depicts death as part of the natural cycle of change which is not always justifiable or explainable. Lesley is another of Cather's Persephone figures who embodies commitment to home, family, and duty and who is finally sacrificed to Death. But, youth endures, and twenty years later the new school teacher at Wild Rose School is one of Lesley's former students; the young superintendent is also "a wideawake, breezy girl" who is "not in the least afraid of life or luck or responsibility."[29] Although "The Best Years" is colored by nostalgia for those times "when we're working hardest and going right ahead when we can hardly see our way out" (p. 136), Cather reinforces her belief in life as the great teacher and death as part of the lesson.

In her other late story, "Before Breakfast" (1942), Cather again addresses the issue of lost youth. In her portrait of the successful but aging businessman Henry Grenfell, Cather describes a reawakening of interest in life, sparked by a glimpse of youth and eternal beauty. This reawakening has been variously described as an optimism in the rebirth of civilization, a reestablishment of man's relationship with nature, and a proclamation that life will perpetually renew itself.[30] Cather describes a situation which lends itself readily to the Christian myth of the resurrected spirit, but the dominant imagery of the story reaches back to her earlier pattern of classical myth. Cather's careful interweaving of the Venus image into the account of Grenfell's rejuvenation indicates that she had not abandoned her interest in classical ideals and reinforces her conclusion that "Plucky youth is more bracing than enduring age" (p. 166).

In developing "Before Breakfast," Cather keeps before her readers the Venus image, which is as important to the story as is the great natural solitude which Grenfell finds on his island retreat, a place very similar to

---

29. Willa Cather, "The Best Years," in *The Old Beauty and Others* (1948; rpt. New York: Vintage Books, 1976), pp. 128-129. All further references to short stories in this collection will be cited parenthetically in the text by page.

30. John H. Randall, III, *The Landscape and The Looking Glass* (Boston: Houghton Mifflin Co., 1960), p. 340; Dorothy Tuck McFarland, *Willa Cather* (New York: Frederick Ungar Publishing Co., 1972), p. 134; David Stouck, *Willa Cather's Imagination* (Lincoln: Univ. of Nebraska Press, 1975), p. 236.

Cather's own retreat on Grand Manan Island. Shortly after awakening on the first day of his visit to the island, Grenfell stares, with calm detachment, into the eastern horizon. There he discovers the "white-bright, gold-bright" planet Venus (p. 144), drifting through rosy clouds. Not unlike the hare in his timidity in confronting a world where desire is absent, Grenfell feels separated from and untouched by the "Merciless perfection" and "ageless sovereignty" (p. 144) of the passion which Venus represents. She awaits, indifferent and aloof, like the comely geologist's daughter whom Grenfell has already dismissed as "Sweet, but decided" (p. 146). For this dyspeptic middle-aged man, life as "theoretical head" of his household involves only signing checks and appearing at dinner. None of the ardor of love, none of the passion of Aphrodite Pandemos, is part of his world. Although Grenfell acknowledges that Venus has done her stunts since time began and will continue to perform them, he believes himself as far removed from this part of the human experience as he is from the morning star.

Yet, Cather indicates that Grenfell's passion is strong, though submerged. The geologist's daughter, as the embodiment of the inhuman Venus, has sensed for a year that Grenfell deeply loves this island. Venus' own flower, the wild rose, serves as a hedge about his cabin. Grenfell is not cold, like his sons, and his "never quite satisfied desire" (p. 157) is not the stomach's hunger. Perhaps in recounting Grenfell's skills as a hunter, Cather wishes her readers to see the young Adonis, devotee of Aphrodite, triumphant in physical prowess and dedicated to the sensual satisfaction of the hunt. Adonis' story is like Grenfell's, for both predict the "singing of dirges over the effigy of...dead youth."[31] Adonis, not heeding the warnings of Venus, is responsible for his own death. Grenfell, marrying for position and intoxicated by his own vanity, is responsible for his own spiritual death. Grenfell has found Venus' gifts treacherous, and happiness with his wife Margaret only an illusion.

Were Cather to leave Grenfell in this condition, his morbidity and despair would be a far cry from her contention in *The Song of the Lark* that desire is all. It is little wonder that Grenfell, after closing out the disturbing

---

31.   Mark P. O. Morford and Robert J. Lenardon, *Classical Mythology* (New York: David McKay Co., 1971), p. 102.

sight of the stars in the night sky, finds the planet Venus so "serene, terrible, and splendid" (p. 158). His impassioned dreams are hers, dreams which he no longer recognizes as his own and can only glimpse through his reading of Shakespeare, Scott and Dickens. By rushing into the primeval forest, Grenfell expands his search for the lost passion for life. Like the fallen giant spruce, Grenfell wants to believe that the sap still runs within him, that he, like the young Adonis, can be resurrected by beauty. This rebirth, he thinks, might come from a new-born light which had been "asleep down under the sea and was just waking up" (p. 160).

At this point in Grenfell's story, Cather uses the Venus image to greatest advantage. Finding himself in the changeless environs of his secret cove, Grenfell seems like the old white birches which, having crept along the ground in the wrong direction, now burst into leaf when reaching the sunshine. Grenfell is ready for a revitalization long before he spies Professor Fairweather's daughter on the beach. Cather depicts this beautiful young woman, who is unconscious of Grenfell's presence and absorbed only in herself, as no other than the indifferent and remote Venus. It is Aphrodite Urania or the Celestial Aphrodite whom Miss Fairweather represents and not the lustful daughter of Dione and Zeus. She is Botticelli's Venus landing at the shore after her birth, a painting which art historian Ronald Lightbown describes as celebrating the beauty of the female "for its own perfection rather than with erotic or moral or religious overtones."[32] Like the "Birth of Venus," Cather's description paints an impersonal celebration of love: "She opened her robe, a grey thing lined with white. Her bathing-suit was pink. If a clam stood upright and graciously opened its shell, it would look like that" (p. 164). Cather, who was undoubtedly acquainted with Botticelli's work, captures in words the image of ethereal Aphrodite, recently born from the foam of the sea and representing idealized femininity. Botticelli's Venus displays the rosy glow of her skin as she begins to step from her light brown clam shell, whose interior is lined with white. In a bay edged by grassy headlands and lighted by golden, divine light, the queen of love makes her first landing on the shore of the real world. She is outside the time-bound

32.   Ronald Lightbown, *Sandro Botticelli* (Los Angeles: Univ of California Press, 1978), I, p. 89.

world of petty men; she is part of the eternities which Grenfell "kept in the back of his mind" as an "escape-avenue" (p. 147). The parallel of Grenfell's experience to that depicted in Botticelli's work cannot be accidental. This is Cather at her best, equating religious and mythic images with a work of art. She draws her mythic image from a painting which Lightbown describes as "suitable for country retreats to which the owner escaped from business, heat or plague of the town to recreate himself with tranquillity and pleasures of a rural retreat."[33] So, it was with Cather as she spent her final summers in her cottage at Grand Manan.

Grenfell's immediate reaction, though, is that Miss Fairweather is a "Crazy kid" who is unaware of the danger of the sea. With a rush of adrenaline, Grenfell is ready to come to this goddess' rescue. But she, like Uranus' daughter, emerges triumphant from the sea. Cather writes, "She had gone out, and she had come back" (pp. 165-166). With her return, hope returns to Grenfell's world, but this hope is more than that life will go on. The persistent Venus imagery points to a hope renewed. Love, which Grenfell thought was drowned in the frigid and rushing waters of modern life, survives and is eternally present. When Cather writes that "something had sharpened his appetite" (p. 146), she is not referring to an awakened physical appetite alone. Grenfell has moved beyond the love of Aphrodite Pandemos, which begins with a sensual desire for a beautiful thing or person. He has stepped into Botticelli's canvas and has moved to a "generic conception of beauty which is wondrous, and pure, and universal."[34] The eagerness for life which Grenfell displays as he returns to the cabin is not an impassioned love in the traditional romantic sense. Cather is not writing a love story. Indeed, desire is all, and Grenfell rediscovers the power of youthful desire, not in the eternal and unchanging presence of nature, but in the materialization of Venus herself. Through such sublime love is his resurrection attained. The implications of Cather's story assume both mythic and religious proportions.

"Before Breakfast" is, then, much more than an example of Willa Cather's stories in which, as David Daiches says, "Everybody...who is worth

---

33. Lightbown, I, p. 86.
34. Morford and Lenardon, p. 116.

anything escapes or tries to escape from the modern world."[35] "Before Breakfast" is a celebration of life and love, of hope renewed. Perhaps for the ailing author the story was a self-prescribed remedy. Grenfell is never really alone in his musings and despair; the immortal beauty of Venus is omnipresent. But, as Grenfell discovers, this beauty is only there when somebody is prepared to see it, and only the seeker will find it.

Cather's last stories and novels, therefore, suggest that human fate is not inimical to eternal beauty. This concept she reinforces primarily through a pattern of Christian imagery and through Catholic themes. Yet, Cather can, and does, integrate images from classical myth when they serve her purpose. In making her truce with the modern world, Willa Cather found in both the Christian rock and the Greek Parnassus a defense against the decay of beauty, the distortion of values, and the deterioration of civilization itself.

---

[35]   David Daiches, *Willa Cather: A Critical Introduction* (1951; rpt. Westport, CT: Greenwood Press, 1971), p. 173.

BIBLIOGRAPHY
Primary Sources

Editions of works by Willa Cather:

Alexander's Bridge. Introd. Bernice Slote. 1912; rpt. Lincoln: Bison Book-Univ. of Nebraska Press, 1977.

April Twilights (1903). Introd. Bernice Slote. Rev. ed. 1968; rpt. Lincoln: Bison Book-Univ. of Nebraska Press, 1976.

April Twilights and Other Poems. New York: Alfred A. Knopf, 1923.

Collected Short Fiction 1892-1912. Ed. Virginia Faulkner. Introd. Mildred R. Bennett. Rev. ed. Lincoln: Univ. of Nebraska Press, 1970.

Death Comes for the Archbishop. New York: Alfred A. Knopf, 1927.

Five Stories. New York: Vintage-Random House, 1956.

The Kingdom of Art: Willa Cather's First Principles and Critical Statements 1893-1896. Ed. Bernice Slote. Lincoln: Univ. of Nebraska Press, 1966.

A Lost Lady. Centennial ed. 1923; rpt. New York: Borzoi Book-Alfred A. Knopf, 1973.

Lucy Gayheart. New York: Alfred A. Knopf, 1935.

My Antonia. 1918; rpt. Boston: Sentry-Houghton Mifflin Co., 1954.

My Mortal Enemy. Introd. Marcus Klein. 1926; rpt. New York: Vintage-Random House, n.d.

Not Under Forty. New York: Alfred A. Knopf, 1936.

Obscure Destinies. 1932; rpt. New York: Vintage-Random House, 1974.

The Old Beauty and Others. 1948; rpt. New York: Vintage-Random House, 1976.

One of Ours. New York: Alfred A. Knopf, 1922.

O Pioneers!. Boston: Houghton Mifflin Co., 1913.

The Professor's House. New York: Alfred A. Knopf, 1925.

Sapphira and the Slave Girl. New York: Borzoi Book-Alfred A. Knopf, 1940.

Shadows on the Rock. 1931; rpt. New York: Vintage-Random House, 1971.

The Song of the Lark. 1915; rpt. Lincoln: Bison Book-Univ. of Nebraska Press, 1978.

The Troll Garden. Ed. James Woodress. 1905; rpt. Lincoln: Univ. of Nebraska Press, 1983.

Uncle Valentine and Other Stories: Willa Cather's Uncollected Short Fiction 1915-1929. Ed. Bernice Slote. Lincoln: Univ. of Nebraska Press, 1973.

Willa Cather in Europe. New York: Alfred A. Knopf, 1956.

Willa Cather in Person. Ed. L. Brent Bohlke. Lincoln: Univ. of Nebraska Press, 1986.

Willa Cather on Writing. New York: Alfred A. Knopf, 1949.

The World and the Parish: Willa Cather's Articles and Reviews, 1893-1902. 2 vols. Ed. William M. Curtin. Lincoln: Univ. of Nebraska Press, 1970.

Youth and the Bright Medusa. 1920; rpt. New York: Vintage-Random House, 1975.

Secondary Sources

Writings about Willa Cather:

Arnold, Marilyn. *Willa Cather's Short Fiction*. Athens: Ohio Univ. Press, 1984.

Bartlett, Alice Hunt. "The Dynamics of American Poetry-XI." *The Poetry Review*, 16 (Nov.-Dec. 1925), 405-414.

Bennett, Mildred R. "The Childhood Worlds of Willa Cather." *Great Plains Quarterly*, 2 (Fall 1982), 204-209.

——————. "How Willa Cather Chose her Names." *Names*, 10 (1962), 29-37.

——————. *The World of Willa Cather*. Rev. ed. Lincoln: Univ. of Nebraska Press, 1961.

Bloom, Harold, ed. *Modern Critical Views: Willa Cather*. New York: Chelsea House Publishers, 1985.

Bois, Bessie de. Rev. of *The Troll Garden*, by Willa Cather. *Bookman*, 5 Aug. 1905, p. 612.

Brown, E. K. *Willa Cather: A Critical Biography*. 1953; rpt. New York: Avon Books, 1980.

Burch, Beth. "Willa Cather's *A Lost Lady*: The Woodpecker and Marian Forrester." *Notes on Contemporary Literature*, 11, No.4 (Sept. 1981), 7-10.

Charles, Sister Peter Damian. "Love and Death in Willa Cather's *O Pioneers!*." *College Language Association Journal*, 9 (Dec. 1965), 140-150.

Cooperman, Stanley. *World War I and the American Novel*. Baltimore: The Johns Hopkins Press, 1967.

Daiches, David. *Willa Cather: A Critical Introduction.* 1951; rpt. Westport, CT: Greenwood Press, 1971.

Field, L. M. Rev. of *One of Ours*, by Willa Cather. *International Book Review*, Jan. 1923, p. 58.

Fox, Maynard. "Symbolic Representation in Willa Cather's *O Pioneers!*." *Western American Literature*, 9 (1974), 187-196.

Fryer, Judith. *Felicitous Space: The Imaginative Structures of Edith Wharton and Willa Cather.* Chapel Hill: The Univ. of North Carolina Press, 1986.

Gelfant, Blanche H. "The Forgotten Reaping-Hook: Sex in *My Antonia*." *American Literature*, 43 (March 1971), 60-82.

Giannone, Richard. *Music in Willa Cather's Fiction.* Lincoln: Univ. of Nebraska Press, 1968.

Gleason, John B. "The 'Case' of Willa Cather." *Western American Literature*, 20 (Winter 1986), 275-299.

Helmick, Evelyn (Thomas). "The Broken World: Medievalism in *A Lost Lady*." *Renascence*, 28 (Autumn 1975), 39-46.

_____. "The Mysteries of Antonia." *The Midwest Quarterly*, 17 (Winter 1976), 173-185.

Hutchinson, Phyllis Martin. "Reminiscences of Willa Cather as a Teacher." *Bulletin of The New York Public Library*, 60 (June 1956), 263-266.

Jacks, L. V. "The Classics and Willa Cather." *Prairie Schooner*, 35 (1961), 289-296.

Jones, Howard Mumford. *The Bright Medusa.* Urbana: The Univ. of Illinois Press, 1952.

Lee, Robert Edson. *From West to East: Studies in the Literature of the American West*. Urbana: The Univ. of Illinois Press, 1966.

Lewis, Edith. *Willa Cather Living: A Personal Record by Edith Lewis*. New York: Alfred A. Knopf, 1953.

McFarland, Dorothy Tuck. *Willa Cather*. New York: Frederick Ungar Publishing Co., 1972.

Moers, Ellen. *Literary Women*. Garden City, NY: Doubleday and Co., 1976.

Murphy, John J. "The Dantean Journey in Cather's *My Mortal Enemy*." *Willa Cather Pioneer Memorial Newsletter*. Special Literary Issue, 30 (Summer 1986), 11-14.

—————. "Euripides' *Hippolytus* and Cather's *A Lost Lady*." *American Literature*, 53 (March 1981), 72-86.

—————. "Willa Cather's Archbishop: A Western and Classical Perspective." *Western American Literature*, 13 (1978), 141-150.

—————, ed. *Critical Essays on Willa Cather*. Boston: G. K. Hall and Co., 1984.

—————, ed. *Five Essays on Willa Cather: The Merrimack Symposium*. North Andover, MA: Merrimack College, 1974.

O'Brien, Sharon. "Mothers, Daughters, and the 'Art Necessity': Willa Cather and the Creative Process." In *American Novelists Revisited: Essays in Feminist Criticism*. Ed. Fritz Fleischmann. Boston: G. K. Hall and Co., 1982. 265-298.

—————. *Willa Cather: The Emerging Voice*. New York: Oxford Univ. Press, 1987.

Olson, Paul A. "The Epic and Great Plains Literature: Rolvaag, Cather, and Neihardt." *Prairie Schooner*, 55 (Spring/Summer 1981), 263-285.

Pearson, Carol, and Katharine Pope. *The Female Hero in American and British Literature*. New York: R. R. Bowker Co., 1981.

Randall, John H., III. *The Landscape and The Looking Glass*. Boston: Houghton Mifflin Co., 1960.

Rapin, Rene. *Willa Cather*. New York: Robert McBride and Co., 1930.

Reaver, J. Russell. "Mythic Motivation in Willa Cather's *O Pioneers!*." *Western Folklore*, 27 (Jan. 1968), 19-25.

Rev. of *Alexander's Bridge*, by Willa Cather. *New York Times*, 12 May 1912, p. 295.

Rev. of *My Mortal Enemy*, by Willa Cather. *Dial*, 27 Jan. 1926, p. 73.

Robinson, Phyllis C. *Willa: The Life of Willa Cather*. New York: Holt, Rinehart and Winston, 1983.

Rosowski, Susan J. *The Voyage Perilous: Willa Cather's Romanticism*. Lincoln: Univ. of Nebraska Press, 1986.

—————. "Willa Cather's American Gothic: *Sapphira and the Slave Girl*." *Great Plains Quarterly*, 4 (Fall 1984), 220-230.

—————. "Willa Cather's Pioneer Women." *In Where the West Begins*. Ed. Arthur R. Huseboe and William Geyer. Sioux Falls, SD: Center for Western Studies Press, 1978. 135-142.

—————. "Willa Cather's Women." *Studies in American Fiction*, 9 (Autumn 1981), 261-275.

—————, and Bernice Slote. "Willa Cather's 1916 Mesa Verde Essay: The Genesis of *The Professor's House*." *Prairie Schooner*, 58 (Winter 1984), 81-92.

Sergeant, Elizabeth Shepley. *Willa Cather: A Memoir*. New York: J. B. Lippincott Co., 1953.

Slote, Bernice, and Virginia Faulkner, eds. *The Art of Willa Cather*. Lincoln: Univ. of Nebraska Press, 1974.

Stauffer, Helen Winter, and Susan J. Rosowski, eds. *Women and Western American Literature*. Troy, NY: The Whitston Publishing Co., 1982.

Stewart, G. B. "Mother, daughter, and the birth of the female artist." *Women's Studies*, 6, No. 2 (1979), 127-145.

Stewart, Grace. *A New Mythos: The Novel of the Artist as Heroine 1877-1977*. St. Alban's, VT: Eden Press, 1979.

Stofer, Kathryn T. "Gems and Jewelry: Cather's Imagery in *My Mortal Enemy*." *Willa Cather Pioneer Memorial Newsletter*. Special Literary Issue, 30 (Summer 1986), 19-22.

Stouck, David. "Cather's *Archbishop* and Travel Writing." *Western American Literature*, 17 (May 1982), 3-12.

—————. *Willa Cather's Imagination*. Lincoln: Univ. of Nebraska Press, 1975.

Swift, John N. "Memory, Myth, and *The Professor's House*." *Western American Literature*, 20 (Winter 1986), 301-314.

Whicher, George F. "In the American Grain." In *The Literature of the American People*. Ed. Arthur Hobson Quinn. New York: Appleton-Century-Crofts, 1951. 900-913.

Woodress, James. *Willa Cather: Her Life and Art*. 1970; rpt. Lincoln: Univ. of Nebraska Press, 1982.

—————. *Willa Cather: A Literary Life*. Lincoln: Univ. of Nebraska Press, 1987.

Yongue, Patricia Lee. "Willa Cather on Heroes and Hero-Worship." *Neuphilologische Mitteilungen*, 79 (1977), 59-66.

Classical Literature and Mythic Studies:

Atchity, Kenneth John. *Homer's "Iliad": The Shield of Memory*. Carbondale: Southern Illinois Univ. Press, 1978.

Barnes, Hazel E. "The Hippolytus of Drama and Myth." In *Hippolytus in Drama and Myth*. Lincoln: Univ. of Nebraska Press, 1960. 69-123.

——. *The Meddling Gods: Four Essays on Classical Themes*. Lincoln: Univ. of Nebraska Press, 1974.

Diel, Paul. *Symbolism in Greek Mythology: Human Desire and Its Transformations*. Trans. Vincent Stuart, Micheline Stuart, and Rebecca Folkman. Boulder, CO: Shambhala Publications, 1980.

Downing, Christine. *The Goddess: Mythological Images of the Femine*. New York: Crossroad Publishing Co., 1984.

Euripides. *Euripides I*. Ed. David Grene and Richmond Lattimore. New York: Washington Square Press, 1967.

Eydoux, Henri-Paul. *In Search of Lost Worlds*. Trans. Lorna Andrade. New York: Hamlyn, 1972.

Friedrich, Paul. *The Meaning of Aphrodite*. Chicago: The Univ. of Chicago Press, 1978.

Grigson, Geoffrey. *The Goddess of Love: The birth, triumph, death and return of Aphrodite*. London: Constable and Co., 1976.

Henderson, Bernard W. *Five Roman Emperors*. 1927; rpt. New York: Barnes and Noble, 1969.

Hesiod. *Hesiod: The Homeric Hymns and Homerica*. Trans. Hugh G. Evelyn-White. Ed. T. E. Page, and others. Cambridge: Harvard Univ.Press, 1936.

Higham, T. F., and C. M. Bowra, eds. *The Oxford Book of Greek Verse in Translation*. Oxford: The Clarendon Press, 1938.

Homer. *The Iliad of Homer*. Trans. Richmond Lattimore. Chicago: The Univ. of Chicago Press, 1970.

—————. *The Odyssey*. Trans. Samuel Butler. New York: Washington Square Press, 1965.

Horace. *Carminum Libri IV*. Ed. T. E. Page. New York: Macmillan and Co., 1964.

Jacobson, Howard. *Ovid's Heroides*. Princeton: Princeton Univ. Press, 1974.

Kerenyi, C. *Eleusis: Archetypal Image of Mother and Daughter*. Trans. Ralph Manheim. Bollingen Series 65. Vol.4. New York: Pantheon Books, 1967.

—————. *Zeus and Hera: Archetypal Image of Father, Husband, and Wife*. Trans. Christopher Holme. Bollingen Series 65. Vol.5. Princeton: Princeton Univ. Press, 1975.

Lucretius. *Lucretius: The Way Things Are*. Trans. Rolfe Humphries. Bloomington: Indiana Univ. Press, 1968.

Makowski, John F. "Persephone, Psyche, and the Mother-Maiden Archetype." *Classical Outlook*, 62 (March-April 1985), 73-78.

Morford, Mark P. O., and Robert J. Lenardon. *Classical Mythology*. New York: David McKay Co., 1971.

Neumann, Erich. *The Great Mother: An Analysis of the Archetype*. 2nd ed. Trans. Ralph Manheim. Bollingen Series 47. Princeton: Princeton Univ. Press, 1963.

O'Brien, Joan. "Who Was Hera Before Zeus Tamed Her?" Illinois Classical Conference, Urbana, IL. 12 Oct. 1985.

Ovid. *Heroides*. Ed. Arthur Palmer. Hildesheim, Germany: Georg Olms Verlagsbuchhandlung, 1967.

_____. *The Heroides or Epistles of the Heroines, The Amours, Art of Love, Remedy of Love, and Minor Works of Ovid.* Trans. Henry T. Riley. London: George Bell and Sons, 1887.

_____. *The Metamorphoses*. Trans. Horace Gregory. New York: Mentor-New American Library, 1958.

_____. *Selections from the Ars Amatoria and Remedia Amoris of Ovid.* Introd. Graves Haydon Thompson. 1952; rpt. Ann Arbor, MI: Edwards Brothers, Inc., 1958.

Serviez, Jacques Boergas de. *Lives of the Roman Empresses*. New York: William H. Wise and Co., 1935.

Smith, William. *A Smaller Classical Dictionary of Biography, Mythology, and Geography*. New York: Harper and Brothers Publishers, 1882.

Vergil. *The Aeneid*. Trans. Patric Dickinson. New York: Mentor-The New American Library, 1961.

Vergil. *Eclogues, Georgics, Aeneid I-VI*. Vol. I. Trans H. Rushton Fairclough. Ed. T. E. Page, E. Capps, and W. H. D. Rouse. New York: G. P. Putnam's Sons, 1929.

Other Sources Cited

Brown, E. K., and J. O. Bailey, eds. *Victorian Poetry*. New York: The Ronald Press Co., 1962.

Burne-Jones. Introd. John Christian. London: Arts Council of Great Britain, 1975.

Carter, Everett. *Howells and The Age of Realism*. New York: J. B. Lippincott Co., 1954.

Goodrich, Samuel Griswold. *Peter Parley's Universal History, on the Basis of Geography*. 2 vols. Boston: American Stationers' Co., 1838.

Kipling, Rudyard. *Kipling: A Selection of His Stories and Poems*. Ed. John Beecroft. Garden City, NY: Doubleday and Co., 1956.

—————. *The Seven Seas*. New York: D. Appleton and Co., 1897.

—————. *Soldiers Three, The Story of the Gadsbys, In Black and White*. Garden City, NY: Doubleday, Page and Co., 1927.

Lewis, R. W. B. *The American Adam: Innocence, Tragedy and Tradition in the Nineteenth Century*. Chicago: The Univ. of Chicago Press, 1955.

Lightbown, Ronald. *Sandro Botticelli*. 2 vols. Los Angeles: Univ. of California Press, 1978.

Mendelssohn, Felix. *Elijah*. Op. 70.

Morris, William. *The Collected Works of William Morris*. Vol. V. Introd. May Morris. New York: Russell and Russell, 1966.

Nordenskiold, G. *The Cliff Dwellers of the Mesa Verde, Southwestern Colorado, Their Pottery and Implements*. Trans. D. Lloyd Morgan. Chicago: P. A. Norstedt and Soner, 1893; rpt. New York: AMS Press, 1973.

Phaidon Book of the Opera: A Survey of 780 Operas from 1597. Trans. Catherine Atthill, and others. Oxford: Phaidon Press Limited, 1979.

Rosenthal, Donald A. *Orientalism: The Near East in French Painting 1800-1880.* Rochester, NY: Memorial Art Gallery of the Univ. of Rochester, 1982.

Werner, Eric. *Mendelssohn: A New Image of the Composer and His Age.* London: The Free Press of Glencoe, 1963.

Index

298

STUDIES IN AMERICAN LITERATURE